girl HUNTER

ALSO BY GEORGIA PELLEGRINI

Food Heroes: 16 Culinary Artisans Preserving Tradition

girl HUNTER

REVOLUTIONIZING
THE WAY WE EAT,
ONE HUNT AT A TIME

Georgia Pellegrini

Da Capo
∞
LIFE
LONG

A Member of the Perseus Books Group

Designed by Brent Wilcox
Set in 11.5 point New Caledonia by the Perseus Books Group

Library of Congress Cataloging-in-Publication Data
Pellegrini, Georgia.
Girl hunter : revolutionizing the way we eat, one hunt at a time /
Georgia Pellegrini.—1st Da Capo Press ed.
     p.   cm.
Includes recipes index.
ISBN 978-0-7382-1466-5 (hardcover : alk. paper)—
ISBN 978-0-7382-1539-6 (e-book)
1. Pellegrini, Georgia.   2. Pellegrini, Georgia—Travel.
3. Women hunters—Biography.   4. Hunters—Biography.
5. Hunting—Philosophy.   6. Food habits—Philosophy.
7. Cooking (Game)   I. Title.
SK17.P46A3 2011
799.2082092—dc23
2011035209

First Da Capo Press edition 2011
Published by Da Capo Press
A Member of the Perseus Books Group
www.dacapopress.com

Da Capo Press books are available at special discounts for bulk
purchases in the U.S. by corporations, institutions, and other
organizations. For more information, please contact the Special
Markets Department at the Perseus Books Group, 2300 Chestnut
Street, Suite 200, Philadelphia, PA, 19103, or call (800) 810-4145,
ext. 5000, or e-mail special.markets@perseusbooks.com.

10 9 8 7 6 5 4 3 2 1

For T. Kristian Russell

Without you, there would be none of this.

Contents

So long as there is lead in the air, there is hope.
—THEODORE ROOSEVELT

Prologue

"Oh my Lord, oh my Lord," Hollis whispers.

In the next field we can barely make out a set of dark crimson tail feathers moving through the high grass. We move quickly toward the wild turkey, along the levee with our backs bent low, in single file, three of us: a farmer named George Hollis, a man they call "the Commish," and me. We are an odd group, me half their size, trying to keep up in too-large-for-me, full army camouflage that I borrowed from my brother's closet—remnants from the days he played paintball with his adolescent friends. The others are in proper hunter's camouflage with 12-gauge shotguns slung over their shoulders, a couple of plastic turkey decoys dangling from their backpacks, turkey callers clenched between their teeth. They climb up the hill beside the field; I stumble after them in the oversize rubber boots that they bestowed upon me to save me from the snakes. We sit panting behind a tree trunk while Hollis unwraps a piece of camouflage fabric attached to plastic stakes and positions it in front of us as a blind. We wait.

"Okay," the Commish says. "This bird's gonna get to meet Miss Georgia. He's gonna have Georgia on his mind . . ."

You may be wondering how I ended up here. It was a series of serendipitous introductions, really, a divine aligning of the stars that introduced me to a man named Roger Mancini, a larger-than-life entrepreneur from the Arkansas side of the Mississippi Delta. I had cooked for him from time to time in Nashville, where we have mutual friends, and always found myself reaching deep into my bag of four-star tricks to impress a man so worldly, yet so distinctly a product of the American South.

During one of those dinners, as I glazed a series of Roger's freshly hunted wild duck breasts with orange gastrique, he overheard me telling a friend that I wanted to hunt. "Hold on now, Georgia," he said as he sauntered over with a wide-eyed, soulful look, a cigar pressed between his thumb and forefinger, which he pointed at me now, saying, "I've got just the man to teach you. My first cousin; we call him 'the Commish.'"

Roger went on to explain that "the Commish" takes his nickname from the governor-appointed position he has held for many years: commissioner of fish and game for the State of Arkansas, and that he would be honored to introduce me; and then, in the same breath, he moved past me, intent on finding three perfect tomatoes for the Panzenella Salad he had been talking about for some time. It was then that his wife, Betsy, leaned over to me, a glass of Bollinger balanced in her left hand, and said conspiratorially, "Down there, the Commish is a bigger deal than the president of the United States."

Many months later in early spring, I was introduced to the Commish at an Arkansas hunting camp, the night before a turkey hunt. He was sitting on a tree stump, holding a large Styrofoam cup filled with ice and whiskey in one hand, and cradling a thick cigar in the other, staring into the fire with a serious expression.

He looked up as they introduced me to him, paused, then offered me a drink and a seat by the fire. He had silver hair and his face bore the faint traces of his Lebanese ancestors who had first inhabited this place a century ago.

"You ever shot a gun?" he asked, still staring into the fire, his voice settling onto his words like molasses.

"Um, no, not really," I said, glancing sideways, feeling the other men at the camp peering at me curiously.

"This twenty-gauge should work pretty well," he said, opening the shotgun leaning against his chair to look down the barrel. "My daughter Ashley learned on a four-ten because it doesn't kick, but it's hard to kill anything with it. The first thing you gotta decide, do you want an automatic or an over an' under, which is a double barrel—the classic hunting bird gun. Quail hunters, they all shoot over an' unders, that's just kinda the old European influence. For you I would use a twenty-gauge. It's a good turkey gun if you can get 'em close."

"Okay, that sounds good," I say, wanting to fit in as much as possible but clearly failing simply by the way I looked in my button-down shirt and J.Crew blue jeans.

We didn't talk much after that. We just sat there and sipped from our Styrofoam cups and chewed on the crushed ice.

"I'll pick you up at five tomorrow morning," he said as I finally got up to leave.

Then he paused and gave me a sober look from his dark eyes through tinted spectacles.

"Are you sure 'bout this?" he asked.

"Yes, I'm sure," I said, my voice unrecognizably high pitched.

"A' right then. I'll see you tomorrow," he said.

Now through the turkey caller set between his tongue and the roof of his mouth, just twelve hours later, George Hollis lets out the cluck of a female turkey. The male gobbles back from the brush across the field. George calls again and the old turkey calls back again.

"He's responding well," I whisper.

"You know what you're supposed to say?" the Commish asks.

"What?" I ask.

"He's gobblin' his ass off."

Hollis chuckles.

"You're hanging out with a bunch of old men now; you gotta remember that," the Commish says.

As he speaks, a thin red and black head appears through the clearing on the opposite side of the field. I put my head down into the barrel of the gun and look through the scope to get a better look.

"It's such a little head they have, though," I say, my voice shaking. "How am I supposed to hit it?"

"You don't have to get it exactly on him. You just get it close and the spread of the shell pellets will do the rest," the Commish says.

I feel my hand tighten as the old turkey begins to strut toward the plastic decoys that Hollis has dropped onto the field. The bird has begun his mating march—stepping forward regally with his wings behind him, displaying the purple and green shimmering colors of his tail feathers, his red wattle and long, wiry beard swaying to and fro. He keeps coming forward, step by adrenaline-inducing step, but then instead of going toward the decoys to my left, he suddenly moves right.

"Hold on," the Commish says. "Just hold on a second." I obey, my head and heart pounding in unison.

"Get your head down on the gun," he continues. "Can you see the red dot on the end of your shotgun?"

"Yeah," I reply. But I can't see the turkey. "What happens if I miss the first shot?" I whisper, trying to veil my rising panic.

"Don't worry about it," the Commish says, guiding my gun as I look through the scope like a blind man in a maze, with no idea of what is beyond the camo blind or where the ol' gobbler is doing his dance. I see nothing but the makeshift fence, the cluster of trees and the field, and beyond that the Mississippi, the color of mercury, moving languidly in the distance.

There is a moment of stillness and utter silence when the world seems to be on mute, and then suddenly, hardly 10 yards away, the turkey appears in my scope, so close he is almost in my face. I let out a gasp.

"Do you see him? Do you see him?" the Commish whispers, showing the first signs of real emotion since I've met him.

I lean forward and look down the rib of the shotgun toward the red dot at the tip of the barrel, and position it on the head of the bird only a few yards away, my hands shaking, my heart feeling almost certainly too large to fit in my chest. I wait for my breath to become at least a bit more steady, I squint, and then I slap the trigger. The sound echoes through the woods and the field below us and I feel a thrust into my right shoulder as the gun kicks back. The ol' gobbler jumps into the air, in a moment of confusion, levitates higher, toward the trees, and then finally . . . out of sight.

I look at the Commish and feel my cheeks turn hot.

Hollis jumps out of his seat and howls, "Is that a turkey hunt or what?!" as I sink my head down further in embarrassment.

"What did he do there, Georgia?" the Commish asks, grinning.

"He gobbled his ass off," I say, suppressing a smile. Hollis howls with laughter.

"That 'responding well' works in upstate New York, but down here it doesn't. We're not letting you go back to be a Yankee; you're from the South now, Baby. Anyone who can put on camo and go hunting with a bunch of rednecks is my kind of girl."

It was at that moment, my cheeks burning with a strange new cocktail of shame and exhilaration, a feeling of determination rising slowly in my chest, that I knew I had just been indoctrinated into a brave new world.

Little did I know, this was just the beginning.

*Civilized life has altogether grown too tame, and, if it is
to be stable, it must provide harmless outlets for the impulses
which our remote ancestors satisfied in hunting.*

—BERTRAND RUSSELL

The Beginning

Watching the orange bobbin float by under the willow tree was a kind of pleasure I didn't know existed until it stopped. Feeling the soil slip under my nails was, too—especially when it ended with a fat worm between my fingers. The bobbin bounced just so over the tiny rivulets of the creek, beneath my feet dangling from my regular boulder. I can still recall the pangs of glee I felt as a six-year-old when the trout pulled on that orange bobbin, and the tug-of-war we played as I pulled on the line and the trout's brassy color began to reflect the light. The fish pulled my rod down in a sharp arc and its white belly flopped and its dots sparkled and shined and my father's hands came down to help me reel it in.

I foraged, too, inspecting mushroom guidebooks with scholarly interest; and I painted, using only wild berries and crushed grass as my ink. I hung from vines until they fell and then made vine wreathes that I studded with dandelions and rosehips. I shoveled chicken manure and collected eggs, and made dolls from dried cornhusks. I made jams, as taught to me by an old woman who lived on the bank of the Hudson River, and soon declared myself the Wild Raspberry Queen. I pickled green tomatoes and climbed apple trees to get the very finest fruit. I learned the names of plants with my great-hunched-over-aunt as my guide—and helped her protect her budding flowers from an overabundance of marauding midnight deer—on the land we called Tulipwood.

My mother, on the other hand, was the perennial standard bearer of animal welfare. She was known to bring road-kill deer home in the trunk of her car to give them a proper burial, and to nurse in her home office ailing chickens from our coop. It wasn't uncommon to trip over a diaper-clad bird named Lorenzo on my way to the kitchen.

During grade school I often visited the Fairy stream and sat on Indian rock. I collected salamanders and slipped them into my pockets for no reason other than their fluorescent green bodies enchanted me.

I preferred not to wear shoes. Or if I had to, then I preferred not to wear anything *but* shoes. Sometimes I'd sit outside and play the cello in the grass, with just shoes on.

Once, I made the mistake of saying that school was too easy, which prompted a trip from Tulipwood in the Hudson Valley to Manhattan, which prompted a uniform fitting, which prompted early-morning commutes to a rigorous girl's school in the city. Soon I was penning history notes next to Ivanka Trump by day and shoveling chicken manure by night.

Suddenly I was hopping back and forth between two worlds, divided only by the George Washington Bridge and sizeable trust funds. Suddenly I was spending time with kids during the week who had drivers in sleek black town cars, and on the weekend I was riding along in my dad's old black stick-shift pickup to get horse manure from the dump.

The seams of my home life began to unravel as I got older. I moved farther away from manure and raspberry jam on the quest for prestigious degrees and prestigious jobs, which were the logical next step after Manhattan prep school. They took over: the heavy books, the ivy walls, the promises of success and fulfilled potential; and I took the path of least resistance into a corporate life. It was a life that nourished my bank account but never my soul, and I found myself looking up one day, while on the trading floor of Lehman Brothers, and saying, "This can't be the answer." I wanted to smell fresh air again, to feel the dirt in my fingernails, to collect eggs and stir ruby-colored jam in a pot and watch it grow thick. And so I left, with the taste of hope in my mouth and soon-to-be worthless stock options in my bank account, determined to nourish my soul again.

Two years later I found myself only miles from Wall Street, but a world away, working at an award-winning farm-to-table restaurant on a Rockefeller estate. I had just graduated from the French Culinary Institute and had given up my apartment on Sutton Place in favor of a rented solitary room in Westchester, with no hot water. I had left behind the trappings of the city—the cars and bars and boys—and traded in my laptop for a set of good knives.

The funny thing was that I was working the same hours that I had as a financial analyst, but I was now feeding the same people with whom I had once crunched numbers—feeding them such things as delicately smoked trout, carefully plucked baby greens, dainty golden beets—creating small, precious flights of fancy in the center of big white plates. I was throwing out (or at least composting) anything that didn't look perfect enough to conjure a certain kind of money from their wallets. Sometimes I wondered how far from the dens of Wall Street I had really come.

One morning the chef gave me an unusual order. Pointing out over the sloping hill of the estate at a herd of turkeys drifting and pecking through the morning, he told me that I was going to slaughter five of them for the kitchen. With this assignment came a revelation. Although I had always eaten meat, and even considered myself an adventurous meat eater—embracing the strange cuts and unusual parts found in outdoor markets and Asian butchers—I had never killed an animal with my own hands. A thin, clear piece of fishing line in my hands had always played the intermediary. But if you knew the chef I was working for, you would know that there was no going back.

I put on a clean apron and walked up a sloping hill, where they stood at the top, calm and stunning, feathers fanned out, their high-pitched gobbles echoing into the woods and over the creek. I stood paralyzed as the other cooks chased them down. There was indeed that proverbial window through which I momentarily peered and contemplated life as a vegetarian.

But there was blood in the meadow that morning. One person pinned down a bird while another cut its windpipe. We held the five down until their bodies went limp, then carried them by their feet back down the hill, past the woods where a 900-pound pig named Boris snorted in his pen; he, too, would soon become part of a Bolognese. I stopped just outside the kitchen doors of the restaurant, grasping my bird's gray feet. I dunked her body in boiling water and plucked her. White feathers filled the air and floated off like a cloud in the sunlight. I thrust my hands deep into her cavity. It was still warm. I slid my hands high up the inside of the breastbone and felt the windpipe and heart and gizzard and intestines and pulled them out in one handful. I severed her feet and head and removed the yellow gland at her tail. I sliced open the gizzard and pulled out the sack of grain she had eaten that morning, the grain still whole. I spread it back out onto the field for the other turkeys to eat.

That day, I used every edible part of the animal and treated it with integrity from the field to the plate. The experience awakened a dormant, primal part of me, and more so, it made the kind of sense to me that I could feel deep in my marrow. As I went on to work in other four-star restaurants in New York and in France, I still wanted to know more, and soon found myself going one step farther down this path, away from the grocery aisle and into the wild.

The Girl Hunter

In Roman mythology, the master of the hunt was the goddess Diana. She was praised for her strength, athletic grace, beauty, and hunting skills. In Freemasonry, she was a symbol of sensibility and imagination, of poets and artists. Shrines were erected in her honor; stags followed her wherever she went; she ruled the forest and the moon.

I like to think that Diana's influence has never entirely waned, that hunting was never just about men getting together in the woods. Hunting is an extension of our being both humans and animals—our first work and craft, one of our original instincts.

We are what we are—omnivores. We were meant to participate in nature rather than keep it at arm's length. I see evidence everywhere that we have become so self-conscious in nature that we now designate areas where those "wild" traits are allowed to be expressed, to the point that the wilderness has become the last great zoo. And it turns our natural human instincts into an abstract condition, rather than a natural human state. Humans have less potential in these contrived landscapes than they do in places, cultures, and behaviors closer to our evolutionary beginnings. Modern life conceals our need for diverse, wild, natural communities, but it does not alter that need.

Often in response to this people tell me, "I don't think I could do it." The good news is that you don't have to. But if you want to feel what it is like to be human again, you should hunt, even if just once. Because that understanding, I believe, will propel a shift in how we view and interact with this world that we eat in. And the kind of food we demand, as omnivores, will never be the same.

Now that I have revealed the cornerstone of my food philosophy, I am going take you on a wild and often bumpy ride from field to stream to table.

In a single year, I set out to discover if it is truly possible today to live off the best your hands can produce. Is it possible to eat only the meat that you kill? And is that kind of kill more humane than the rest of it? This is my road trip, my ride on the back of an ATV chasing wild hogs along the banks of the Mississippi; my dove hunt with beer and barbecue; my visit to the birthplace of the Delta Blues, a cigar and Scotch at dusk, smoked hog and molasses, all in the name of knowing and understanding what it means to be an omnivore in this modern world that we live in.

The people that you meet along the way—the men, and the occasional woman—were generous with their invitations and all of them were my teachers. Their names have been changed to protect their privacy and respect their generosity. You'll see the good, the bad, and the ugly on this journey, including my ill-advised fearlessness, and hopefully will learn as I learned. Most important, you'll see the transformation of a stiletto heels–wearing girl who, yes, lived close to the land while growing up, but had never truly *lived close to the land*. You'll see it's possible for absolutely anyone, no matter how strapped to city life, to change, to become more one both with nature and with being human.*

The pleasures of eating are trumpeted loudly in today's society and that is a wonderful thing: But the pleasures of *knowing* what occurred on the journey from the field to the table are just as important, because the food tastes so much better that way. . . .

---

*In addition to the story, you'll find recipes at the end of the chapters, and at the end of the book you'll find some "gravy" that delves into the basic stocks, sauces, and marinades so fundamental to any cooking. There are notes in the gravy section on how wild animals can be interchanged with ones you find in the store, so that you can make all of these recipes without a trip to the woods.

I do not hunt for the joy of killing but for the joy of living,
and the inexpressible pleasure of mingling my life however briefly,
with that of a wild creature that I respect, admire and value.

—JOHN MADSON

1

The Beginning and the End

They say you always remember your first time. For me it was that turkey hunt four years ago, early on a Saturday morning deep in the Arkansas Delta, in a place they call the Village. It was after a spring night spent drinking aged Scotch and smoking cigars on a wide veranda with some of the most gregarious and unpretentious Southerners I had ever encountered. They were well-heeled country folk who liked to live large and take no prisoners when it came to what they stood for and the life they prized. Good food was a huge part of that life, and on that particular evening before the hunt, there were rows of silver-haired men smoking cigars, mud caked to their leather boots, before a granite table bearing endless stacks of cheese and freshly baked bread, and a mound of salad that could feed a regiment. Meats—cacciatorini, salami, ham, pork belly, catfish, and other delectables, too—were piled high on platters, and, of course, we had collard greens with white macaroni, and chips and dips. And there was plenty to wash it all down: red wine, beers in large tubs with ice spilling out over the edges, and then the whiskey before the meal and after, too, when everyone moved gradually into the smoking room by the fireplace and the guitars emerged, and the loose, hard notes of the blues drifted beautifully overhead in a haze of Cuban cigar smoke, a sort of bacchanal to welcome in the warmth of spring and summer and, more important, the start of turkey season.

After I missed my first turkey in the Delta, I spent many afternoons in a shooting range at home among fathers and sons, blasting clay pigeons, while an elderly man named Walter gently adjusted my stance and raised my elbows just slightly and taught me what it meant to get my head down on the gun. Now in retirement, Walter released clay pigeons at the trap range as his pastime, and we had a Friday afternoon date of sorts. It was among these kindly men and their adolescent sons that I learned to "pattern" a shotgun, to make sure the spread of the pellets was even on a target, and that not all ammunition was called bullets. It was with Walter and my other unlikely tutors that I learned shotgun ammunition was called shells; and rifle ammunition was called cartridges; and a 20-gauge shotgun was lighter than a 12-gauge, and they continued to become lighter as the numbers went up. It was also where I learned to sight in a rifle to make sure the scope was accurately mounted, and that I could spend years studying all of this and still not know it all. So I just figured out what I needed to know, and after trying out all the guns like Goldilocks, decided that a 270-caliber rifle and a 20-gauge shotgun were *just right*.

Now still, so many seasons later, so many hunts later, the arrival of the wild turkey in spring marks the beginning of certain things for me, and also the end. The earth has begun to warm; I can smell it just as much as I can feel it. It is the last hurrah of the hunting season, when the earth erupts in color and rain. The light starts to come up along the edge of the trees to the east earlier than it has for months, and I can hear the sounds of nature slowly rolling out of bed—rustling, squeaking, groaning, stretching.

There is so much waiting in a hunter's life, so much silence and space between the lines, and in that space a whole world exists. It is rare to know how much time passes by while you are in this world, but wild turkeys mark the end of your time there, because they are the last big hunt before the season ends and the long summer months begin.

Now, as I drive along the Sonoma California coast toward a midmorning turkey hunt, that is what I think about, that this is the end for a while. It is the last chance to hear the owls agitate the turkeys at daylight—and to hear the turkeys gobble back as the house wakes up.

My hunting partner is a man named Sean who was born and raised on the Sonoma coast. His girlfriend, an enthusiastic follower of my blog, has volunteered him to me and so he waits for me warily in Bodega Bay, leaning against the end of his pickup, watching the salmon boats come in. He is tall and lean and in his early thirties. He is dressed in beige canvas workpants, heavy boots, and a faded T-shirt that suggest he wears these every day, as if they have become part of his very form, an extension of his lifestyle. Sean is an expert underwater hunter—he often dives for his food, fetching abalone and salmon with a spear among the great white sharks of the Pacific. Through the years he became such an expert at underwater hunting that he began to lead expeditions in the Pacific and in Mexico. It was his ever-growing passion for eating what his own hands could procure that eventually led him to hunt on dry land as well. Hunting was a process of discovery that became a natural extension of his lifestyle.

"It just felt so natural to me. It made sense," he says as we drive along the winding road in his truck. "I grew up fishing with my dad, but it wasn't until I befriended some locals here who took me under their wing, that I started hunting game. And then it became the primary source of my meat eating. I don't have a taste for store-bought meat anymore."

Befriending the local landowners was essential. Sean admits that the ranch families here are very different than he is, in many ways, in terms of their values and politics. But they discovered that they had something to offer each other—Sean could teach them about hunting in the sea, and they could teach him about hunting the lush Sonoma land. As he says this we turn into a dairy farm to meet one of these locals, Marcus Scruggs, whom Sean describes as a "man's man."

Scruggs looks as if he could be a street fighter—scrappy, medium height, with a permanent scowl etched into the contours of his face. He gives me a keen once-over before he begins to talk, a look that I have gotten more times than I can count by now. "Are you ready to hunt some turkeys?" he asks with more than a hint of skepticism. "Yep," I reply. He walks away without responding.

The three of us squeeze into Scruggs's two-seat pickup and drive to a local sheep dairy to seek out wild turkeys. "I'm a coyote hunter," Scruggs says as we drive. He stops several times to survey the rolling hills with his binoculars, to see if there are any coyotes lurking among the cattle. By day, and when he is not coyote hunting, Scruggs builds bridges. But there's something about coyotes that really get him talking.

As we turn into the sheep dairy, a large tom, a male wild turkey, fans his tail in the field next to the truck. "That's a beauty. Look at that beard," Sean says, eyeing the cluster of wiry feathers that grow from a male turkey's chest.

"Yeah, it is," Scruggs says. "The domestic birds these days are like Orange County women. Their breasts are really big but at some point you have to ask yourself why."

I decide not to shoot the ol' tom. It doesn't feel very sportsman-like without some exertion on my part. Besides, I think he is too close to the road. So we drive further into the dairy land.

The air is wet as we drive past steaming piles of sheep dung, through the perfume of eucalyptus, then high into the green hills. Finally we come to the rounded peak of a short grass hill, and we slow to survey the scene. As we step out to walk, the sky is changing, and dark clouds are stacking.

"It won't rain," Scruggs says. "You need a south wind for it to rain."

We walk farther, through the sweet dirty smell of hay and past an occasional cow blocking the muddy road, running wildly ahead of us, then off the road in a frenzy of flying saliva and guttural snorts.

In the silence of this alternate wilderness, you almost see the gentle rhythm as things happen—condors descend majestically on their prey, squirrels run frantically, golden eagles hang-glide above our heads, dipping and then reemerging with rabbits clutched in their talons. It all unfolds like a well-thought-out ballet, a logical pattern of energy being transferred from one organism to the next.

And then it begins. "Jakes!" Scruggs shouts in a whisper, grabbing my shoulder and spinning me around, binoculars suctioned to his eyes. I feel a heavy stillness, thick and promising, as I step higher onto the hill and see three jakes—the young male turkeys, the best-tasting wild turkeys you can hope to hunt during a California spring, when hens are off-limits and old turkeys are tough.

"They don't have very big beards," Scruggs says, squinting through his binoculars again.

"I don't care about size," I say. He looks at me and gives me that keen once-over again.

"You don't?" he says with an eyebrow raised.

"No."

He pauses to contemplate. "Okay, then follow me."

The three of us walk farther along the green pasture and tread along the edge of a gully, watching them from the shadows of the brush, languidly selecting insects and digging for worms with their undeveloped spurs, moving through the clover and crabgrass. One jake begins his mating march—dragging his wings behind him, fanning his colorful tail feathers, making a low spitting and drumming sound like a gong. He keeps dancing forward, like some fine-feathered Fred Astaire.

Sean and Scruggs begin to fall behind as I creep along the brush. In part it is because they expect me to shoot now. (For some reason, men always expect me to shoot earlier than I ever do.) But I keep crawling along the bushes with one of Sean's 12-gauges clenched in my hands. It takes a long time to move just a few yards. I freeze again and again as the jakes look straight at me. Some say that if their sense of smell were as acute as their sight or hearing, we would never be able to catch them.

Wild turkeys are the ultimate test for a seasoned hunter. They teach you things—that the hunt itself is the great thing, not the amount of game you take home. There are many times when you leave the woods empty handed, and all you can do is salute an ol' gobbler for outsmarting you.

I keep inching along, watching the jakes' dark crimson tail feathers move through the high grass, as they flex their muscles for the hens they hope to attract. When I reach a small clearing in the brush, where the hill meets the gully, I finally sit and watch them strut. I don't know where Sean and Scruggs are anymore; my head is a kaleidoscope of adrenaline mixed with visions of turkey Tetrazzini.

I feel my hand tighten on the shotgun as they begin their regal dance. I raise my right knee just slightly to stabilize my shot. Then two jakes move toward each other in the clearing, their identical silhouettes bobbing in the sun. And as two of the heads come together and become one, I slap the trigger of my shotgun and the silhouettes disappear.

Sean and Scruggs appear at my side, and I hear Sean shoot as the third jake runs up and over the crest of the hill.

"She got two!" Scruggs says somewhere behind me as the adrenaline quiets its coursing hum and stillness overtakes us.

"I think one of them was Sean's," I say. As I approach I can see the jakes now, lying in the tall crabgrass right where I had last seen them.

Scruggs shakes his head. "Two in one shot."

I can see that they are young, their beards not fully developed and their spurs rounded rather than sharp. Despite their youth, they are heavy, very heavy, as I lift them by their leathery feet and carry them off the field, their crimson feathers fanned out and enveloping me like parachutes for the world to see. "She got two," I hear Scruggs say again behind me, that skepticism in his voice gone now. "I think one of those was Sean's," I repeat. But he ignores me. "So where are we hunting next?" he asks.

Back at Sean's house we take the two turkeys into a wooded area and begin to pluck them, a few feathers at a time so that the skin doesn't tear. Sean's girlfriend, Ree, bursts through the kitchen doorway, her long, curly brown hair flying in her wake. She is ecstatic at our success, wanting to know the details and snapping photos as we pluck.

"Do you want to have this experience?" I ask her, smiling. "Yes!" she says, rolling up the sleeves of her plaid shirt. I step away from my half-plucked bird and let her pluck.

"Whoa," she says after a few plucks. "It's not that I'm grossed out . . . it's just that I definitely come from a grocery store kind of family."

Next we sever the wings at the first joint, then the head and feet. We cut a slit below the tail and remove the intestines, heart, and gizzard in one handful. From the top we cut another incision and remove the crop, all of the grain the bird has eaten in a day. "Eww," Ree says. "But in a good way."

In this moment, with the turkey warm in my hands, it all feels strangely familiar. Like the beginning. Like the very first time I killed a turkey on the softly sloping hill of a restaurant, the moment I felt the warm heart of a turkey in my hand and realized what it meant to be an omnivore. That was the moment that led to this one, the moment that made me a hunter.

There have been so many other moments between then and now, so many strange, primal, and transformative experiences. But I know much more now than I did that day when I harvested a domestic broad-breasted white with only a knife and my hands. Even though I had spent many hours at a stove, learning the highest forms of culinary creativity in esteemed restaurants, it was nothing like the education I found in the woods. I know now that turkeys, when given freedom in the wild, are like ghosts—if they're not vocal, you'd swear there aren't any within 100 miles. I know that subtle changes in barometric pressure or the weather make animals act differently. I know that distinct natural feeling of tapping into my original human instincts. Today I am much closer, perhaps as close as I will ever be, to where my food comes from, but it wasn't always this way. In fact, getting here it was more difficult than I expected.

Wild Turkey Schnitzel
Serves 6 to 8

Schnitzel is an Austrian breaded cutlet, thin and fried. The Austrian woman who first cooked it for me served it with lingonberry sauce, but it would also go well with cranberry relish or your favorite chutney. It could also be served with gravy, mashed potatoes, or on a sandwich with tomato sauce.

    1 turkey breast, cut thinly into slices, on the bias against the grain
    1 cup all-purpose flour
    1 teaspoon dried oregano
    1 teaspoon garlic powder
    1/4 teaspoon red pepper flakes
    1 egg
    1 cup panko
    1/2 teaspoon paprika
    1/2 cup grape seed oil (see Note)
    Salt and pepper
    1 lemon, cut into wedges
    Cranberry relish (page 228) or lingonberry sauce

1. Set three plates and one wide bowl on the counter. Place a sheet of plastic wrap on the counter and lay one turkey cutlet on it. Lay a second sheet of plastic over the turkey and pound it gently with a rolling pin, meat pounder, or wine bottle until it is thin and even. Set the cutlet on the first plate. Pound the remaining cutlets and add to the first plate.
2. Place the flour, oregano, garlic powder, and red pepper flakes on the second plate and mix. Place the egg in the bowl and beat it lightly with a fork. On the third plate, combine the panko and paprika.
3. Heat the grape seed oil on medium heat in a skillet until a sprinkle of flour into the oil sizzles. Lay a turkey cutlet first into the flour mixture, then the egg wash, then the bread crumbs and place directly in the hot oil. Cook for about 2 minutes on each side and transfer to a rack set over a sheet tray or paper towel. Sprinkle with salt and pepper to preserve the crispness. Serve immediately with a wedge of lemon and cranberry relish or lingonberry sauce.

Also try: wild boar, antlered game, upland game birds, rabbit, duck

Note: Throughout this book, you'll notice my singular affinity for grape seed oil. This is a holdover instinct from my days in professional kitchens. Grape seed oil, like other vegetable oils and unlike olive oil, has a relatively high smoke point, which makes it good for cooking. But what I like most about grape seed oil is its light, clean taste that is less assertive than that of many of the other oils and therefore doesn't affect the flavor of the final dish. That said, you can use other vegetable oils if they are what you have on hand. If you are looking to simply "finish" a dish post-cooking, high-quality extra virgin olive oil is best.

Wild Turkey and Oyster Stew
Serves 8

This dish is a play on spring and all of the wild ramps and fresh peas that pop up during the turkey season. If you can't find wild ramps in your area, green garlic, green onions, or leeks are a nice substitute. The key is to use the fresh spring ingredients indigenous to your area. This is also a great way to use the carcass and leg meat of the turkey, which can be tougher and is best cooked for a longer time. In addition to cubing the leg meat, you can add the carcass with the breasts removed and let the meat fall off into the stew, then remove the carcass at the end of cooking.

1 head of garlic
1 tablespoon olive oil
6 tablespoons butter
All-purpose flour
Salt and pepper
2 cups wild turkey leg meat, cubed, plus leg bones and carcass if available
1 cup ramps, green onions, or leeks, sliced into 1-inch lengths
1/2 cup poblano pepper, diced
1 cup oyster mushrooms
1 cup dried shiitake or porcini mushrooms
2 slices lemon
3 bay leaves
1 cup Marsala
6 cups turkey stock (page 214)
2 cups leafy greens, such as kale or Swiss chard, chopped
1 cup fresh peas
1 cup fresh flat-leaf parsley leaves
1 cup raw oysters, either canned or freshly shucked, then diced
2 tablespoons Worcestershire sauce

1. Preheat the oven to 350°F. Place the head of garlic in tinfoil and drizzle with olive oil. Close the tinfoil and place in the oven. Cook until the cloves are soft, about 1 hour. Remove from the oven and squeeze the cloves out of the garlic skin. Mash with a spoon on a cutting board and set aside.
2. Melt half of the butter in a large heavy-bottomed stew pot over medium heat until it is frothy and bubbling. Dust the turkey with flour, salt, and pepper and brown in the butter on both sides, about 5 minutes total. Transfer the turkey to a plate and set aside.
3. To the same pot, add the remaining butter, ramps, poblano pepper, and mushrooms. Season with salt to help release the juices and let sweat until tender, about 5 minutes more.
4. Add the turkey, roasted garlic, lemon, and bay leaves and cook for 2 minutes more. Sprinkle with 1 tablespoon of flour and stir for 1 minute to cook the flour. Deglaze with the Marsala and cook until reduced by half. Add the stock and bring to a simmer. Cook, covered, for 1 hour, and in the last 30 minutes, add the peas, greens, parsley, and diced oysters. Finish with Worcestershire and salt and pepper to taste.

Also try: upland game birds, rabbit, squirrel

Whiskey-Glazed Turkey Breast

Serves 4

Turkey feathers are quite easy to pluck as long as you do just a few at a time so the skin doesn't tear. It is better to leave the skin on, because attempting to remove it while the feathers are still on can result in a feathery mess. If you don't have skin on your turkey breast, simply layer it with bacon or lard before cooking. It is essential that you brine the breast meat before cooking it. I have a friend that uses a brine of simple filtered water from the sea, which has ample salt, then after 24 hours, switches to a bath of unsalted purified water. Or if you're not feeling quite as adventurous, you can also use homemade brine.

   6 tablespoons butter
   1 turkey breast, skin on and brined (page 220)
   Salt and pepper
   8 to 10 strips of bacon, or equivalent in lard (for breasts without skin only)
   1 cup turkey stock (page 214)
   3 tablespoons honey
   6 tablespoons whiskey
   1 tablespoon grated orange zest
   2 tablespoons freshly squeezed orange juice
   1/2 teaspoon cayenne

1. Preheat the oven to 325°F. In an ovenproof skillet or Dutch oven, heat 2 tablespoons of the butter until it begins to bubble. Sprinkle the skin of the brined turkey breast with salt and pepper. If the breast is without skin, wrap it with bacon or lard and fasten with toothpicks or kitchen twine as needed. Place the breast skin side down in the butter, sprinkle the underside with salt and pepper, and let the skin brown for about 5 minutes. Turn it over and add the stock. Cover with foil or a lid and transfer to the oven.
2. In a separate skillet, melt the remaining 4 tablespoons of butter over medium heat. Whisk in the honey until well incorporated. Add the whiskey along with the orange zest and juice and cayenne and whisk together. Turn the heat to low and let the glaze reduce by half. Turn off the heat and set aside.
3. Once the turkey has cooked for 10 minutes, brush with half of the glaze and re-cover. Roast for 20 more minutes, brush with the remaining glaze, leave uncovered, and increase the temperature to 400°F. Cook for 15 to 20 minutes more, or until the internal temperature reads 140° to 150°F.
4. Remove the turkey from the oven, cover with foil for 10 minutes before slicing, and serving.

Also try: upland game birds

Swedish Turkey Meatballs   Makes 4 small portions

This is a traditional Scandinavian dish that is comforting and rich. The addition of lingonberry sauce at the end gives it an underlying sweetness, while the yogurt gives it a tang. The meat and gravy is ideally suited for mashed potatoes, which makes this hearty dish especially good for fall turkey season.

6 tablespoons butter
1/2 cup finely diced shallots (you can use a food processor for this)
4 cloves garlic, minced (you can use a food processor for this)
1 pound ground turkey leg meat
1 whole egg
3/4 cup bread crumbs
1/4 cup sherry
1 tablespoon Worcestershire sauce
1/2 cup chopped fresh parsley
1/4 teaspoon ground allspice
1/4 teaspoon ground nutmeg
1/2 teaspoon ground cardamom
1/2 teaspoon sea salt
1/2 teaspoon freshly ground pepper
3 cups turkey stock (page 214)
3 tablespoons all-purpose flour
1 tablespoon lingonberry sauce or red currant jelly, plus more for serving
1/4 cup plain yogurt

1. In a skillet on medium heat melt 2 tablespoons of the butter until it bubbles. Add the shallots and garlic and sweat over low heat until soft and translucent, about 4 minutes. Sprinkle with a pinch of salt to help release the moisture. Turn off the heat and let cool for 5 minutes.

2. In a mixing bowl, combine the turkey, egg, bread crumbs, sherry, Worcestershire sauce, parsley, allspice, nutmeg, cardamom, salt, and pepper. Add the cooled shallot mixture and incorporate.

3. Shape the turkey mixture into 1-inch balls and place on a sheet tray or plate. You should end up with about twenty meatballs.

4. Heat the turkey stock in a small pot and bring to a simmer, then turn off the heat and set aside.

5. In the skillet, melt the remaining 4 tablespoons of butter over medium heat. Cook the balls for about 1 minute on each side, just so they are browned but not cooked through. Depending on the size of your pan, you may need to cook them in batches so as not to overcrowd the pan. With a slotted spoon or tongs, transfer to a clean plate.

6. Once all of the meat has been browned, use the pan juices to make a sauce. Whisk in the flour until it is thick and clumpy and let cook for a few minutes while you whisk. A thick paste will form. Next, whisk in the warm stock a little at a time until you have a light brown sauce.

7. Let the sauce thicken slightly, then return the turkey meatballs to the pan. Cook, uncovered, over low heat for 10 minutes, stirring occasionally, until the sauce reduces further. Turn off the heat and whisk in the lingonberry sauce and yogurt. Serve immediately with additional lingonberry sauce on the side.

Also try: wild boar, antlered game, upland game birds, rabbit, squirrel, duck

No, I'm not a good shot, but I shoot often.
—THEODORE ROOSEVELT

2

The Village

Every year, as hunting season begins in the heat of an Indian summer, my first hunt is in the Village.

While I drive on the thin line of blacktop through the southeast portion of Arkansas, the mist gets thicker as the earth slinks away from the sun. There is something elemental here, evidence of a once vibrant life that's passed. Many things are half-collapsed. I see overturned trucks and pervasive rust. Some towns come and go with each flutter of the eye, and some linger a little bit longer . . . like McGehee, a town that emits a sudden flash of light in the gray night; where far back in a cornfield is a football stadium so bright and so polished that for a moment it is the most gentrified city in the south. The stadium is full, containing 3,881 townsfolk and all of their pride. And then I see why—a rough-hewn crooked wooden sign on my right, hand painted by a townsman, announces that in the next thirty seconds, I will be passing through the home of the Owls, the State Football Champions of Arkansas.

Along the lake is a house that smells of cooking, and a housekeeper named Betty, who is still repairing the ravages of the night before as the sun sets again. Men sit in antique lawn chairs, regarding the mystic order of the heavens, wondering what part of it all is theirs. Their families are called the Mancinis and the Berberas and the Pagonis, the descendents of the Italian and Lebanese immigrants that came to this place in search of wealth.

On the great lawn beside the lake, a black barrel smoker slowly rotates the bodies of twenty-five chickens, their juices dripping, their skin bewitched to a dark gold. Whiskey and thirty-year-old Châteauneuf-du-Pape appear from the depths of the cellar. There are ribs soaked in apple juice, cooked until the edges are rendered to a caramel crust, and tabbouleh and hummus, and crawfish corn muffins to honor the visitors from New Orleans, and a porcelain bowl of baked beans as sweet as candy and musty with hickory smoke.

In every direction are the flickering embers of lighted tobacco floating across sun-weathered eyes, smoke-flavored conversations, and a man injecting an imagined noun with the wave of his hand. On the mantel, a Bundt cake drips with sticky white icing.

Roger Mancini leans his shiny head back on a green antique lawn chair, his teeth clamped firmly down on the cigar protruding from the side of his mouth. He is conveying his wisdom to some young men who lean in intently: "Don't be wishin' you were fishin'," I hear him say. He turns to listen to his Italian neighbor Nero play his guitar, making up lyrics as he goes. They take turns; Roger interjects a few, then Nero returns. And then more people come and sit and sip and sing, and a few others play, too, and it sounds like poetry.

Across the great sloping lawn, the boys on a party barge can be heard howling in the distance, an octave too high, weaving along the lake between the cypress trees suspended on the surface of the water.

Inside, one of the wealthiest men in Arkansas sits at the long mahogany table and tilts his head back and looks up at the ceiling. He will spend five months of this year on his boat, drifting through the Southern Hemisphere, and the rest in this unknown village, deep in the Delta.

Cassidy walks in with a bag of bread from his commercial bakery in New Orleans, and the Commish glides in and out with the rib grease on his hands. He is a man of few words, but when he does talk, people pause to listen.

When you leave this place to find sleep, you always go kicking into the night, through the bug swarms in the pool of a single fluorescent streetlight, the hound dogs prancing after you with saliva spraying from their jowls. And you look at the clock and it is one. And almost immediately afterward, you look at the clock and find it is five. And you climb out of bed with the taste of whiskey still in your blood and quickly swallow some instant coffee and a banana.

This is the rhythm of the Arkansas dove hunt. This is how I always find it year after year, untouched by time. Dove hunting is a social affair, to be sure, and so I imagine there are many variations on the same theme around the country on this day, the opening day of dove season.

The Commish always arrives ten minutes early in his white pickup. It is one thing in life you can rely on. His truck is full of gear that changes only slightly, depending on what is available to hunt. But it always contains the cooler, full of ice, water, Gatorade, Coke, and beer. And there are many articles of camouflage, from chairs to hats to rubber boots. And there is a dog named Humphrey, a golden Lab who likes to put his tongue to the wind as we drive swiftly along the dirt road in the unquiet darkness of the morning.

The Commish is fifty-eight and is both a planter and a banker. He oversees a chain of banks, and owns and operates thousands of acres of farmland. As we drive along the road together, the flatland and rich alluvial soil are partitioned—700 acres here, 600 acres there—and a lot of what you see is his. In the Village, people are many things at once—a planter and a lawyer, a storeowner and a doctor. This is how people have always forged a life for themselves along the great Mississippi Delta.

When the first pioneer farmers entered the Mississippi River Valley, they found a formidable and forbidding world of dense forests and swamps that evoked a primeval world. There were enormous stands of oak, gum, cottonwood, hickory, pecan, elm, pine, and cypress, some more than five hundred years old.

These early-nineteenth-century farmers carved out plantations and small farms for themselves and set out on a long struggle to cultivate the Delta—a struggle that meant controlling floods, draining swamps, and clearing the land. The land along the powerful Mississippi River was continually crushed by heavy floods, including the most devastating Great Mississippi Flood of 1927, which changed lives for generations. Running in some places to a depth of 100 feet, the flooding also left behind even richer soil.

This place has always been a slowly cascading sequence of anomalies; a place where people fought the elements and the river for decades to become great established families, transforming their lives from hunting panthers in the overgrown cane jungle that engulfed their plantations, to attending European opera festivals—this place would come to be known as the Alluvial Empire. There was a time not long ago when cotton was king and the settlers of this region were considered "the aristocrats of the earth."

The Mississippi River and its wild chocolate waves at once created great wealth and great destruction for those who fought to tame it. Above all, the river perpetuated the plantation system, which prospered in the antebellum period but finally collapsed under the pressure of the Great Depression and World War II. Sharecropping replaced slavery after the Civil War, as Chinese and then Italians migrated in hopes of owning land. They had a cashless economy that relied on the rise and fall of cotton to fuel commerce, keeping many tenant farmers dependent on landowners.

The contemporary Delta remains a product of its plantation heritage. There still remains a modern form of sharecropping, now called tenant farming. But no one lives in the few remaining old plantation homes that glide by our window as we drive, because no one can afford the rent—another reminder that poverty runs deep here, as does old wealth.

The Delta has one of the lowest population densities in the American South, sometimes less than one person per square mile. The demographics are the same as they were before the Civil War. This is one of those preserved places, its authenticity both inspiring and heartbreaking at once. It is where you make your own destiny and you make your own food.

The Commish talks most when he is on his way to a hunt. He will tell you things, such as why his state is so poor. "Farming methods have changed," he says quite simply. "And the population declined as the farming methods changed from human hands to mechanized labor." The young people leave, too, reducing the state income and increasing illiteracy and unemployment, leading inexorably to extreme poverty.

When we arrive, the other trucks are parked in a cluster on the outskirts of the field, all the boys and men stand in their camouflage, yawning and sluggish, and sucking in hot coffee. The Commish stops and rolls down his window to check on them, then continues on, along the dirt road, his truck tossing clay in its wake.

He finds a promising patch of land and sets up two small folding chairs in front of a field of dead sunflowers, facing the cotton—millions of milky white balls of it that begin to glow iridescently as the orange sun rises, turning the boys in the distance into black silhouettes.

We sit in silence and watch the sunrise and feel the orange heat on our faces and the bubbles of Diet Cokes on our tongues.

"You know what time it is?" the Commish says.

"What time?" I reply.

"Cigar time."

I begin to smell the strands of sweet tobacco as the sun begins to tear through the field, and the doves begin to flutter in. They descend, silently, sparingly, toward the wheat that has been scattered by the farmers to sweeten the field. Killdeer weave in and out of the doves and I try not to mix them up as I swing my shotgun and slap the trigger.

Dove hunting centers around their feeding patterns: Doves feed in the morning at sunrise, and in the late afternoon, and because this marks the beginning of hunting season in many states, you will see many hunters out twice per day at first, satisfying their thirst after the eternal spring and summer drought.

"Do you remember your first hunt?" I ask, while we watch the sun rise.

"My first hunt was a dove hunt with my dad and his friends. I was probably five or six years old," he says. The Commish talks about doves and hunting and life, in equal parts words and silence, in between the crisp report of his Benelli shotgun. He is one of the rare people who can say just as much with silence as with words.

"Any highway is like a buffet line for doves," he finally says out loud, as Humphrey retrieves and drops a dove into his palm.

What he means is that all of the fields, now in their most fertile state, are a distraction for the doves, which draws them elsewhere and sometimes makes the sit-and-wait method less successful, as the doves dip in and out of the vast buffet of farmland sandwiched on either side of the thin line of blacktop cutting through southeast Arkansas. This season, though, is expected to be one of the best dove seasons ever.

"The dove population is up this year because of a dry spring and summer, which increased their nesting success," he says. "We usually plant sunflowers, which doves love to feed on. Some harvested agricultural fields are great places to hunt during certain times of the season. Water holes are great afternoon spots, also."

But for most hunters like the Commish, any hunt is about the experience itself, sitting here and watching the sun rise with his dog and his cigar, not really the amount of game they take.

"My wife has always viewed hunting as 'the other woman,'" he eventually says.

We sit for hours, or maybe minutes, longer; time passes differently here. As the doves are fetched one at a time and added to the pile,

this hunt feels strangely anticlimactic. It is beautiful here, it is peace-
ful (save for the blasts into the sky), but am I allowed to sit like this
when I hunt? Don't I have to experience a little pain? I think about
this as tendrils of cigar smoke float by and the Commish asks me
about the book I am writing, and about my father.

"He's a vegan," I say.

"A who?"

"A vegan."

"What's that?"

"Someone who doesn't eat meat or dairy or other animal products."

"I never heard of that," he says, letting out another shot and sending Humphrey darting into the cotton field.

In the end, the sun casts shadows onto the theatrical faces of the
fading sunflowers, as we fold up the chairs and carry our gear to
the truck.

We congregate with the boys and men back where we left them
and begin to clean the birds. The men puff on cigars and a few of the
boys raise their eyebrows at me as I begin to pluck a dove. It is most
common to breast the small birds and toss the rest. But when I tell
them I am a bit of a purist, they pluck, too. And I show them how to
gut the bird and cut off the gland at the tail and they watch intently
and begin to pluck some more, and then we form an assembly line
and soon have fourteen plucked doves among us.

As we drive away, the air smells of burning rice straw, and the fields
are a vision of black and gold stripes. I begin to notice that some people walk along the sides of the infinite roads because they don't have
cars. The Commish doesn't react because it is such a familiar sight.
He tells me about the time he met the Horse Whisperer, an Australian
man who walked the roads all the way from Nashville and could tame
a wild horse in an afternoon. But even an anomaly like that is com-
monplace here.

We go to breakfast at LJ's, the only place to go, where the bathroom soap is thinned out with water, and the morning soap opera
plays on mute; where an elderly couple sits side by side reading the

paper, and a pair of curly-haired mother-daughter clones sit across from each other, eating their pancakes in silence.

Cassidy and Peter sit at the end of our table, eating a morning cheeseburger and talking about the best sausage maker in town, Jimmy Little.

The Commish extends his arm slowly to reveal his watch from under his sleeve, then brings it to his face and squints his dark eyes through rimless glasses. "Jimmy Little's funeral is in ten minutes," he says as if announcing the price of corn.

The table is silent again as we eat our western omelets and greasy, succulent hash.

The rest of the day in the Village consists of a deep afternoon nap and a visit with Roger Mancini in his antique workshop; and then the Commish heads over to his farmland, where one of his workers has a photographic memory and will recite the baseball scores from the last twenty years if you ask him to.

But then at night, the stage lights up again, the lake reflects the moonlight like one thousand angry diamonds, the glasses jingle, and the cigars smoke.

The walls of Roger Mancini's smoking room resound with the sounds of Faulkner as he imparts his wisdom to the young people again, a kind of wisdom that will linger with them for days after. "If it's not of substance, it will never be a success. Nothing in history has been," and "Be happy with what you're doing," and "If the world can live without Winston Churchill, they can live without me," and then howling laughter as someone says, "This wine is so good that if it was any better, God would have kept it for himself!"

We sit around the mahogany table again and eat dove putach, a traditional Italian stew filled with tomatoes and wine and whole doves. And then beer-battered fried dove breast, and then cold poached dove and pears in brandy.

"This meal makes me want to learn to shoot better," someone says. "My plate looks like a biology class," someone else says, chuckling as he wipes the vestiges of putach from his plate with a piece of Cassidy's bread. "We're suffering from extreme comfort."

It is not recorded when this lake became a lake. Some suspect it was when the Mississippi River changed course and the forces of erosion cut the bend in her flow, forming a crescent-shaped lake. This is the place where it all began for me and the place I keep coming back to. It is where I missed my first turkey and where I tasted my first hog slowly smoking in a dome-shaped grill. It is a place of such sweet sadness, of nostalgia, of blues pioneers, and in some ways of hope for what could be. It is a place some people like to ignore because it doesn't smack of success and commerce. But it is a place that can change the meaning of success for some; where you can still find comfort in the simplest of things—in the wild tonic of the rain, and the salty crunch of a simple fried dove harvested with your own hands on an orange morning and consumed in the same night. It is a place where time moves differently, a place where you can settle into a deep vinous sleep.

It is all so easy, so deceptively easy, to hunt and gather and live well here if you have means. It is because this place, of all the places I've ever met, is untouched by time. It is easy to live off the land when you have no other choice. In a way it is choice that plagues our modern food system, our expectation that there will be seven kinds of peanut butter on the shelves of the grocery store, and twelve brands of boneless, skinless chicken breast in the refrigerated aisle. And I wonder if living off the land successfully is possible anywhere but in the Village.

Beer-Battered Fried Dove Breast
Serves 6 to 8

Doves are one of the easiest birds to pluck and so can easily be kept whole. But if you simply like to breast your dove, as many people do, this recipe is simple and requires only ingredients that are usually on hand anyway during a dove hunt—birds and beer. The beer and baking powder give the breast a puffiness and a crunch. It is the perfect complement to that rich liver flavor dove tends to have. I recommend a sweet-and-sour or barbecue dipping sauce (see pages 226 and 227), though the battered dove is also nice just as it is.

    30 dove breasts, bone in
    4 cups vegetable or grape seed oil
    2 cups all-purpose flour
    1 tablespoon baking powder
    1 teaspoon salt
    1 (12-ounce) can beer
    Salt and pepper

1. Rinse the dove breasts under cold water until the water runs clear. Pat the breasts dry with paper towels and set aside on a plate.
2. In a medium-size pot wide enough to hold about eight dove breasts at a time, heat the oil over a medium flame. The wider your pot, the more vegetable oil you will need to completely submerge the dove breasts.
3. In a large bowl, combine the flour, baking powder, and salt. Slowly whisk in the beer until the liquid is uniform and the consistency of thick syrup.
4. Using your fingers or a fork, dip one breast in the batter until it is uniformly covered. Dip one side of the breast in the hot oil to see if it immediately sizzles. If it doesn't, wait for the oil to get hotter. Keep testing with the same dove breast, then add more battered breasts, enough to cover the bottom of the pot.
5. Once one side of the breast is golden brown, turn it over and cook the other side until golden brown, 5 to 7 minutes total.
6. Set a wire rack over a sheet tray. Remove the breasts from the pot with a slotted spoon and place them on the rack. Sprinkle all sides with salt and pepper to help retain the crispiness for serving.
7. Repeat until all the dove breasts are cooked, and serve immediately.

Also try: brant, coot, duck, gallinule, goose, grouse, prairie chicken, partridge, pheasant, pigeon, ptarmigan, quail, rail, snipe, turkey, squirrel, rabbit

Poached Dove and Pears
in Brandy Sauce

Serves 4, as an appetizer

This starter is cool and light, but with a hint of fall, like Labor Day or an Indian summer. It is perfect when temperatures can still be hot, and the rich, heavy game recipes aren't quite suitable yet. Brandy and vermouth round out these sweet and gamey flavors—the vermouth is subtle and rich and the brandy, which you light on fire, gives it all a caramel finish. The blue cheese adds the salty tang and the mint ensures that it is fresh and not too cloying. There wasn't a speck left in the bowl after my fellow hunters and I sat down to dinner.

 10 to 15 dove breasts, peeled from the breastbone
 2 cups ripe pears, peeled, cored, and quartered
 1 cup vermouth
 1/2 cup brandy
 1 tablespoon thinly sliced fresh mint
 2 tablespoons crumbled blue cheese
 Freshly ground black pepper

1. Place the dove and pears in a wide saucepan or sauté pan. Pour in the vermouth and poach, uncovered, at a low simmer for 10 minutes, turning over halfway through.
2. Add the brandy, light it with a match, and let the alcohol burn off.
3. With a slotted spoon, remove the pears and dove from the liquid and transfer to a bowl. Reduce the remaining liquid by half and pour it into the bowl.
4. Chill in the refrigerator for at least 30 minutes.
5. Before serving, add the mint, blue cheese, and pepper to taste. Toss and serve.

Also try: brant, coot, duck, gallinule, goose, grouse, prairie chicken, partridge, pheasant, pigeon, ptarmigan, quail, rail, snipe, turkey, squirrel, rabbit

14-Dove Putach   Serves 8 to 10

This is my take on a very traditional Italian dish made frequently in the Mississippi Delta region. Most people there have memories of putach made by their mother, grandmother, or great-aunt. It works with many kinds of meat, but what makes it a true putach is the vinegar and rosemary base. People add their own elements from there—crushed tomatoes, potatoes—I have even seen the addition of Cajun sausage. My version on a warm September afternoon went like this:

    2 tablespoons grape seed oil
    14 whole doves, plucked, gutted, feet trimmed, and wings cut at first joint
    2 cups red wine
    2 large onions, chopped
    3 cups button mushrooms, quartered
    10 to 12 gloves garlic, crushed
    1 sprig fresh rosemary
    1/2 cup fresh basil leaves
    1/2 cup red wine vinegar
    1 (6-ounce) can tomato paste
    3/4 cup diced tomatoes
    1/3 cup Worcestershire sauce
    4 cups water
    2 tablespoons red pepper flakes
    1 cup peeled and chopped carrots (optional)
    4 cups potatoes that have been sliced 1/2 inch thick and quartered (optional)

1. Preheat the oven to 250°F.
2. Heat the oil in a Dutch oven or heavy-bottomed oven-safe pot. Brown the doves on all sides and then deglaze with the wine, scraping up the bottom of the pot with a spatula. Add all the remaining ingredients except for the potatoes.
3. Cover the liquid with parchment or tinfoil so that the surfaces are touching. Then cover the pot with a lid. Place the pot in the oven and braise it for 2 hours, then raise the oven temperature to 300°F and braise for 2 more hours. This time will vary depending on your meat, so keep checking it to see if the meat is falling off the bone. That is when it is ready.
4. At the 3 1/2-hour point, add the potatoes and cook until tender. Remove from the oven and let cool slightly before serving. Serve over pasta, rice, or good bread to lap up all of the juices. It will taste even better the second day.

Also try: pigeon, quail, squirrel, rabbit, and many other meats

Just let me live my life as I've begun!
And give me work that's open to the sky;
Make me a partner of the wind and sun
And I won't ask a life that's soft and high.

—BADGER CLARK, cowboy prayer

3

Hunting the Big Quiet

The remote places that have fewer food choices tend to be the same places that create choice for the rest of the country. The people raise the cattle and the corn and ship it off, and in their free time, these men can almost always be found in a deer stand. Not many places are as far removed as the Village, but I know of at least one more: the home of a ranching family in West Texas who, after reading my website, sent me a note inviting me to taste a local delicacy called javelina. Javelina were named *jebeli* (Arabic-Spanish for "wild boar") or *jabalina* (Spanish for "spear," due to their spearlike teeth) by early Spanish explorers because of their similar appearance to the swine of the Old World. The only native piglike animal in the United States, javelina, technically speaking, are not pigs—they are peccaries. If I can manage to hunt one, the ranchers said, the challenge is to make it actually taste good. They aren't sure it can be done.

And so I go to West Texas, where the air presses down heavily over hay fields and railroad tracks, so that I can hear the pressure of the silence. The canyons turn pink and then orange to the east and to the west, and the twinkle of the railroad shines brighter, offering to take you out of here and dump you onto the streets of Los Angeles in sixteen hours or less. West Texas has a way of making you feel like a runaway. It is a place where the javelina run wild, along the edges of America.

But as the pink sky darkens over that perpetual iron streak of rail leading off to the horizon, and things turn gray, West Texas becomes pure romance. The landscape uncovers a powder blue trailer and a blaze orange truck cab lying in the grass. The silence is so loud it begins to hurt, and reality becomes heightened.

The town of Alpine appears after a long, unvarying canvas. It is where people go to escape the light and find the stars; where the bricks of the buildings glow and the strip of Main Street resembles the set of a western. The old hotel with its peeling pillars emits a yellow stored-up light, while the cars glide by and their lights wink red. The air is inky and it smells like iris.

Around a dark corner and through a dim sidewalk, Jim McMillan waits under the golden porch light of his restaurant. The restaurant is one of many arms of his father's enterprise that Jim now oversees. His family got their start in silicone, made their way south by way of Michigan, and arrived in Texas, where they bought ranches. Then they opened restaurants just because they needed a place to eat. And they kept making silicone.

Inside the restaurant, the wooden paddles of the ceiling fan spin slowly, stirring up the quiet. Dried-out chaps hang on the wall next to signed movie posters from the *Streets of Laredo* and *Rough Rider*, two of the many westerns filmed at Jim's ranch. Horse saddles adorn the corners of the room. Sweet women in aprons sweep in and out with platters of jalapeño grits and rare meat arrayed along their arms. A couple whispers in a corner; a cowboy cuts into his rib eye in another.

Jim is young and grave, but will demonstrate bursts of vigor when you talk to him about ranching or cattle or hunting. "My dad had the biggest impact on my hunting experiences," he says, eating a salad in a room full of steak.

"When did you start hunting? I ask.

He lists the big game animals at a man's fingertips in West Texas and tells me the stories of his worldly hunts: "The first big game animal was an axis on the YO ranch and a black bear when I was nine. When I was eleven, my father took me to Africa. Our professional hunter was Tony Henley and you couldn't have asked for a better teacher. He was a student of Africa; grew up in Kenya and knew every bird, antelope and bush across Botswana. And I can't forget Jim Hancock and Jack Demetruck. Both gentlemen took me hunting countless times, west of Fort Worth, before I could drive. We spent many mornings in a duck blind together."

Jim went to ranching school in Texas and will tell you about his field trips to ranches around the country, which he likens to investment-bank field trips in business school. It was there that he learned how closely intertwined ranching and hunting really were, and that many ranches rely on both to earn money.

I scrape the last grits from my plate, and we leave the warm room and step out into the waning light on the golden porch scattered with matching newly fallen leaves. I follow him by car on the dirt road to the 8,000-acre ranch that he calls "headquarters." It is partitioned into patches that have been tamed and rendered livable, and patches that are simply managed by hired cowboys on horseback. Where the patches meet are metal gates to keep the two separate. Beyond the gated living quarters, mountain lions and mountain goats mingle; inside the gate, where the patches are prettied up with manicured sod and hammocks and blue slate walkways, a bit of civility is maintained.

In the pebbled driveway, where my car skids to a halt, three semi-blind javelina snort and root in the barrel cactus, their eyes little beads of light. The dry grass crunches under my feet outside the gate as I leave them snorting in the driveway. Gnats flicker across my eyelids as I walk through the gate and onto grass as smooth as silk.

The guest rooms are appointed with glossy wood and more horse saddles and pictures of dignitaries and celebrity outdoorsmen that have slept here. The moths coat the screen door looking in. The air smells of burnt sugar, and the coyotes howl good night.

The morning air is marked by the drifting scent of hazelnut coffee and breakfast burritos that Jim prepares in his fluorescently lit kitchen. We eat quietly in the shadows of the taxidermy perched in the rafters above. Everything else is inky—the sky, the mountains, and the silence.

Down by the barn, we climb into the triangular dune buggy, and I cover my face with a cloth as the cold wind starts to whip. The motor labors as we move higher and higher into the canyon—stopping once at a pen to check on a single white goat left as a trap for the mountain lions—the black wind blanketing our faces in bitter cold. When the rocks and terrain become too unruly for the dune buggy, we leave it behind and continue on foot. We cross a creek fed from a natural spring, and as we do, the sky turns from black to a deep royal blue, and the smell of whitebrush, an aromatic Texas flower, gets stronger. So, too, does the burn on my ankles as the cactus stickers needle in through two layers of socks.

Jim glides up like a long-legged Barbary sheep and I trail behind, gingerly picking my steps on uncertain ground. At the top of the canyon, a set of boulders, like neatly stacked bubbles, juts over the deep valley, 500 feet below. Jim sits and dangles his legs down, taking out his binoculars to watch. "This is the best it's looked in a long time," he says to himself. It has rained 30 inches this year from July to September, rendering the mountains a patchwork of green.

He looks down at the base of the mountains where the javelina root and to the oak trees where they forage. He sees three deer instead, camouflaged in the rocks. "Look for white asses," he whispers.

The sky turns yellow, then red, and the light sharpens across our eyes. We wait for the black, short-haired javelina with their rodent pig features and their hot meaty smell, on their way to bed after a nocturnal feast. But they don't come.

The sun now high, we leave to climb back down the mountain, the cactus needles collecting on my ankles until I no longer feel them individually but as a widespread throb.

On the dune buggy, we pass the ranch cattle; their white and yellow heads peer up from the matching switch grass. They look at us, young and curious, with white eyelashes set upon glossy eyes, and jump back as we drive through.

This ranch gets its income by cultivating two kinds of meat, one that is hunted and one that is farmed. There are tax incentives for ranchers to keep these cattle. Jim used to keep as many as three thousand cattle on their ranches, but this fall he will ship only two hundred to the feedlot. He will get $1.10 per pound, and at 700 pounds per cow, it is still more money than they make from having hunters pay to hunt their ranch.

Once shipped, the cows will put on 3 pounds per day by eating corn up in the Texas Panhandle, and in ninety days or less they will reach 1,200 pounds and be ready for slaughter. Before they go to the Texas Panhandle, the cows will be injected with multiple vaccines, because they are about to enter into a world they have never seen before—leaving the pink canyons of West Texas for a dry, teeming feedlot often housing more than eighty thousand head of cattle. Their immune systems have to be prepared. There, they will meet other cattle from Hawaii and Florida, cattle that have been on an even longer journey, because it is cheaper to bring the cattle to the feed than the feed to the cattle. These cattle will convert feed to meat at a rate of seven to one.

If the cattle ate only grass, it would take longer to bring them to that weight, so long that they may not even be graded beyond hamburger status by the USDA—thirty months old is the cutoff.

And so it begs the question I ask him next: "Why do they have to get to twelve hundred pounds?" And Jim answers with the simple facts—that we used to be much less efficient with them. We used to slaughter them at 700 pounds. But our feedlots also used to also be smaller, with more farmers running their own little operations. Now the feedlot is condensed, in a place where there is dry air and thus less disease. And because there is less space, more meat has to be mined from each animal. The simple laws of space, crossed with supply and demand, turn the cattle into nothing more than a meat-based commodity.

He says that now even young calves are often sent to feedlots early and fed extra roughage with cornflakes, because the roughage makes them grow and the corn makes them fat.

"The banks prefer it that way," he says.

"Why?" I ask.

"Because it's easier to count your inventory in a feedlot than in a pasture." He smiles and shakes his head.

And in that moment, I look to my right and see three black creatures lumber through the tall straw. I slide out of the dune buggy and pull back the bolt action on a high-velocity .22–250 caliber rifle (it can travel at 4,000 feet per second, according to Jim). I listen to the cartridge slip into the chamber, and walk sideways into the tall, cream grass. The javelina move right and stop, then start again, then stop to root once more. They are mostly blind, and one stops to stand there and stare. I stare back through the scope of the rifle into its little black eyes and realize I've never stared my food in the face before. I feel the metal of the trigger on the pad of my index finger and wonder if it is fair for me to press it. I wonder if I had to work hard enough for this. I wonder if I had to exert myself enough, whether my throbbing ankles are enough, and whether this scope and just a bit more pressure on the metal trigger is a fair match for the semiblind javelina. Then I wonder how javelina taste, and that unconscious desire to know and taste adds pressure to the trigger, and I hear a thunderous sound and feel an intense pounding in my upper chest and a sting in my throat. I automatically flush red and apologize for missing. Jim looks at me funny but a tad bored. It turns out I have very unceremoniously killed a javelina. Unceremonious for Jim, because this is all business for him, but for me it is anything but unceremonious. It is immense, significant, and *it is so much meat.*

It was an instant shot in the neck, so I didn't ruin the meat. The black piglike creature is 40 pounds, fat and brown, and smells like mesquite. And almost as quickly as I shot it, we field dress it: I take a sharp knife and insert it just under the belly skin and pull up toward the rib cage, making sure not to puncture the bladder on the way, then pull out the guts, making sure not taint the meat by an accidental knick of the intestines, and leaving the remaining matter in the grass for the coyotes and mountain lions.

More than anything I don't want to waste a single morsel. I even inquire about what I can do with the hide, as we drive my javelina to the barn and hang it on a hook by its Achilles tendons, and, each taking a side, begin to skin it with two small knives until we have made it to the head, which we twist off with one strong, opposing motion. Jim power washes it with a hose and we let it drip dry, leaving it to compose a pink puddle on the cement floor of the clapboard barn. The hide sits on the cement floor, too, looking like an outfit the javelina has just slipped out of. But a call with the local taxidermist determines that javelina are shedding their hair for the season and aren't good candidates for a preserved hide. Even so, I conjure up recipes in my head, determined not to waste my first javelina, determined to show Jim and his family that it can taste good.

While the javelina drips, I take the dirt road to town and find lunch and some local intrigue at a roadside saloon. Here there are bandanas of every kind, on the women, too; and long, silver mustaches that hang below the lower lip. There is denim and European taxidermy, and outside are picnic tables with lovers' initials carved into the surface for all of eternity to see.

A diesel whistle blows on the railroad tracks in the distance, and the inside of the saloon echoes it with a roar as the football game goes the right way. The cowboys at the picnic tables tap their cigarettes against the black trays and eat pulled pork sandwiches that have soaked through their bottom buns. An old man stares in between the particles of dust, past all of us to something else.

A flaking pool table sits in the center of it all, its balls scattered into the webbed pockets. A cowboy scrawls on a postcard, peering over his brown paper bib, as he chews on his brisket. Another sits and rolls a cigarette, delicately licking the edges of the wrapper with focused precision. One man, with the red-lined skin of a Native American and stick-straight, shoulder-length hair, removes his cigarette pack from the rafters where he keeps it hidden.

They talk to me about javelina and how they like to cook them. The pulled-pork maker says he likes to cook them in chili; the cigarette roller calls them "desert rats"; the red-skinned man says, "They look just like my ex-wife." I listen to their low, rolling voices and watch their eternal staring through the smoke and dust of the picnic tables, and their mustaches of every kind, and the ashtrays and bandanas, and the slow sips of beer, and the denim and the spurs.

When I return to the ranch, I walk through an orchard of pecan trees and old movie relics to the barn, where the javelina is now cooling inside a refrigerator. I stand with Jim at the butcher block and finish the work of taking the javelina apart, the motions of which are familiar to me from my professional kitchen days—first the tenderloins, then the legs and shoulders, then the backstraps, those luscious thick strips of meat on either side of the spine, then the ribs, which have to be sawed apart. It is an orderly affair, and I feel like I am a butcher shop pro, until I notice that I am unwittingly shod in flip-flops and my toes are speckled in blood.

At night, the air smells like iris again, and the moon is just a thumbprint on the black sky. The air becomes hot and meaty while I cook the tenderloin and backstrap of the javelina for Jim and his mother. She is as sweet and comforting as a glass of warm milk in the evening, and I watch them eat javelina—for their first time—marinated and tangy and a bit chewy, too, and they actually like it.

The next morning, I say good-bye with 20 pounds of frozen javelina in my suitcase. I drive on the dirt road and back through Alpine. I see the cowboys at their picnic tables, and the old man staring through the particles of dust. And soon, there is almost nothing again, just ranch after ranch, covered in ocotillo and yucca and capped with mountains so wide that it is as mesmerizing as seeing where the horizon meets the sea. It is land that is porous and vast, but full of odd images—like pronghorn antelope, or men crossing borders, or abandoned trailers that buckle like caterpillars in the desert grass. It is a time encapsulated, containing the essence of simplicity and pure freedom.

The fate of the javelina in my suitcase is very much the same as the cattle I left behind at the ranch; it is also the same as my fate. But it is the journey to that place that is utterly different. Or perhaps more important, it is just that I stared into those small black eyes and understood fully what I was about to do. I paid the full karmic price of the meal. And now I am taking it through airport security with me on the way to the next hunt and the next meal.

Braised Javelina Haunch Serves 4 to 6

Braising is a great technique for many cuts of meat with a lot of muscle tissue, which almost every game animal has because they roam freely. The process of slowly cooking the meat at a low temperature over a long period of time helps break down the muscle and collagen, making a tender and sometimes buttery texture. This kind of meal is best served with crusty bread or some other grain to help soak up the juices.

2 haunches (4 to 6 pounds total) of javelina
1 (750 ml) bottle red wine
12 juniper berries
16 peppercorns
1 cup cider vinegar
2 teaspoons salt
4 bay leaves
8 sprigs fresh thyme
1 medium-size onion, peeled, cut in half, and stuck with 4 cloves, 2 on each half
3 medium-size carrots, sliced thinly
1 stick (8 tablespoons) butter

1. Combine all of the ingredients except the butter in a large, nonreactive container and marinate for 48 to 72 hours in the refrigerator, turning the meat every 8 hours so it marinates evenly.
2. Remove the meat and wipe it dry. Strain the marinade.
3. Preheat the oven to 300°F. Meanwhile, in a Dutch oven or large, heavy-bottomed pot, melt the butter over medium-high heat. Brown the meat on all sides, about 10 minutes.
4. Add the strained marinade to the pot and transfer the pot to the oven. Cover the meat and liquid with a piece of parchment paper or tinfoil and then with a lid.
5. Cook for 1 1/2 to 2 hours, basting every 20 minutes with the remaining marinade, until the meat is tender and easily falls off the bone.
6. Transfer the meat to a heated platter, cover with tinfoil, and let sit for 20 minutes so the juices retreat into the meat. Serve with the pan juices.

Also try: wild boar, antlered game

Adobo Javelina Backstrap
Serves 4 to 6

Javelina has a naturally smoky flavor, and there are ways to use that to your advantage. Adding more smoky flavor in the form of a marinade is one of them. All of the javelina is lean, even more so than wild boar, so when using an already lean cut like the tenderloin or backstrap, it is important to brine it first. The difference it makes is worth the wait.

> 2 javelina backstraps or tenderloins, brined (see page 219)
> 1 chipotle chile pepper in adobo sauce, finely chopped, with about 1 or 2
>   teaspoons of the sauce
> 1/3 cup cider vinegar
> 4 garlic cloves, minced
> 1 tablespoon brown sugar
> 1/2 teaspoon dried oregano
> 1/2 teaspoon dried thyme
> 4 tablespoons olive oil

1. Place the loins in a resealable plastic food storage bag with all of the ingredients except 2 tablespoons of the olive oil. Refrigerate for 1 hour and up to 4 hours.
2. Remove the meat from the refrigerator and allow to come to room temperature for 20 minutes.
3. Tie the backstraps with kitchen twine so they are uniform in thickness, as you would a roast, wrapping the string around, making a loop, and pulling it through. If you are using tenderloins, tie them together using the same method.
4. Preheat the oven to 350°F. Heat a large, ovenproof skillet and when hot, pour in the remaining 2 tablespoons of olive oil. Sear the tenderloins until golden brown on all sides, about 4 minutes. Transfer the skillet to the oven and roast for 12 to 15 minutes longer, until the backstraps reach an internal temperature of about 145°F.
5. Remove from the heat and set on a plate. Cover with tinfoil and let sit for 20 minutes before slicing to serve.

Also try: wild boar, antlered game (doesn't require a brine)

Javelina Chili

When butchering an animal, there are always meat scraps that don't quite make it into any particular cut. This is especially true with the more muscular bits. Those can all be collected and frozen in plastic bags, well labeled. Once you have enough, you can put the frozen scraps through a meat grinder, or dice it finely and use it for chili. Any kind of meat will work in this recipe, but it is an especially good combination with javelina because of the natural mesquite flavor of the meat. This chili will taste even better the second day, and even better the day after that. It will also freeze well in smaller portions.

4 tablespoons grape seed oil
3 1/2 pounds javelina, ground
4 garlic cloves, chopped finely
1 cup finely chopped onion
1 bell pepper, seeded and diced finely
1 (15.5-ounce) can red kidney, pinto, or similar beans
1 (8-ounce) can tomato sauce
2 cups hog stock (page 213) or antlered game stock (page 213)
3 tablespoons chili powder
2 tablespoons ground cumin
2 teaspoons paprika
2 teaspoons dried oregano
2 teaspoons sugar
1/2 teaspoon ground coriander
1 teaspoon hot sauce
1/2 teaspoon sea salt

1. In a large saucepan, brown the meat in the oil, breaking up the meat and stirring with a wooden spoon.
2. Add the garlic, onion, and pepper and cook over medium heat for 5 minutes, continuing to break up the meat.
3. Add the remaining ingredients and mix well.
4. Bring to a boil, then lower the heat and simmer, covered, for 2 hours.
5. Taste and adjust the seasoning to your liking, adding more hot sauce and salt and pepper as necessary.

Also try: wild boar, antlered game, turkey, ground or diced finely

Pulled Javelina
Serves 10 to 12

This is an ode to the cowboys in Alpine and the pulled pork truck that sits outside their saloon. The spices can be adjusted and experimented with, but the final product should always be paired with a tangy slaw and something spicy and pickled, for the real experience. Every smoker is different, so you may have to adjust the smoking time, depending on how your smoker operates. Javelina won't shred quite as easily as domestic pork, but it should shred reasonably well when it is done.

    1/2 cup molasses
    1 cup kosher salt
    1 quart water
    2 shoulders (3 to 5 pounds total) of javelina
    1 teaspoon cumin seed
    1 teaspoon fennel seed
    1 teaspoon coriander seed
    1 tablespoon chili powder
    1 tablespoon onion powder
    1 tablespoon garlic powder
    1 tablespoon paprika
    1 teaspoon cayenne
    1 teaspoon ground allspice
    1 tablespoon dried oregano
    1 tablespoon mustard powder

1. Combine the molasses, salt, and water in a plastic brining bag or nonreactive container. Add the shoulders and let sit in the refrigerator for 12 hours.
2. Remove the meat from the brine and let rest on a rack in the refrigerator for at least 1 hour and up to 24.
3. Place the cumin, fennel, and coriander in a spice grinder and grind until fine. Transfer to a small mixing bowl and combine with the remaining ingredients.
4. Preheat a smoker to 210°F. Sprinkle the cumin mixture evenly over the shoulders and then pat onto the meat, making sure as much of the rub as possible adheres. Wearing latex gloves will help you to get more of the mixture to adhere to the meat.
5. Place the shoulders in the smoker and cook for 5 to 7 hours, maintaining a temperature of 210°F. Begin checking meat for doneness after 5 hours of cooking time. The meat is done when it falls apart easily when pulled with a fork. Once done, remove from the smoker and set aside to rest for at least 1 hour.
6. Pull meat apart with two forks and serve as a sandwich, with pickled jalapeños, coleslaw, and tangy dressing.

Also try: wild boar

When you have shot one bird flying you have shot all birds flying.
They are all different and they fly in different ways but the
sensation is the same and the last one is as good as the first.

—ERNEST HEMINGWAY

4

Grouse and Other Creatures

Montana seems like a logical, almost necessary stop. I think of this state as more entangled with nature than almost any other in the lower forty-eight, being as it is one of the last in the nation with more animals than people. If I want to experience raw nature, then this must be the place, and so I accept an invitation from a friend of a friend to go bird hunting—a "blind hunting date" of sorts. It begins in an airport full of camouflaged men whose bellies are very large and whose hair is very silver. They are clad in their favorite uniform for the fall and winter months, and they will wear it religiously as they carry the fruits of the hunt in their cars on the long drive home.

Montana is sky country, with hills and plains that glisten crimson and mustard in the light. Strong winds send the cars wobbling around the road kill and rotting carcasses, speeding past black velvet cows mingling on great green fields that seem to stretch forever onward until they meet the purple snow-capped mountains.

If there is no ceiling in the sky at night, the Milky Way is extravagant in Townsend—an ungentrified, undepressed town where the folks are regular. There is an ample supply of gas stations in Townsend, ice boating on Canyon Ferry Lake, and mule deer grazing on alfalfa like cattle.

In a board and batten cabin atop a hill, a thin sixty-year-old man named Wilbur listens to Italian lute music and sips a serious Cabernet in sixty-dollar stemware from which he refuses to sip standing up, for fear it will break.

There are bachelor-size things inside: a very small skillet; a small bowl of cashews on the slate counter; glass vases full of speckled pheasant feathers, each plume a token of his achievements; and a full bar of fine brandies, ports, and vermouth. Next to the bar are seven-dollar wineglasses from Ikea, should you wish to drink standing up.

He heats the cabin solely with a woodstove, often taking the temperature of the room to demonstrate how well he has insulated his house. He likes to write letters to politicians.

But Wilbur spends so much time with his fourteen-year-old English pointer that he generally interacts with people the same way he does with his dog—in single-word orders or replies. Except when he talks about hunting: "I imagine going bird hunting for the next decade. It's endlessly interesting to me," he says, pacing the room in wool moccasins and green corduroy. "It's a lark. I'll go fifty days a year. In the fields, you're predatory, exploratory, interested. I think it's sort of my roots showing in some ways and I think it's the real thing." He hides his small brown cigarette expertly as he talks, but the smell of cloves he exudes betrays him.

There was a time when he was a boy, that he lived in Montana. But he left it behind in the sixties to deal in fine art in Berkeley, when the university was in full dissident bloom. He walked in poet circles, went by his initials—like T. S. Eliot—always had good seats for the symphony, ate at Chez Panisse in the seventies when lunch was $3.50, and could tell a good Époisses cheese from a bad. Now in retirement, he is on a quest—trying to become a Montana man again.

In the morning, as the moon is dying and the air smells of burning mountain mahogany, we drive together toward the Golden Triangle. It is a patch of land to the north blanketed in succulent wheat and tall cover grass that the birds enjoy.

"Do you remember your first hunt?" I ask.

"I started hunting in earnest at ten before I had a license or hunter safety, for which you had to be eleven," he says, driving cautiously, sometimes mysteriously stopping short in the blue and orange morning "The first bird I ever shot was a prairie chicken while sitting on my uncle's lap. By the age of fifteen when we were all driving, we all started hunting on our own including before school and after school all the way up until the end of duck season in early January. It is still an undiminished pleasure for me. And I would come back to Berkeley with all of this frozen game, and I'd have these dinner parties and everybody was just instantly converted. Even just your basic deer roast. I had a whole circle of people who just begged to get re-invited to that menu. And ditto the grouse and the pheasant."

As the sun rises higher, we can begin to see the silhouettes of mule deer grazing on the roadside. There are sometimes hundreds leading to the fir trees in the distance.

"Wow. There are *so* many deer," I say marveling at the herd on the planes.

"The deer problem has gotten really out of hand in states like Montana," he says. "Right up against these mountains is just overrun. You're driving down the streets and they're just hanging out. It just takes about two years for them to completely adapt in the habitat, and they have gone back and forth for the last decade on what to do about them."

Game numbers overall are greater now than they were one hundred years ago. At the beginning of the twentieth century, there was no game licensing or game seasons. There was market hunting—a way for people to make money by selling their game to restaurants, which depleted game animal populations to very low numbers. Regulation began in about 1920. It became illegal to serve hunted wild game in restaurants, which means that any game meat on a restaurant menu today has been bred and farmed just like the cow, the pig, and the chicken.

The fish and game departments now closely monitor the wild animal populations, determining when and how long the seasons should be, asking hunters to supply tooth and blood samples, and monitoring the changing dynamics of sprawl—where urban landscapes interface with outdoor environments.

"I want to go on record that it's a myth that whitetail are better tasting than mule deer," Wilbur says, breaking the silence. "It's not true."

Wilbur's friend Kurt waits for us at a crossroads in the parking lot of a boarded-up saloon, looking elegant and tall in his suspenders and shoulder-length silver hair. His dog, a French Griffon Fauve de Bretagne named Red Elvis, is urinating on a post. We consolidate the contents of our cars into one and drive farther north toward Canada, to meet a farmer named Sammy Field who will loan certain people his farmland to hunt on, in exchange for his favorite bottle of whiskey.

As we drive the whiskey toward Sammy, the great brown mountains turn liquid in the delicate morning sun. Farther north they become buttes, mountains with missing tops that the Native Americans once worshipped in their vision quests. Before the advent of steel-tipped arrows and lances, Indians on the high plains who hunted the bison for food and warmth enticed the herds to the edge of these buttes and instigated a stampede to force them over the edge.

Over time, as we drive, the land grows more arid and orange, and the sky seems to sink lower and lower until the cloud-filled canyon blends with the snowcaps in the Rocky Mountain front. High above an eagle flexes his wings and pushes them toward his back like a diver, dropping for a rodent into the great blank plane. There are flashes of black stripes as we drive past the perfect rows of wheat stubble, studded with the occasional pyramid stack of tightly wrought rolls of glossy hay.

Old Sammy Field, wearing overalls, with protruding whiskers and disheveled hair, meets us on the corner of a dirt road in his red pickup, 100 yards from his double-wide trailer home. He has the land wealth for something far greater, but he spends most of the days with his cows anyway, and regardless, what's the point? Sammy Field cares more about being anti-ostentatious.

The truth about bird hunting in Montana is that it requires knocking on doors like a Bible salesman, to see if the owners will let you shoot on their land. The public owns the game, but the landowner controls access to it, heightening a certain discord. There are government incentive programs here to encourage landowners to share their land, but too many hunters abuse it. Bad hunters turn farmers off, and so they don't maintain the habitat that supports the birds. The modern farmer plays an important role in the fate of so many wild game birds—whether a pheasant will be exposed to predators or not is determined by whether the farmer maintains its habitat or plows down the tall cover grass. In turn, the hunter plays an important role in influencing the farmer. Although he is caught between a growing human population and a shrinking resource, the hunter's behavior and treatment of the farmer and his land is really what determines his access to the hunting grounds. Wilbur makes these connections religiously and delicately ("I don't overextend my welcome here"), calling on his art house charm. He is meticulous about bringing farmers food and drink from Berkeley's Gourmet Ghetto. But Sammy Field prefers whiskey.

Kurt and I walk in parallel through a field of numbered cows. Number ninety-six is a handsome white bull with red eyelids. Wilbur runs ahead and scrambles down the fingers of the hills. He runs rapidly with his dog Clyde, who dashes forward quietly sniffing the ground intently. Kurt and I walk above on the plain for 3 miles, through the tall brush grass and over the gray sinews of a dried-up creek. The bleached ribs of a dead cow jut through the grass, its remaining bones scattered down the ridge.

In the distance, Wilbur still runs up and down the fingers of the hill, his hands waving maniacally for us to keep up. Kurt doesn't seem to notice. Instead he adjusts his red suspenders and pushes back his long strands of silver-white hair, looking skeptically at the sky and the cloudy western front through the orange tint of his shooting glasses that change color depending on the light.

We walk on through the old barns in the field, where the Hungarian partridge likes to linger. We scare a jackrabbit that speeds through the grass in an undulating sprint.

"Everything is so still," I say looking at the shimmering vast land around us. "The sky feels so low."

"It's a really off year," Kurt says, pausing to smell the air. "It just acts that way."

High rains and late frost in Montana killed the chicks in a cold snap. The rain then grew thick, tall grass that makes the remaining birds hard to see.

It is a challenge even in the best of years. The partridge is an immigrant from Europe, the most abundant game bird in Montana. The pheasant is an immigrant from China, and makes you work and hunt harder than you ever have before; it is, in a sense, the last wild bird. Many animals, from the mule deer to the squirrel, adapt to humans, but the pheasant still has a distinctly wild spirit—it cackles as it hears you and runs off on its springy legs.

The breeze rises sharply and reddens our faces now, then drops low again, and the sky turns phosphorescent as a flash of color paints the wind. We weave in and out of grazing red and black Angus cattle shimmering in the light, beige strands of dried grass dangling from their mouths. They pause to watch us midchew, as if we've just delivered bad news.

In the distance there is a double shot that blows the trees full of life.

"Oh, there he goes," Kurt says shaking his head and smiling. "I just can't keep up with him, so I've stopped trying."

And soon an orange cap rises up from the valley, hands raised high, with a speckled brown and white Hungarian partridge in each. Wilbur has a yellow smile of expectation on his face, as he walks toward us, and we smile and nod in silence.

"I like how animated shotgun shooting is! It's an exploration of the elements," he says, dropping the two Huns not into his game pocket, but into mine, the large pocket built into the back of my jacket and secured with a zipper.

We walk on to new pasture, stepping in puddles along the way. Kurt and I help each other over barbed fences held together by crooked old fence posts. Time passes slowly in a way that tires. The weight of the two Huns against my back gets heavier over time and the winds get higher and drier until I can taste the saliva in my mouth. My body cells begin to tingle. The two dog-man teams run ahead of me, the men relying on the dogs' noses, and they look like the perfect companions. Hunting is in both species' genes.

Many hours pass, and the patchwork of farming properties begin to blend together. The sun now centers itself in the low ceiling of the sky, and the sweet-and-sour smell of cow manure ripens the air. Upland bird hunting in Montana is a game of knowing the bird—knowing that the Hungarian partridge prefers field stubble and weed seeds, that the pheasant likes tall cover in cattails and fescue, that certain grouse will eat exclusively sage. It is also when you begin to see possibility in things you never have before, such as the beauty of a fanned-out half-pecked cornhusk lying in a plain. Up on the corner where the field meets the gravel driveway, Sammy Field is breathing heavily, letting out small puffs of vapor as he kicks a pile of steaming cow dung. It is then that I realize that he is tired, too, and that upland bird hunting is also a bit like a game of chicken. Nobody wants to give up first, admit that his back aches, his ankles itch, or that one of his socks is very wet.

Occasionally we break to pick burrs off the dogs and ourselves, and to eat a boiled egg and a piece of chocolate, and have a drink of water before we try another line of tall grass along the pasture. But eventually there are signs of relief; the sun is covered by cumulus clouds now and I can feel the gentle prairie wind on my face, cooling the sweat on my neck.

We arrive at an improvised junkyard holding a rusted horse buggy, a few rubber tires, and the pale blue shell of a car. We come to a pool of water formed by a thin stream. The dogs stop inside the grass and point, then turn to stone and tremble. A brown hen pheasant flies up in the breeze and snaps to the right along a line of pines. Wilbur yells, "Hen!" to call us all off from shooting. If we only shoot roosters as the law usually requires, we do not harm the pheasant population; a single rooster can fertilize the eggs of twenty hens, in the same way a single rooster is all that is needed for a barnyard full of hens. In the field, sorting the hen from the rooster is a series of split-second decisions. Kurt seems to know almost intuitively what it is going to be and predicts it before it rises from the cover. In part, it is that hens prefer the tall, thick, wet grass, whereas roosters prefer the outer brush. But there is another difference, too.

There is a mystical quality in the rooster as he shoots into the air like a feathered arrow, in all his green and purple splendor. The long spike of his tail feathers taper for aerodynamic flight, and he banks to his side and paints the wind. I hesitate when I see the rooster, in awe of his faultless beauty. You must follow the bead of your shotgun just ahead of him with both eyes open until the bead is just ahead of his beak point, and that is when you slap the trigger.

Sometimes the rooster doesn't fall. Sometimes he will keep flying because he is a rooster and he is mysterious. Sometimes he will leave only a single feather floating to the ground for you to ponder. That is why you hunt the rooster. You must earn him and be taunted by his cackle. You must walk sometimes for eight hours to earn him, and you must hurt a little, and sometimes you must hurt a lot.

The distinctly wild spirit of the rooster means you must spend time respecting him and feel the fear of not finding him, and also the fear of actually finding him, before he will relent and fall. And even after he falls, lest you become too proud, he will sometimes disappear to a place where even the dogs must search forever until they finally catch the scent and seek him out and drop him in your hands, smooth and handsome.

There is grouse, too, the one the Native Americans called fire birds. Grouse rely on forest fires to create highways for their habitats—a mosaic of grasslands interspersed with shrubs and brush-filled coulees. They linger along drainage ditches, surrounded by grain fields, and subsist on native bunchgrass. They snack on buds and berries, on rose hips and wild watercress. The males display their mottled feathers and white bellies and violet neck sacks in their mating dance, stamping their fully feathered three-pronged feet rapidly twenty times per second, rattling their tail feathers, circling and dancing forward, inflating their sacks. The one that does it the best is chosen by the female to mate.

Having traversed the grass cover by midday, there is one last chance for us to take home a bird. It is in late afternoon, at four o'clock when the birds peck at pebbles in the gravel roads to improve their digestion. We drive in the truck along these roads and look for birds through the cracked windshield. The tall grasses beside the road are yellow and creamy in the wind and I can begin to feel all of the stiff and sore and strained parts of my body harden, one by one—I can count them.

"It's an old Montana tradition to shoot a bird out of a car," Wilbur proclaims. "I've shot a lot of birds from out of the car window. You hold the steering wheel with your knees. Are you ready to do it?"

I don't really hear him. Instead I open the window until the air in the truck smells like corn, and I bask in the yellow light on my face and watch the combines in the distance as wide as a highway, trolling along. "That is nice stubble," Kurt says of the hacked-off wheat. But there are no birds. The moon is rising and it is time to leave.

After we bid good-bye to Kurt and Red Elvis at the crossroads of the old saloon, Wilbur and I drive through vacant towns. I can see the shape of an old man in his reclining chair through a pair of glass doors. I see people giving a point salute to one another as they drive. I see wings beating in the trees. I see whitetails everywhere, jumping like snowballs over hillcrests.

There are noses and antlers sticking up above the beds of pickup trucks, and men and their daughters in camo. In some places, the colors are still royal and true before they fade toward dusk and headlights flicker on. Where the Missouri River is dammed at Canyon Ferry Lake, the water reflects the light in its ripples. We turn right over the railroad tracks and up the steep dirt road and meet Wilbur's neighbors, retired transplants from Minnesota, cleaning an elk in their driveway. They are warm and sweet and accept an invitation to come for dinner. They are bringing elk, caribou, and mule deer to go with our quarry. We creak up the hill, my muscles anticipating the bubble bath and my stomach aching for the roasted bird, bathed in butter and brandy. As we come into the driveway Wilbur says, somewhere far off, "Be prepared for his cream sauce."

The cream sauce is wonderfully creamy, with mushrooms and elk underneath. And there is an intoxicating medley of apples and squash from the Minnesota neighbors' garden, pressed and stirred together in one dish. And there is wine, one glass, worth seven dollars, filled partway for when we want to stand, and one sixty-dollar glass filled partway for when we want to sit.

We stand and sip, and the Minnesota wife talks in her sweet Minnesota voice, and suddenly, just as I begin to drift into the warm reverie of the moment, I feel something strike my rear end. I turn my head, red-cheeked, knowing instinctually what has just transpired, but not wanting to believe it. Wilbur walks by briskly swinging his wet, grease-stained dish towel with a look of sheepish amusement. For a second I am reminded of the misogyny I found so tiresome while working for four-star chefs in New York and in France. And I recall the jacked-up Lehman Brothers traders, giving me a little tap when they were feeling particularly high on life or a little lonely after a long day at the office. Naively I assumed I had left this behind, that the home of an eccentric Berkeley art dealer who hunted for food was far from these other places. Before I began hunting, when it was merely an idea in my head while neatly tucked into my urban lifestyle, this was the kind of act I imagined happened among men who lived in the backwoods, who were self-proclaimed rednecks that held burping contests, the kind of men Wilbur proclaimed he, too, looked down on. Except that my experience in the backwoods had never fulfilled that stereotype. In fact, it had done everything to contradict it. I stand here thinking how fascinating it is to me, really, that *he* was the one to bring out the ass-slap.

Wilbur, utterly unaware of his transgression, resumes his post at the table. I pause and put down the seven-dollar wineglass, as the neighbor chirps in her singsong voice, then lean in to the table and pick up the sixty-dollar wineglass and stand back against the counter. I look at Wilbur, raise my glass with a wink and take a nice big sip, and watch the wave of panic wash across his face.

Partridge with Pancetta in Orange Brandy Sauce   Serves 4

Maybe it was the Montana air, or the fact that I had walked for so many hours and so many miles to earn it, but sitting down to eat this was a revelation. The sweetness and the saltiness and the dripping fat and the most tender breast meat I had ever sunk my teeth into, all made the perfect combination. It will work with other bird meat, but I like to think there is something about the small tender white meat of the Hungarian partridge that made the experience. I recommend keeping the breast-bone in whatever meat you use, whenever possible, to help the meat stay moist.

Marinade:

  Zest of 1 orange
  1/2 cup freshly squeezed orange juice
  Juice of 1/2 lemon
  1 teaspoon salt
  1/4 cup brandy
  1/4 teaspoon dried tarragon
  1/4 teaspoon dried parsley
  1/4 teaspoon dried rosemary
  1/4 cup olive oil
  1/8 teaspoon freshly ground pepper
  4 partridge, butterflied, bone in

To Cook:

  4 round, thin slices pancetta
  4 tablespoons cold butter, cubed
  4 thin slices orange, cut from the center

For the Marinade:

1. With a whisk, combine all of the marinade ingredients in a baking dish. Place the meat breast side down in the mixture. Marinate for 3 to 4 hours, turning over every hour.

To Cook:

1. Preheat the oven to broil. Place one orange slice on each breast that is sitting in the marinade and then cover with pancetta. Fasten them with a toothpick on each side.
2. Add the cold butter to the baking dish with the marinade and place in the oven. Broil the birds breast side up, basting every 5 minutes, for 25 to 30 minutes. Remove the breasts and let them rest on a plate for 10 minutes. Put the baking dish back in the oven and let the sauce reduce for 5 minutes more. Serve immediately.

Also try: prairie chicken, pheasant, turkey, rabbit

Whole Pheasant Poached in Juniper Sauce   Serves 2

Poached pheasant should be on everyone's bucket list. Luckily it is now available in grocery stores, if you aren't able to harvest one with your own two hands. It is sweeter, softer, and more tender than chicken. It is a bird born to be poached. It would be a good idea to have some fresh ravioli or tortellini on hand to serve as a bed for this pheasant and its broth.

1 whole pheasant, skin on or off
6 pieces bacon or pork fat, cut into 1/4-inch-thick strips
1 tablespoon grape seed oil
3 shallots, minced
1/4 cup vermouth
12 juniper berries, crushed
1/4 cup gin
4 cups game bird stock (page 212)
2 tablespoons butter
Salt and pepper

1. Drape the bacon over the bird and truss the bird with kitchen twine, toothpicks, or a combination, so the fat is fastened to the bird.
2. Heat the oil in a heavy-bottomed ovenproof pot with a lid. Brown the bird on all sides, about 10 minutes, until the bacon fat is well rendered. Be careful not to turn the bird if the bacon sticks to the pot, otherwise it will tear. Instead let the bacon render and crisp until the bird can be easily rotated. Once the bacon has been crisped, remove the birds from the pan and set aside.
3. Add the shallots to the pan and let sweat until soft. Add the vermouth to the pan and deglaze. Scrape up any brown bits from the pan with a spatula.
4. Add the juniper berries and gin. Lay in the pheasant and pour the stock over it. Cover and cook for 30 to 35 minutes.
5. Remove the pheasant from the pot and peel off the bacon. Reduce the sauce and whisk in the butter. Season with salt and pepper to taste. Quarter the pheasant and add it back to the broth. Serve this dish in shallow bowls with fresh ravioli as a bed for the pheasant.

Also try: prairie chicken, partridge, quail, turkey, squirrel, rabbit

Apple Wood–Smoked Pheasant   Serves 2 to 4

Smoking is a great technique for a whole bird that is unblemished and worthy of a table centerpiece. Because game birds dry out quickly, it is necessary to brine the pheasant first. This also works very well with birds that have redder breast meat and ones with a thicker, fattier skin, such as a speckled goose or mallard. As for smoking wood, this recipe calls for apple wood, but more important, use a wood that is local to your region. In the South, it's pecan; in the Southwest, it's mesquite; in Washington state, it's apple wood; in the Midwest, it's hickory.

Brine:

   4 cups water
   1/2 cup white wine vinegar
   1/2 cup brown sugar
   1/4 cup granulated sugar
   1/4 cup salt
   1/2 tablespoon mustard seeds
   2 cloves garlic, crushed
   1 tablespoon crushed black pepper
   2 sprigs fresh thyme
   1 bay leaf

To Smoke and Serve:

   1 whole pheasant, skin on or quartered pheasant, skin on or off
   Goose or duck fat or smoked bacon strips
   Barbecue sauce (page 227) (optional)

To Brine:

1. Combine all brine ingredients and bring to a boil.
2. Remove from the heat and let cool.
3. Add the bird and submerge, covering with a plate or some other weight so it stays completely submerged in liquid.
4. For a whole bird, refrigerate in brine for 8 hours; for a quartered bird, refrigerate for 4.
5. Remove and pat dry and let rest on a rack in the refrigerator for at least 3 and up to 24 hours before cooking.

To Smoke and Serve:

1. Stabilize the smoker at a temperature of 200°F, using apple wood chips.
2. Cover the bird with fat or strips of bacon. You may need to secure it with toothpicks or kitchen twine. Smoke the bird for 45 minutes, turning once.
3. Slice against the grain and serve with barbecue sauce, or serve cold on a sandwich.

Also try: dove, grouse, prairie chicken, partridge, goose, duck, coot, pigeon, ptarmigan, quail, rail, turkey

Grouse with Cabbage and Chestnuts

Serves 4

Grouse meat is dark red with a rich game flavor. Ruffed grouse have the strongest game flavor, which in my opinion is wonderful. The meat of the older birds can be tough and all of it will dry out easily if you are not careful. More than any other game bird, grouse need to be kept moist while cooking. This is best done with the help of goose fat and bacon. The French always viewed grouse legs as bitter and I notice that many people still use them solely for stock or gravy. At the very least, give the young ones a chance and try them whole sometime.

4 grouse, whole and skin on
Salt and pepper
Juice of 1 lemon
4 tablespoons goose fat or butter
8 to 12 slices bacon
1 medium-size red or white cabbage, sliced thinly
1 tablespoon sugar
1 cup apple cider
1 cup roasted and diced chestnuts (see Note)

1. Rinse and dry the birds thoroughly and season them with salt, pepper, and lemon juice inside and out.
2. Melt the goose fat in a large skillet and brown the birds slowly on all sides.
3. Remove the birds from the skillet. Wrap each in a few slices of bacon and secure with a toothpick or kitchen twine. Set aside on a plate.
4. Add the cabbage to the skillet containing the remaining fat. Sprinkle the cabbage with sugar and salt and let it brown slightly. Deglaze with the cider.
5. Lay the birds back in, breast side down. Cover tightly and simmer slowly over low heat for 45 minutes.
6. During the last 15 minutes of cooking, turn the birds breast side up and add the chestnuts.
7. Let rest, covered in tinfoil, for 10 minutes before serving. Serve the birds whole on a bed of stewed cabbage.

Also try: dove, prairie chicken, partridge, pheasant, pigeon, ptarmigan, quail, rail, turkey, squirrel, rabbit

Note: To roast chestnuts, score on the back with an X, roast in a 450°F oven for 10 minutes, then shell and peel.

A peculiar virtue in wildlife ethics is that the hunter ordinarily has no gallery to applaud or disapprove of his conduct. Whatever his acts, they are dictated by his own conscience, rather than by a mob of onlookers. It is difficult to exaggerate the importance of this fact.

—ALDO LEOPOLD

5

Calamity Jane

I promptly leave Wilbur's home the next morning in a mad dash for Billings Airport, where I return my rental car. Afterward I walk to a hotel near the airport to wait for my next hunting companion, Stan Jones, who is driving up from Wyoming to meet me. Stan owns a grass-fed beef operation and had followed my blog for quite some time. He even sent me beef samples at one point to demonstrate how much better grass-fed beef can be.

A stack of books sits in the lobby of the hotel—several copies of a biography of Calamity Jane—and the hotel clerk hands me one and tells me to keep it. I sit there fingering through the pages, enthralled. Calamity Jane was a heroine of the plains. Some say that she acquired the name because she warned men that to offend her was to "court calamity." In light of the prior evening's events, I find it wildly captivating.

I read it while I wait for Stan, who has been in touch with me for a year and a half, plying me with hints of his hunting prowess, sending me pictures of his elk hunts, teasing me for missing out. He has been persistent, and I have always been curious about Wyoming. Like Montana, it has always sounded so well balanced with nature. Stan had used the term *we* a lot when he referred to his business, and sent me photos of my accommodations on the ranch. His grass-fed beef business is advertised as being part of the largest ranch in the country, owned by Native Americans. The photos and videos of the place were beautiful. I wanted to meet some members of the tribe and talk to them about their tradition of hunting and how it intersects with a grass-fed cattle operation in a place where the feedlot system is king. Historically, Native Americans were the ultimate hunter-gatherers, yet now they were raising beef. Here was evidence of how far we humans experienced an agricultural revolution in which farming gradually replaced hunting and put us on a path to a more sedentary life. By cultivating crops that were most productive, we had simplified our diet into a few basic commodities—mostly corn, soy, and grains. I wanted to learn more about Native American history on this land and get their perspective on this point in time. And I wanted to set my eyes on a cattle ranch comprised of hundreds of thousands of acres. So I agree to drop in for an elk hunt with Stan after my time in neighboring Montana.

Stan and his young son arrive in Billings in his pickup, and we cross the border into Wyoming. He is tall, red haired, and balding, with a ruddy face and an overly groomed moustache that suggest he is younger than he looks. He wears faded blue jeans and a collared shirt with his logo embroidered on the left shirt pocket. "That's where Lewis and Clark floated down," he says, pointing out the sights along the empty roads, as I scribble notes diligently. What I notice more than anything, though, is how barren the land suddenly becomes, how vast and empty it is.

Wyoming was never meant to be a state. If Ulysses S. Grant had had his way, the land would have been split among Idaho, Montana,

Colorado, and South Dakota. But the citizens of Wyoming put more people on the official rolls than actually inhabited the state. They began naming babies before they were born, and they were the first to give women the right to vote because they needed all the voting power they could get. Even today, however, it is sparsely populated; Wyoming is a place of survival, not one that concerns itself with the nuances of our industrial food system. It is hard to grow food here at all because of the high desert climate. If you have the willpower and the fortitude, you can make it work. The people of Wyoming choose to persevere and that is what makes them unique. They like to say that you go through Wyoming to get somewhere else; it's not where you put down roots.

If you want to be alone, in lucid silence, under a sky of gray putty, as vast as Texas and Montana, but darker and more ominous, come to Wyoming. It is one of the last places in America where you can drive on a two-lane blacktop road for hours and not see a soul. The sky never appears to move, nor does anything underneath it. I have been anxious for more open sky for a long time, and here it is.

But just as I begin to bask in it all, things begin to unravel. That evening, my accommodations turn out to be in Stan's home; and via e-mail, my research assistant kindly suggests to me that Lewis and Clark had never, in fact, been through the land we now call Wyoming. It also seems strange when Stan says he doesn't own a knife with which to field dress an animal. Or a single piece of blaze orange clothing so as not to get shot by an eager hunter trekking the mountains on opening day. And it seems more than strange that he hasn't purchased a license to hunt—it cost me about $250 for an elk tag. When we leave one morning to hunt the elk on his friend's cow pasture, it is a last-minute decision. We have to stop at Walmart on the way to get a knife. All of these flags should, and do, make me nervous. But Stan is still jovial and enthusiastic, and what about those pictures of his elk hunt he'd sent? This is Wyoming, land of people who hunt and gather from the moment they step out of the womb. I want to have this experience, I have paid a lot for this experience, but also . . . where am I? I'm not sure I could find my way out of here without his help.

There is just a sliver of moon as we leave Walmart and drive along the north fork of the Shoshone River. This is the geographical zone that I am to hunt in, according to my elk tag. But Stan begins to look confused. "We're looking for a buck-and-rail fence," he says, over and over again. "My night vision is bad, ever since I had that Lasik surgery."

Stan stops and starts his truck like the hiccups. He puts his high beams on, and as he does I can see the reflection of the headlights on a herd of elk, their eyes like orange coins in the black morning air. The eyes wink at random and some of the elk run across the road in front of us, then float up into the fissures of the mountain. Stan is unfazed and indicates so with a burp. Then he drives his truck into the ditch along the buck-and-rail fence toward the remaining elk herd, to keep them in their place.

Once he is satisfied that they will stay where he wants them to, he drives down the road a little ways, to the area where his friend's land begins. He parks his truck on the bare edge of the road and we sit in darkness. Once in a while, the speed of a passing car shakes us. I can smell the cold steel bullets for his handgun on the seat, more potent as I grip my seat tighter with each passing car. When it is lighter and the mountain silhouette grows dark against the blue sunrise, we climb out of the truck and gather our gear and begin to walk into the field quietly and quickly. We crawl under an electric wire and lean against a wooden fence to wait for the light. With the range finder, I look to the herd of elk and see that miraculously some of them are still in their place 166 yards away.

"I don't have night vision; I can't see them," Stan says loudly.

The light rises further until at last Stan sees the elk. And once he sees them, he begins running directly toward the herd as they stand next to the road, barreling into the green field like a hunger-crazed bear. I watch through the rangefinder as they look at him, their orange-coin eyes blinking, and I think I see them laugh. The elk turn away and look toward the mountain, jump the fence, and spring into the crevices and out of sight. Stan lumbers back, hunched over, breath steaming from his nostrils.

"We boogered 'em out!" he says.

I don't even know what to say, so I say nothing instead.

We walk along the edges of the Yellowstone River, hoping to see more elk, but they've all gone up the mountain. Stan dials his cell phone, and talks loudly, piercing the cold morning air with questions to his friend about where there might be more elk. As he does, an unfamiliar truck turns into the road, and a man rolls down his window and asks Stan a question. As it turns out, this land I am hunting is not his friend's land at all. We are officially poachers.

I kneel down to tie my shoe and hide my face, then walk toward the truck while Stan smoothes it over with anemic jokes. This ranch belongs to the Diamond Match Company, and they don't allow hunting here. If I had shot one of those elk, I could have spent six months in prison.

As you might imagine, Stan's grass-fed beef business turns out to be a completely separate entity from the land the Native Americans own, and that ranch is very, very far away.

So now on the second evening in Wyoming, I sit in this vast stretch of desert mountain land, in a bedroom full of pink ruffles, dolls, and children's books, in his home that seems to be without a real address, with no cab companies and no car service for 100 miles, wondering how to leave. That is when Stan calls me and tells me our next hunt will be on horseback and to come fit the saddle to my height. The possibility of filling my elk tag is alluring; I want there to be a silver lining in this trip. But mostly, I want elk jerky.

So I walk down the dusty road toward the horse corral, where Stan huffs and puffs as he pulls the saddles out of the truck and tightens the buckles.

"Did you get a sandwich?" he asks suddenly.

"A sandwich?" I asked.

"Yeah, for tomorrow. You want to eat, don't you? This is when I expect the guest to think," he says.

I fit my saddle, ride the horse in a few small loops, then take off the saddle and bridle. Stan shimmies onto a horse, too, and the horse bucks violently.

We put the horses in a corral for the night, and he asks me to feed them. I try to open the gate at the end of the haystacks while he drives a combine full of hay toward me, but the gate, which is really only a vague separation between two wooden posts, is bound tightly with rusted old wire. This gate hasn't been opened in years, which means that these horses must not eat very often or they don't spend a lot of time at Stan's place.

"Are you lost?" he asks.

"No, your gate is wired shut," I reply. "Would you like me to get some wire cutters?"

He continues to mutter. But after the wires are cut, the hay ends up in the corral and the horses eat. And now in the dark, I feel my way down the long gravel road to the house, make tuna fish sandwiches, and go to sleep.

It is so hard to leave your sleep on cold black mornings during hunting season, but it is even harder when you feel dread, the kind that causes you to wonder what disaster may befall you in the hands of a reckless hunter. But I motivate myself with the thought of filling my elk tag, as I slide out of bed and throw on layers of camo and denim. I walk down the long dirt road to saddle the horses again, who are as spooked as I am as Stan draws near. I climb into the truck that hauls the horses and lean my head on the cold glass to look at the stars. I watch Andromeda and can almost see her get bigger and bigger, feasting on the stars around her.

"Are you usually this talkative?" Stan says, conjuring up a wad of phlegm and spitting out the window.

We climb the narrow winding dirt road to the top of Rattlesnake Mountain, and after an hour, come to the end at 10,000 feet. There are two signs. One on the right says NO TRESPASSING, PRIVATE PROPERTY. The one on the left says PUBLIC PRESERVE, NO HUNTING, WOOD CUTTING ONLY.

"We can't hunt here," I say.

"What do you mean, we can't hunt here," he says, more of a statement than a question. He walks over to the sign, and there is silence for a few minutes. Then he walks back and begins to lead the horses out of the trailer.

"So what is the plan?" I ask, hoping to slow him down.

"Well, I'm goin'," he says.

"But the sign says that we can't hunt here," I say again, the anxiety making my voice higher, a round lump forming and rising with it.

He stands with his hands on his hips and his head cocked and paces around and sucks his teeth and grumbles. "In all my life I've never seen anything like this. Humans have exceeded their carrying capacity," he says. He stands in front of the sign for a few minutes more. I wait, hopeful, and notice the sign for grizzly bears.

"I understand the jargon now," he says finally, and proceeds to finish saddling the horses.

"What jargon?" I ask.

"It's just that side of the sign that we can't hunt on, but we'll go through on the other side," he says.

I pause, considering Calamity Jane. This is when I should channel her. This is when I should lasso Stan with a rope, tie him up, put him in the trailer, and drive us back down the mountain. But instead, I stuff my rifle deep into the leather holder strapped to my saddle and mount with the lump even higher in my throat. Although I would prefer to eat meat from McDonald's than procured this way, I am at a 10,000-foot elevation, with no other sign of life, warning signs for grizzly bears, and no way out. I mount the horse in calm desperation and follow Stan the Man.

I look down at my white horse with his albino eyes. I can feel his lungs heave out against my shins like a steamship. I know I can count on my horse's eyes in the dark, more than mine; this is a strange feeling. I take some comfort in knowing that he probably feels the same way about the man on the horse next to me. They both let out grunts and snorts of displeasure.

As the sun rises, our shadows appear on the ground like giant finger puppets, and I can see the snow scattered on the Rockies above like powdered sugar on a Bundt cake. The light flickers and the heat of the sun on my eyelids gets warmer. Soon a sky of blue marble above us shines down on the snow and the twitching muscles of the horse's albino body. The silence is so vast that I would be able to hear one thousand pins dropping into the dehydrated cliffs of grass. There is no sign of life, hardly an insect, not even the contours of a melting track on the snow. But there are the ghosts of animals jumping across the hills, disappearing when I blink. And then I start to hear the reverberations of familiar sounds, echoing as they leave my head into the great room of silence. And then I start to hear the sound of reality, the voice of the man in the other saddle on the other horse.

"Did you bring toilet paper?" Stan asks riding ahead of me and sucking his teeth.

"No," I reply.

"You don't think you're going to need it?" he says, harassed and red faced.

"No, as a matter of fact, I don't think I will!"

"I have some you can buy off me," he says without grinning.

We ride higher into Monument Mountain, in silence mostly, except when he proclaims that humans have ruined his environment, about toilet paper, and how the world has overrun its carrying capacity.

The horse trots and walks at its discretion, and I bounce higher off the saddle with every step. I can feel the small muscles on my back come alive and work, and my inner thighs begin to ache as I twist them inward and hold my feet in the stirrups. We ride higher, toward a boulder of limestone jutting into the sky, and guide the horses, slipping and snorting, to it.

My two-legged companion gets off his horse and ties him to a tree, and I do the same. He begins to walk away toward the limestone boulder and announces he's hungry. And so I open the saddlebags and retrieve our tuna fish sandwiches and walk toward the limestone boulder, too.

At the top of the boulder, we scan the sides of the mountains and the thick pines for elk, lying in the afternoon sun. But there are no signs of life, hardly a bird. It is just utter silence, save for the sound of Stan sucking his teeth.

We eat our tuna fish sandwiches and some dried blueberries and Stan retrieves a Butterfinger from the depths of his pockets. He then lies back on the rock, tips his hat over his head, and descends into a snoring sleep.

I lean back on the rocks, too, and look at the blue marble sky. I close my eyes and a gold veil comes across them and flickers off. I take shallow breathfuls of the thin air and dream of nothing.

After some time, the motor of a fly wakes me. I begin to wonder how Stan planned on getting an elk out of here were I to shoot one in this place where it is forbidden.

I suppose that a poacher is most like the Paleolithic man. He helped himself to what a leopard stored in a tree, and what nature had to offer. Hunting was an expression of man's first instinct and his first craft, with no limitations other than his own physical and mental strictures, both of which were challenged and expanded as he honed his craft. It must have been very freeing to play only by the rules of your own moral compass.

The modern manifestation of that philosophy was Walter Earl Durand—a mountain man in Wyoming after the Depression. From an early age, he lived with ease in the wilderness and could hit almost any target at any time. He resisted the transition requiring hunters to have a license and a season to hunt and was eventually arrested for poaching elk. To him, it defied the natural human condition.

Although there are many rules governing hunting today, there is still the essence of Durand in hunting—it is still my own morality that guides me as a hunter and meat eater. The great outdoor writer Aldo Leopold once wrote, "A peculiar virtue in wildlife ethics is that the hunter ordinarily has no gallery to applaud or disapprove of his conduct. Whatever his acts, they are dictated by his own conscience, rather than by a mob of onlookers. It is difficult to exaggerate the importance of this fact." The problem with this, though, is that some people have a very weak moral compass.

When explorer John Colter left the Lewis and Clark expedition, he came down through Wyoming and got into trouble with the Indians while traveling through Yellowstone. He vowed to himself that if he ever got out of that mess, all he wanted to do was go home and die in his own bed. And that is exactly what he did.

In this moment, watching Stan snoring peacefully on a limestone rock, I begin to understand that sentiment thoroughly.

Stan wakes up with a snort and a Butterfinger burp, takes the scope of my gun, and peers through it to scan the horizon for elk, grinding the wooden stock of my rifle against the limestone. But there is nothing.

In the end, he agrees with my suggestion that it is time to go down. We begin back down Monument Mountain, leading each of the horses by rope for 3 miles. All the while, Stan talks about "his baby," his grass-fed beef operation. He says that one ordinary burger patty has the DNA from two thousand cows, and how there is "no accountability" because ordinary ground beef is produced in so few locations.

It is hard to listen to Stan. Not because what he says is inaccurate, but because he has made himself into a victim. Calamity Jane was never a victim. Stan loves the story of his failure as a grass-fed beef farmer in cattle country, where every other feedlot farmer is a success.

Of course, there is some real truth to Stan's narrative. He is one of only a few farmers in Wyoming who raise cattle entirely on grass. He grows the grass organically and lets his cows eat it until they are sent to slaughter at an organically certified slaughterhouse. Most beef production has a huge carbon footprint. Fertilizer is a petroleum product; a lot of fertilizer is used to raise the feed corn and a lot of fuel is used to get the cattle to the feedlot. So Stan's heart is in the right place, but his business model is terrible. And the truth is that while he whines that he "cannot take a Super Bowl ad out for organic beef," there are other grass-fed beef operations that are successful.

Unlike grass-fed operations, most of the other cattle in Wyoming are sent to feedlots where their rations are controlled by "feed science." They are fed more carbohydrates and less roughage. And because of the increased carbohydrate, the cow's rumen, which becomes a four-legged fermentation vat, grows more sugar than the rumen can stand. And because it is growing more sugar, it produces more bacteria, and that bacteria starts to ulcerate the rumen. It is as if there is beer brewing in their stomachs. So the big feedlots add antibiotics to the feed to reduce the bacteria count in the rumen. That is how O157:H7 appeared—a fatal form of *E. coli* that came strictly from feedlots, and is resistant to antibiotics.

Four companies—Cargill, JBS, Tyson, and Smithfield—control over 90 percent of this meat system across the world. It is a system that relies heavily on nitrogen and corn. After World War II, nitrogen fertilizer developed because nitrogen was left over from TNT, and we realized that if we put it in the soil, the plants would flourish better than they ever had. This was the advent of nitrogen fertilizer—a wartime commodity. After the war, it was disseminated to farmers, which led them to stop spreading manure as natural fertilizer, and opt instead to simply send the cows to dusty, centralized feedlots.

I tell Stan no more elk hunting. "I have a lot of writing to do." He seems perfectly fine with it, or at least that is what I gather from the burp. I ask him if I can borrow a car for "research," and he says fine, and so I spend a day away from my two-legged friend and explore this empty state and its great brown mountains.

I drive from 4,000 feet in elevation to 5,000 feet, through the Big Horn Desert, slowly past vast ranches owned by big companies or big individuals. I pass Heart Mountain, where the rock on top is 300 million years older than the rock on the bottom, prompting geologists to study it for the past hundred years. There are mountains all around me, to the south and to the east. The Big Horns tie together at the bottom through the Wind River Canyon like a big parched bowl. Now less than 30 miles from one of the world's largest volcanoes at Yellowstone Lake, I move past pregnant cows and a range of wild Spanish horses.

I ride through the north fork of the Shoshone River, named after one of the poorest of Indian tribes. I drive through the town of Cody, named after William "Buffalo Bill" Cody, a horse rider and trick shooter who was also a real estate developer and showman who built the Wild West Show and took it all over the world. Calamity Jane was one of his performers. Buffalo Bill was also a hunting outfitter, one of the first people to take people hunting as a business, and his clients included Theodore Roosevelt and the prince of Monaco. He was an entrepreneur of the Wild West and formed the town of Cody when Yellowstone became a National Park, in 1872.

Past Cody, there is only one road across what the Shoshone called "the land of the stinky water." It is the road to Yellowstone, where the geysers and water emit the smell of sulfur. I pass a V shape in the canyon where the sun never shines, and see herds of mule deer with dark, wet beads for eyes and shiny Rudolph noses.

On the road are volcanic rock formations that look like crystals, and pine trees that are gray ghosts, ravaged by the pine beetle and wildfires. But despite the vast land, some houses are still clustered together, perhaps for scarce resources, or perhaps because even when given the space, we humans still desire one another's company in the end.

The east gate to Yellowstone is lovely and simple. A ranger tells me everything I could want to know with an animated enthusiasm. She hands me pamphlets and maps and the receipt for the steep entry fee, and it begins to feel strangely like my childhood trip to Disney World. But the drive is beautiful, the dead trees are stark, the snow-capped mountains look fierce, the grand lake glistens, and the blacktop winds gently between the falling rock zones and the water. Ravens carve the sky with their wings and stop at parked cars with their beaks open, beckoning for a morsel. Signs warn people against playing with the animals, and visitors with heavy camera equipment are parked on the roadside. The rivers and lakes in the forest look like pools of oil. Swans dip their necks in it, and duck tails point high to the wind.

At the famous geyser named Old Faithful, a chipper man uses the microphone with extreme regularity, announcing which geyser will go off next. People rush down the boardwalk and stand with their cameras poised. Two ladies watch from the comfort of their Chevy Tahoe, eating popcorn. I sit in silence, eating a sandwich with curious components, and wonder—has nature become one big stadium? Yellowstone is a wilderness that can be seen from the comfort of your car, a series of scenes that can be taken home with you from the gift store. This worries me.

This is supposed to be one of nature's great triumphs, a place where people can experience the natural world in its purest form. I wonder if it is too late, if the notion of "nature" has become so alien to us, that living off the land is only a romantic notion and not a realistic one. I wonder if Nature has become the last great zoo, an inaccessible place.

On the drive out of Yellowstone, a herd of bison block the road, close enough to reach out and touch. They seem stoic and unimpressed with mankind. Farmers raise bison now—restoring prairies with the native grasses for the bison to eat. It is cheaper because the sun fuels the soil, rather than nitrogen fertilizer, and the bison, which are more mobile than cows, spread the native seed with their dung. Bison meat is nutrient rich, leaner, and subtly sweeter than beef, and bison farmers say that a single bison expends about one barrel of oil during its life, compared to a single cow, which burns eight barrels. Once upon a time, there were 75 million bison roaming the western plains of North America. They were a staple food for Native Americans, who used their hides for teepees, their bladders to store fat, and their partially curdled milk as a form of yogurt.

In the movement to settle the west and transplant the Native Americans onto reservations, U.S. settlers hunted the bison so fiercely that by the end of the nineteenth century, only eight hundred living bison could be identified in North America.

Today there are 500,000 bison in North America. And though they are being raised by ranchers now, there are still fewer bison slaughtered in the United States in a single year than beef cattle in a single day. What makes bison most intriguing as an alternative to cattle is that they are inherently wild and are survivors. They are the only terrestrial North American mammal to have survived the Ice Age and our modern agrarian system of domesticating animals. Whereas they previously had been hunted with abandon, they are now quietly going about their lives under the radar.

Back near Cody, I have my last meal with Stan. I don't know it is my last meal until I sit watching him at his dinner table, cooing over his sirloin.

"This is my baby," he says cutting his knife into the medium pink hunk shimmering on his plate.

"That's the thing that I don't think most vegetarians and vegans understand," he says. "The woman is the one that needs the meat. The male does not. And the man that brought home the meat was the one who got chased after. There's no doubt it was that primal. I mean, we didn't grow this brain on our head from eating tomatoes. I mean there's not an ob-gyn doctor that's not going to load you up with iron. All the stuff that's in meat—if you're not eating it, you're in trouble."

Then he nags me to say that his is the best beef I've ever tasted. In this moment, the spirit of Calamity Jane grabs hold of me and I know I, somehow, have to go.

I get up and make a brief phone call midmeal in the pink frilly bedroom, then conjure up all that I learned in ninth grade drama class when Mrs. Turner cast me as Abigail in *The Crucible*. I channel it all, the angst, the outrage, the drama as the townsfolk were burned at the stake for their witchcraft, and I emerge from the bedroom with tears streaming down my face and exclaim, "I have to go!" It was an Oscar-worthy performance, one I'm not particularly proud to say I performed, and one that will possibly have karmic implications down the line for the lies I had to tell. But sometimes, you just have to go.

And so I walk down the gravel road where the air smells like dried blood, with suitcase in tow, and I wave good-bye to the cows. I keep on walking away from Stan and his wisdom and his steak. And in a strangely cascading sequence of more phone calls, I arrange for a couple at a car repair shop to drive me to Billings Airport. And in the most beautifully ironic metaphor, they, the kindest of strangers, willing to help an unfamiliar girl escape a barren land, meet me in the parking lot of a McDonald's.

They are sweet and talk to me about cooking and how they had no plans on a Saturday night anyway, other than to go out to dinner at Arby's or McDonald's. And they point out the sugar factories on the road, and the oil refineries, and the single red light of a limestone mine in the middle of the desert at dark, and the smell of sulfur drifting from the Yellowstone River. And she tells me that she loves to bake and has written homemade cookbooks from time to time. I close my eyes and feel the yellow light from the oil refinery drift over my eyelids. The comfort of her voice and sight of it all make my eyes well with happiness. I think about the albino horse, and the rhythm of its steamship lungs. I wonder when I will taste elk harvested with my own two hands. Was this trip a waste? I ask myself. I don't think so. Because as I was taught that very first morning I went turkey hunting with the Commish, it is the hunt that matters, not the amount of game you take. Things are now in high relief for me more than ever before. And just as much as I want to be a hunter, I know the kind of hunter and the kind of human I never want to be, and that is a lesson worth paying for.

Elk Jerky

One of the traditional ways our ancestors preserved meat was by drying it. It is also one of the simplest. Fresh strips of meat were often first soaked in a marinade or brine, then, traditionally, hung to dry in the sun, the attic, or some other dry place. Some people let it hang over a slow, smoky fire, which added flavor and discouraged flies. You can, of course be modern and use the oven or a dehydrator.

   2 pounds elk (lean cuts are ideal)
   2 tablespoons Worcestershire sauce
   2 tablespoons red wine vinegar
   1 tablespoon salt
   1 teaspoon brown sugar
   1 teaspoon red pepper flakes
   2 cloves garlic, sliced
   2 teaspoons cayenne
   1 cup water

1. Put the meat in the freezer for about 30 minutes, until just firm. Slice it across the grain into strips about 1/4 inch thick.
2. Combine the other ingredients together in a bowl and mix well. Let sit for 10 minutes.
3. Add the strips and marinate, covered, in the refrigerator overnight.
4. Preheat the oven to 200°F. Place the strips on tinfoil with the door propped open and dry the strips until they are pliable, 5 to 7 hours.
5. Store in a plastic container for up to 2 weeks.

Also try: other antlered game, bison, turkey, rabbit

Elk-Stuffed Cabbage Rolls

I once met a hearty Wyoming woman who lived in a farmhouse, and her kitchen smelled wonderful. When I inquired about the source of the aroma, she said she was making a pot of stuffed cabbage rolls. This is my version, inspired by the memory of those good kitchen smells. It is cooked in a tomato sauce base, which is the traditional Eastern European way.

    12 cabbage leaves, large and unblemished
    1 pound ground elk meat
    3/4 cup cooked brown rice
    1/2 cup finely chopped onion
    2 garlic cloves, minced
    2 tablespoons chopped fresh flat-leaf parsley
    1 egg
    2 teaspoons kosher salt
    1 teaspoon pepper
    1/2 cup cream
    2 tablespoons Marsala
    1 tablespoon tomato paste
    1 (8-ounce) can tomato sauce
    1 (14.5-ounce) can diced tomatoes, unstrained
    1 tablespoon sugar
    2 tablespoons white wine vinegar or red wine vinegar
    2 garlic cloves, smashed
    1/2 cup water

1. Bring a pot of water as salty as the sea to a rolling boil. Drop the cabbage leaves into the water, cover and cook for 3 minutes. Drain well and set aside to cool.
2. In a large bowl, combine the elk, rice, onion, garlic, parsley, egg, salt, pepper, cream, Marsala, and tomato paste, and mix well.
3. Lay out the cabbage leaves on a cutting board or clean surface and place a twelfth of the elk mixture into the center of each cabbage leaf. Fold the top and bottom edges toward each other, then roll the outer leaves around the filling and fasten with toothpick. Place the rolls in a baking dish and set aside.
4. Preheat the oven to 350°F. In a small saucepan, combine the tomato sauce, tomatoes, sugar, vinegar, garlic, and water and bring to a simmer for 2 minutes, until well blended. Pour over the cabbage rolls.
5. Bake, covered, for 40 to 45 minutes. Remove the baking dish from the oven and carefully remove the toothpicks.

Also try: other antlered game, bison

Corned Elk
Serves 8 to 10

Before refrigeration, people struggled to find fresh meat, especially during the cold-est winter months. The meat they obtained came from hunting and fishing, or through trade. Because fresh meat spoils after a few days without refrigeration, what people could find needed to be preserved. Corning was one way to do it. This consisted of meat laid in a salt brine for several weeks, which allowed it to be stored for much longer.

    4 quarts water
    2 cups kosher salt
    1/4 cup sugar
    1/2 teaspoon cracked black peppercorns
    1/2 teaspoon cracked mustard seeds
    1/2 teaspoon cracked coriander seeds
    1 bay leaf
    2 whole cloves
    4 allspice berries
    2 cloves garlic, crushed
    5 pounds elk brisket
    2 onions, sliced
    Homemade sauerkraut, for serving (page 234)
    Homemade mustard, for serving (page 235)

1. In a large, nonreactive pot, heat and whisk together 1 cup of the water and the salt, sugar, and spices until the salt and sugar have dissolved.
2. Turn off the heat and add the remaining water. Place the brisket in a large plas-tic brine bag and add the brine. If using a bowl, weight the meat with a plate so that it is submerged completely.
3. Refrigerate for 3 weeks.
4. After 3 weeks, remove the brisket from the brine and rinse well. Discard the brine. The elk is now corned and ready to be cooked.
5. Place in a large pot and barely cover with water. Add the onions and bring to a boil, then lower the heat to medium, cover the pot, and simmer for 2 1/2 hours, or until the meat is tender.
6. To serve, slice the meat across the grain. Serve with homemade sauerkraut and homemade mustard.

Also try: other antlered game, bison

Moroccan Elk Stew   Serves 8

This isn't your everyday stew, but it's perfect for the really cold months and for large gatherings when you have a lot of people to feed. It has a Middle Eastern flair, with a little sweetness and a little spice. I like to spoon it over Israeli couscous tossed with a bit of orange and lemon zest, but regular couscous or rice work just as well.

> 4 tablespoons grape seed oil or butter
> 4 pounds elk shoulder or haunch, cut into cubes
> 3/4 cup all-purpose flour
> 1 teaspoon salt
> 1/4 teaspoon ground cinnamon
> 1/4 teaspoon ginger powder
> 1/2 teaspoon freshly ground black pepper
> 2 medium-size onions, roughly chopped
> 4 carrots, peeled and chopped
> 2 medium-size turnips, peeled and chopped
> 3 cloves garlic, roughly chopped
> 2/3 cup dried apricots
> 2/3 cup prunes, pitted
> 3 to 4 cups antlered game stock (page 213)

1. Heat a large, heavy-bottomed pot with oil. In a bowl, toss the elk cubes in the flour. Shake the cubes well and place them in the pot in batches, being sure not to crowd them. Brown them on all sides and transfer to a plate or rack.
2. Put all of the browned meat back in the pan and sprinkle it with the salt, cinnamon, ginger, and pepper. Then add the vegetables, garlic, and dried fruit. Pour in enough stock for the meat to be three-quarters covered, and bring it to a boil. Lower the heat so the bubbles percolate. Cover and simmer gently for 2 hours, until tender.

Also try: other antlered game, bison

Eat the meat and leave the skin.
Turn up your plate and let's begin.

—COWBOY'S GRACE

6

The Upland High Life

By now I am questioning any more of these "blind hunting dates." The next stop on my itinerary is a luxurious ranch in Texas Hill Country, at least according to its publicist who invited me, where I'll be hunting but also be followed around by a photographer and a reporter and a magazine and a camera crew. I feel a bit jaded and not entirely convinced that I won't end up in this woman's pool house in downtown San Antonio, flipping venison burgers for the camera. I call her from Billings Airport and tell her that I'm not so sure. And before I know it, I start to ramble on about cows and bears and elk poaching and a parking lot in McDonald's and how I'm not going to be tricked anymore because I'm Calamity Jane! Something along those lines, anyway. She listens and expresses her horror and sympathy in that Southern female way that I find so comforting. She promises me that this is a beautiful private house for me to stay in, at a real hunting ranch, and I can just rest.

"Okay," I say. "But I'm not getting on any horses."

This Hill Country is a foreign land to me, 1,400 feet high, lush and green, bugless save for the crickets and the dragonflies, and cooler than its slightly southern neighbor San Antonio. It could be a small town in Martha Stewart's Connecticut, with perfectly coiffed horse fences, or in the hills of Marin County California, where the air is slightly damp and smells of burning wood and the roads are dirt. But this Hill Country is in Texas, between a town called Welfare and another called Comfort.

Along Joshua Creek lies a ranch where blazing red cypress trees line up like soldiers along the creek, turning the water crimson. Amber waves of tall grass blur in a band of perpetual motion, and pheasant and grouse dart in and out of the brush. To the north, the quail flit faster than the dragonflies, and to the south, sounds of prized dogs fill the air, yelping at the feeding hour, lapping up their meal after a day spent flushing birds from the fields.

I am here for a "media event" at the ranch—one of a handful selected in the United States for induction into the Beretta Trident program, a kind of Michelin Guide for hunters that rates professional hunting ranches around the world and bestows upon them one to three tridents. A trident rating is an indicator of the experience a hunter might have if she chooses to visit this place.

Cocktail hour is at six forty-five in the owners' residence, where I am greeted by a real African lion frozen in time in a perfectly menacing pose. On the veranda, a stone fireplace burns and mimics the melting sunset and warms the flagstones beneath our feet. The chef appears with a dimpled silver platter of axis venison carpaccio, purple and sweet and bejeweled with vegetable confetti. Across from me, a reporter poised with his notebook sits in a chair made of branches, a tad bewildered and out of his element. A photographer sits languidly on a stone bench, his back to the fire, sipping a merlot. The big Texas husband somehow realizes that I prefer something stronger, fixes a whiskey, and hands it to me diluted with soda and tinkling with ice . . . and after just a few sips offers me more.

Past the veranda, the sky turns into a purple bruise. The Texas wife sits calmly with a pleased smile, her hair velvet black and shiny, sparkling jewelry reflected on her body and blending with the new evening stars.

This is a place where money and tradition collide—where descendents of the five-hundred-year-old *maestro da canne* (master gunsmith) Bartolomeo Beretta dynasty in Brescia, Italy, mingle with newer dynasties from the American Southwest.

There are many components to this place. In part, it is a library that holds classic books and photographs from a hunting honeymoon in Africa, and sterling magnifying glasses carefully laid on a leatherbound desk with its rich mahogany legs nestled into a finely embroidered rug. The Texas *padrone* lifts his hand to one of the shelves, and with one motion pulls its panel back to reveal another door leading to a chamber. He types a code onto the handle of the door, opens it, enters into a room the size of a small Manhattan apartment, and gestures for me to follow him.

The interior walls of this secret chamber are lined with vintage shotguns, old McKay Browns with Turkish walnut stocks, Parkers, delicate and rare quail guns, and a 16-gauge Broses. The guns bear utopian hunting scenes brought to life by countless hours of fine metal work carved in Brescia, so fine that the ducks seem to spring from the steel, dogs chasing birds threaten to run off the locks, and even leaves of the trees are shaded and stir in the wind.

When we return to the surface from the secret chamber, we sit for dinner in a well-paneled room, another grand fireplace warming our backs and a Texas-size chandelier reflecting the candlelight. We eat pork roast, cranberries, spicy butternut squash, and a chocolate soufflé with a sugar crust on top. The big Texas husband tells the story of hunting a "real pissed-off leopard" in Africa, which hunted him the whole time he hunted it, and how the African bushmen spoke in their language of clicks as they chased the leopard through the grass. He tells his stories in the presence of a gallery of bobcats and leopards watching us from the living room, their muscles poised taut for eternity.

"When I'm sitting with men around a fire," says the big Texas husband, "we often ask ourselves, what is it about this that we like so much? And the truth is that we're going *back*. Even though we eat the nice food and wear the nice clothing now, it was only two or three generations ago that this is how we provided food for our families. Now we just have places like HEB Grocery. But with hunting there is still the camaraderie, a series of beautiful things that bonds you. The people you hunt with will always take your call."

Sitting here and listening, I realize there are as many ways to hunt the food as there are to cook it. It wasn't long ago that American companies entertained their clients abroad in the United Kingdom on a traditional walk-up hunt, the European-style driven pheasant shoot, or on a fast-paced Continental shoot, in a quest to feel a part of old-world luxury.

But in true capitalist style, Americans discovered they could experience similar luxury on their own soil for one-third of the price. And so a market was born in the United States. Hunting amid this kind of luxury was no longer just for the leisured class, but for people who had money but limited time; they could now spend a weekend at a place like this. Men could bond with one another and experience that special element of trust that comes with hunting together, more so than from playing a game of golf.

"You'll meet the greatest people in this business," the big Texas husband says, sipping his whiskey. "Multimillion-dollar mergers happen here with men walking behind dogs."

In the morning, I walk the bowl of the Guadalupe River, through bluestem grass and live oaks. The reporter and I arrive at a field with a gamekeeper they call El Hefe. English setters and pointers and

Brittany spaniels yelp from their cages in the back of a truck, eager to begin their daily task of finding and flushing birds. Lacy, a seven-year-old English cocker, walks along El Hefe's side, waiting for Brittany spaniels Stan and Rock to point her in the right direction. When El Hefe says, "Hunt 'em up, Lacy," she dashes forward, the nub of her tail wagging, and weaves in and out of the grass until the birds fly up and shots ring out.

I bring a 28-gauge Beretta to my cheek again and again, as I make my way through my case of number six shot and the air begins to smell of smoking shells. Everyone is silent as Lacy weaves. I watch with my arms alert, and my heart beating just a little bit faster. I can hear the squishing sound of El Hefe's chewing tobacco, as the reporter arbitrarily calls him Bob. But he doesn't care, he just squirts and talks to his dogs. A large tin bath of water has been set in the field for the dogs to cool the Texas sun off their backs. Lacey jumps in and out in one fluid motion. The pointers follow suit, shake and spray without missing a step, and continue to sniff. Hawks fly above me, eyeing their competition. They have already broken up the coveys of birds, causing them to scatter, and the dogs now set out to find the birds individually. There are pheasants with their long tendril tails, and quail so small and fast my eyes mix them with the dragonflies, and when I shoot, sometimes one falls and sometimes one doesn't. The chukar, though, is what I want—a native of southern Eurasia, brought from Pakistan to the United States to be a game bird. I have not tasted a chukar, and the one that appears in the corner of my eye, I miss.

After a lunch of meat and peach cobbler and iced tea, a flusher named Tramp takes over for Lacy. She is black and seems almost shy and she weaves in and out and brings the birds up demurely. There are birds everywhere, so many birds now, but still no chukar appears.

I walk the red rows with a swirl of dogs in front of me, their bodies embroidering the grass. My wool tweed jacket holds in all of the afternoon heat and wets my back, and the dogs continue to weave and stitch, their tongues hanging out in short breaths of expectation. I walk observing all the noises flowing in and out of the grasses, whirring, cackling, mysterious, and always real.

The guttural chirping sounds of the fields repeat in my mind and so do the images of the men I see fishing the Guadalupe River on my way through the fields—men stringing up the Guadalupe bass, bluegill, and catfish.

And then at last, in the iridescent trickles of an afternoon sun, an olive brown figure rises from the left, only 10 yards in front, and crosses my path in a diagonal leap skyward. I swing my shotgun into the sky and squint into the sun, and with a slap of the trigger, my chukar gives unto me. Tramp retrieves it and I hold the bird in my hand. It has a buff-colored belly, bold black and chestnut barring on its flanks, and black lines circling the contours of its eyes, all flowing down its neck and into its chest toward a white throat, covering the span between a red bill and legs.

The most knowledgeable outdoorsmen are often the El Hefes, who have spent a life as hunting guides and understand the nuances of nature better than all of the other humans around them. The El Hefes of the world won't always share this knowledge with you because it is just a part of their existence, and quite honestly, they have a job to do at this type of hunting ranch, leading you through the dance of the glossy fields, guiding you and the dogs toward pirouetting pheasants. But sometimes when you inquire, the El Hefes teach you a bit more than is normally known.

By the late afternoon we switch our prey. I now sit in a deer stand in a small forest with a twenty-year-old guide named Grady who could moonlight as a football player, except that he recites animal facts as a player would game stats. We are waiting for an axis deer, a reddish-haired native of Asia whose meat is fine grained and slightly sweet. Grady instructs me on the need for proper camouflage. "With big game, you always want to break up solid colors, and break up your outline; you don't want to silhouette yourself," he says, squatting on an overturned bucket and peering through a pair of binoculars.

An armadillo and a porcupine waddle through the leaves below my deer stand, just the point of a leather tail and a coat of spikes showing through the dry leaves.

The axis deer, like the pheasant and the chukar—like us—is also an immigrant. The famous Texas YO Ranch began bringing exotics into the United States in the 1950s and '60s and today these include axis, fallow deer, blackbuck antelope, sika, audad, and addax, among others—all of which have naturalized and flourished in range and pasture where they can come and go as they please.

"How do people justify going to Africa to kill a lion for sport?" I ask. "I don't imagine they are eating lion meat for dinner," I smirk.

"Those Africa trips that wealthy men take are actually what keep the animals from going extinct," Grady says matter-of-factly. "And the native tribes do eat the lion meat. For a single animal, thirty to forty thousand dollars goes back into the local economy, which incentivizes the governments to keep the animals healthy. The U.S. is now introducing certain breeds like the blackbuck back into their native African populations, where their conservation practices weren't good enough and there is poaching."

The idea of an "exotic" in a sense becomes relative with time. After all, the white man was an exotic when he first stepped on the soil at Plymouth Rock.

But the notion of importing exotics is far older than the United States. It is the stuff of myth and legend. After capturing the Golden Fleece, mythological Greek hero Jason and the Argonauts discovered pheasant on the return voyage on the Phasis River. (Pheasants derive their name from this river Phasis, now called the Rion.) There, they caught some and brought them home to Greece.

While Grady talks, I peer through the slit in the square wooden deer blind, and see the chalky nose of a young whitetail buck outside, chasing a three-year-old doe in heat, their cottony tails wagging like the spaniels'. But I am in the deer stand not for a whitetail but an axis, and so I wait.

A gray-faced whitetail doe appears next, trailed by a parade of twenty-three wild turkeys, heads bobbing forward and backward, feet stepping purposefully on the pine-needled forest floor.

"Axis deer vitals sit farther forward so you have to shoot really tight to the shoulder blade," Grady says as I peer through the crack and into the flood of evening sunlight.

"Axis deer don't breed 'til they rub out the velvet in their horns and are full horned," he continues in a heavy whisper.

In the distance, beyond the clearing where the whitetails stand and feed, and the turkeys peck, I can hear the high pitched bark of an axis doe, then her soft-pitched mew, like a cow elk's. But she doesn't show herself. By now, the sun has grown murky, too murky to see, and as if to let me know, an axis buck lets out his screaming roar from the woods, telling me to go home.

Grady and I climb down from the deer stand as the stars flicker on, and we begin to walk the twilight path toward the ranch house. Arriving, we find a stone fire pit, and a long table of roasted meats and very fine wine.

"Next time, you'll harvest an axis," he says.

"Why do you use the word *harvest*?" I ask.

"In my mind, it is just like any other harvest because it is food for the table," he says.

In Texas, there are few public hunting sites, and few places that can be leased for less than ten thousand dollars per gun. Large companies are willing to pay large sums to entertain large clients. Experiences like these are hard to come by and are ones that you will remember fondly for the rest of your life. They are the kind you wish will stick like beer-battered pheasant to your ribs. As a result, they also present a moral dilemma. This sort of hunting isn't sustainable as a way of life. It is a sporting event, an opportunity for leisure, even though all of the birds are used for food. Looking at the experience objectively, it isn't where I can go regularly if I want to eat only meat that I've killed with my own hands. In a way, it is much like the aristocratic approach to hunting in the Old World, a way to put on woolen coats and experience what it must have felt to be Catherine the Great as she sat in a well-paneled banquet room, with platters of roasted pheasant and stuffed partridge dangled beneath her nose. This experience is escapist and luxurious, so far from the everyday, or rather, so far from *my* everyday. But it is something I will always recall fondly—the way that one remembers a warm, bright elusive dream.

Braised Pheasant Legs with
Cabbage and Grapes

Serves 4

Unlike a farmyard bird, wild birds have muscular legs, which lend them well to braising. Each bird will be different, depending on variety and age, but the key is to cook them low and slow until the meat is tender and falls off the bone. A good braising green or vegetable can be substituted for the cabbage.

    8 pheasant legs
    Salt and pepper
    2 tablespoons all-purpose flour
    2 tablespoons butter
    1/4 cup diced onion
    2 cups finely sliced cabbage
    1 cup seedless grapes, crushed
    1/4 cup brandy
    2 cups game bird stock (page 212)
    2 tablespoons freshly squeezed lemon juice
    2 tablespoons minced parsley

1. Rinse and pat the legs dry, and season on both sides with salt and pepper. Dust both sides with the flour.
2. In a sauté pan, melt the butter until it begins to bubble. Add the legs, skin side down, and cook until golden brown, about 4 minutes. Turn over, cook for about 1 minute, then transfer the meat to a platter.
3. To the same pan, add the onion and cabbage and sauté until soft and brown, about 5 minutes.
4. Add the grapes and stir. Add the legs, browned side up, and nestle them into the cabbage and onion.
5. Add the brandy and light with a match. Let the alcohol burn off and reduce. Add the stock, cover partially with a lid, and cook at a very low simmer for about 1 hour, or until the meat falls off the bone.
6. Finish with the lemon juice and parsley and more salt and pepper to taste.

Also try: brant, coot, duck, gallinule, goose, grouse, prairie chicken, partridge, chukar, pigeon, ptarmigan, quail, rail, snipe, turkey, squirrel, rabbit

Chukar Pie

A pie is perfect for a medley of game bird scraps that wouldn't necessarily make a meal on their own. This recipe uses a double piecrust, the way you would in a traditional potpie, but you could also use leftover mashed potatoes as your top "crust." This is sometimes referred to as Hunter's Pie. A version of this was sent to me by one of my blog readers, who said his mother in McLeansville, North Carolina, often made it with pheasants, but any game bird or even other game meat will work well.

Crust:

- 2 1/2 cups all-purpose flour
- 6 tablespoons lard (see page 187 to render your own)
- 6 tablespoons cold butter, cubed
- 1/2 teaspoon grated nutmeg
- 1/2 teaspoon salt
- About 4 tablespoons ice water
- 1 egg white, lightly beaten

Filling:

- 3 chukar, fully dressed, or the equivalent in game bird meat (see Note)
- 2 cups game bird stock (page 212)
- 1 medium-size onion, chopped
- 2 cloves garlic, minced
- 3 celery stalks, chopped
- 1/2 cup white wine
- Salt and pepper
- 1 tablespoon butter
- 4 tablespoons all-purpose flour
- 1/4 cup milk
- 1 cup peas
- 3 medium-size parsnips, peeled and chopped
- 3 medium-size carrots, peeled and chopped
- 2 cups spinach or other leafy greens
- 1 teaspoon fresh thyme leaves, picked from the stem

For the Crust:

1. Combine the flour, lard, butter, nutmeg, and salt in a bowl and work it with your hands until sandy and lumpy. The lumps of fat should range from pea to walnut size, which will ensure a flaky crust.
2. Add a few drops of water at a time until the dough comes together but is not too sticky. The amount of water you need will vary, based on humidity. If it is very hot, work quickly. Divide the dough into two disks. Wrap them in plastic and place them in the freezer for about 30 minutes.

3. Remove one dough disk from the freezer, let rest for 10 minutes, then roll out on a cutting board, dusted with lots of flour, until the circle is slightly larger than the size of a 9-inch pie dish. Drape it over your pie dish. Trim as needed, and patch if need be, using a bit of water and extra dough scraps. Put the pie dish back into the freezer for at least 30 minutes, preferably longer.

4. Once the bottom crust is frozen in the pie dish, preheat the oven to 425°F. Bake the crust for 20 to 25 minutes, until it is firm and golden brown. If the dough puffs up at all, simply pat it down with the back of a spoon. You won't need pie weights here because you have frozen the crust. Remove from the oven and let cool.

For the Filling:

1. Combine the chukar, stock, onion, garlic, celery, wine, and salt and pepper in a pot. Bring to a simmer and cook, partially covered, until the meat is loose, about 1 hour.

2. Allow the filling to cool slightly and then remove the meat with a slotted spoon, pull it from the bones, and cut it into bite-size pieces. Set it aside on a plate.

3. Preheat the oven to 350°F. Meanwhile, in a small saucepan, melt the butter and whisk in the flour until it bubbles, 1 minute. Add the milk and whisk until a paste forms, then add the paste to the pot containing the broth and bring to a boil. Stir until the broth has consistency of gravy, about 10 minutes, then remove from the heat.

4. Add the meat and additional vegetables to the broth, along with the thyme. Season with salt and pepper to taste.

5. Add the filling to the prebaked crust. Remove the second dough disk from the freezer, let rest for 10 minutes, then roll it out on a floured surface, until it is about an inch wider than the pie dish. Drape it over the filling. Trim the edges and tuck them under the top crust.

6. With a pastry brush, brush some beaten egg white along the circumference, between the two crusts, and press down gently with your thumb or a fork.

7. Brush the top of the pie with egg white. With a paring knife, cut small vent holes in the center and on the outer edges.

8. Bake at 350°F for 35 minutes, until the crust is golden brown. Serve hot.

Also try: brant, coot, duck, gallinule, goose, grouse, prairie chicken, partridge, pheasant, pigeon, ptarmigan, quail, rail, snipe, turkey, squirrel, rabbit, or a combination of those leftover scraps

Note: To substitute other game birds, 3 chukar = 2 pheasants, 3 grouse, 6 quail, or 12 doves.

Quail en Papillote

Serves 4

Cooking *en papillote* is a very traditional French technique that is designed to trap the flavor and the aroma until it reaches the diner. The protein, traditionally fish, is baked in a parchment envelope sealed with egg white, which puffs dramatically in the oven. French gastronome Brillat-Savarin described the quail as "everything that is most delightful and tempting. One of these plump little birds is pleasing equally for its taste, shape, and its color. It is unfortunate to serve it any other way but roasted or *en papillote*, because its aroma is extremely fleeting, and whenever the bird comes in contact with a liquid, this perfume dissolves, evaporates, and is lost." This method is especially useful when the bird skin couldn't be saved. The juices that develop in the bag serve as the sauce, but you can also serve a beurre blanc (page 228) or other sauce on the side.

2 tablespoons grape seed oil plus additional oil or butter as needed
1/2 cup diced shallots
4 garlic cloves, diced
1 cup sliced white button mushrooms
1/2 cup thinly sliced leeks
1 cup seeded and diced tomatoes
Salt and pepper
4 sprigs fresh thyme
8 tablespoons white wine
4 whole quail
Salt and pepper
2 egg whites, lightly beaten

1. Preheat the oven to 425°F. If you have a convection setting, that is best.
2. In a sauté pan, heat 2 tablespoons of the oil. Sweat the shallots and garlic until they are soft. Add the mushrooms and brown them on all sides. Add more oil or a bit of butter toward the end if the pan becomes too dry. Add the leeks and tomatoes. Cover partially with a lid and cook on low heat until all of the excess liquid has evaporated. Season with salt and pepper.
3. Cut two large pieces of parchment paper in half. Fold each piece in half and cut off the corners, rounding off each edge, so that when unfolded, all outer and inner corners of each piece of paper are rounded.
4. Place a fourth of the vegetable mixture on one rounded half of each piece of

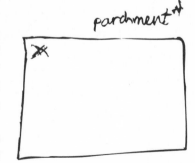
parchment

parchment. Top each with a whole sprig of thyme and moisten with 2 tablespoons of white wine.

5. Season the quail liberally with salt and pepper. Insert a toothpick through the
   legs to keep them together. Then lay one quail over each bed of vegetables.

6. Using a pastry brush, brush the edges of the parchment paper with the beaten
   egg white, and press the edges together to seal. Brush the edges of the folded
   package with the beaten egg white and make a series of short folds along the
   edges. Brush the edges again with egg white and repeat the short folds. Very
   lightly brush the top of each parchment package with oil.

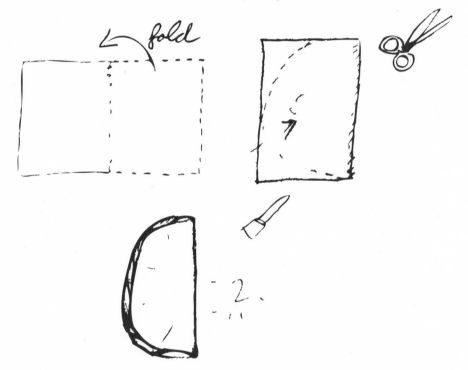

7. Place the *papillotes* on a sheet tray. Bake for 10 minutes, until completely
   puffed and the parchment has browned. Serve the quail in the *papillote* to be
   opened at the table, so that people can enjoy the aroma when they open the
   package.

Also try: any small game bird of similar size

Quail Kebabs

This idea of kebabs was described to me while I was in England, sitting at the fire-side with a lovely woman, at a pub. She is married to a farmer-gamekeeper and is frequently faced with a glut of game birds. This is one of her favorite recipes, no doubt inspired by the high-quality ethnic food that is now prevalent in Britain. You can also add any medley of vegetables to these skewers. These kebabs will also work with a variety of other sauces, such as barbecue sauce (page 227) or sweet-and-sour dipping sauce (page 226).

> 4 quail, quartered, deboned, and cut into large chunks
> 4 tablespoons finely diced green chiles
> 4 cloves garlic, minced
> 1 tablespoon ground coriander
> 2 tablespoons thinly sliced fresh basil
> 2 tablespoons lemon juice
> 1 tablespoon curry powder
> 1 teaspoon red chili powder
> 1/2 cup plain yogurt
> 1 cup coconut milk

1. Combine all the ingredients in a bowl. Cover with plastic wrap and marinate for 2 days in the refrigerator.
2. If using wooden skewers, soak them for 30 minutes first. Then skewer the chunks of meat onto four wooden or metal skewers and barbecue for about 6 minutes, rotating and basting with the marinade once (discard any remaining marinade). Alternatively, you can broil the skewers in the oven, though be careful not to overcook them or they will become dry.

Also try: brant, coot, duck, gallinule, goose, grouse, prairie chicken, partridge, pheasant, pigeon, ptarmigan, quail, rail, snipe, turkey, squirrel, rabbit

Stuffed Quail

This is an elegant dish, and the stuffing is good enough to eat on its own by the spoonful. I suggest deboning the quail first so that the flavors can be scooped up and swallowed together, rather than your having to pick around the bones. The birds become little packages this way, which can be tied off with a strand of green onion or chive if you're feeling particularly whimsical. Deboning may sound intimidating, but there are several good online video tutorials that a quick search will pull up for you. Or you can simply get a good pair of kitchen shears and cut along both sides of the backbone and remove the spine, which will allow you to wrap the quail around the stuffing but keep the remaining bones in.

    10 tablespoons butter
    4 tablespoons finely diced shallots
    4 celery stalks, peeled of outer strings and finely diced
    1 cup white wine
    8 tablespoons finely chopped walnuts
    4 tablespoons dried currants
    4 cloves garlic, diced
    4 tablespoons bread crumbs
    8 tablespoons chopped fresh flat-parsley leaves
    2 tablespoons fresh thyme
    8 quail, deboned if possible
    Salt and pepper

1. Preheat the oven to 350°F. Meanwhile, melt 6 tablespoons of the butter in a small sauté pan and sweat the shallots and celery over low heat, until translucent.
2. Add the white wine and reduce by half.
3. In a small bowl, combine the walnuts, currants, garlic, bread crumbs, parsley, and thyme.
4. Once the wine is reduced by half, stir in the bread crumb mixture and cook until it thickens and forms a paste. Season with salt and pepper to taste and set aside.
5. Distribute a lump of stuffing onto the back side of the breast meat of each deboned quail and wrap the leg meat and breast meat around it until it is sealed. Fasten with a toothpick through the seam.
6. Lay the quail in a cast-iron skillet with 4 tablespoons of butter. Place the skillet in the oven and bake for 12 to 15 minutes, basting the top of the quail with butter three times during the process.
7. Remove from the oven, and remove the toothpicks carefully from each bird. Serve immediately.

In Nature's infinite book of secrecy
A little I can read.

—SHAKESPEARE

7

A Moveable Hunt

As if to prolong my visit in the land of luxury, a college classmate named Annabelle sends me a note inviting me to go hunting with her family in England over Thanksgiving. She had read in an alumni magazine about my newfound foray into the world of hunting and thought I might want to have the traditional British hunting experience.

"It is a really special event and I think that you'd love it," she says.

And so needing very little convincing, a week after Hill Country I drive through the English countryside toward a different kind of high-class hunt, the kind we model ours after.

Two hours north of London, 6 miles to the west of Cambridge, is a village called Ellington. Some say it isn't a village at all but merely a hamlet, with ten brick houses, a church, and a village pub to call its own. The spines of the narrow roads leading here glisten in the fresh evening rain, sodden leaves smack the passing cars, tires spatter through the puddles, and it feels like midnight at five o'clock. I arrive at a row of small brick houses lined up like siblings and glowing behind the spikes of a black iron fence. Where the spikes part to reveal fine gravel, I slow and turn left, and drive into the darkness, between the shadows of great conifers that continue down the row like a suspended reverie.

Past the small brick houses, at the end of the driveway, is a great red mansion in fading brick. A white door frames the silhouette of a woman. Around her neck is a rope of pearls that match her straight, pearl-colored hair. She says her name is Magdalen, and she speaks in an accent that is part high British, part Danish farmer. "Let's leave this wet night behind us," she says, as the mansion swallows us in.

In the drawing room, a large fire is purring, and pristine tea sandwiches are stacked in a pyramid, made of white bread with trimmed crusts, smoked salmon, and cucumber. There is an almond cake, too, dense and delectable. Magdalen pours milk into the bottom of porcelain teacups, their gilded edges twinkling, then dilutes it with very strong tea, exquisitely hot, that steams and blends with the salty salmon on our tongues. The room is pink and tufted. Cream and rose stripes of silk shine from the couch; thick curtains fall heavily from the high ceiling to the ground. The high windows are shuttered from the inside, white and wooden, and latch with a fat wooden arm. The fire cracks and spits, and elegant smiling Annabelle and her husband, Anderson, sit intertwined on one couch while Magdalen sits on the edge of another, talking about pheasants—"They say that the pheasant always walks toward the sun."

Preceded only by the smell of a pipe, puffing its tobacco like a small chimney, Magdalen's husband, Fergus, enters the room. He is carrying a glass bowl of ground pork studded with sage, and he is slowly mixing it with a fork as he walks. In the corner, he sits in a small chair, mixing quietly while we talk and sip, his clear, rimless spectacles stationed at the tip of his nose, the smoke from the pipe rising and mixing with his facade.

When the tea sandwiches and almond cake are finished, we move into the kitchen, where Fergus finishes assembling his pork mixture and peels soft-boiled eggs. He spreads a layer of ground pork on a cutting board, slathers it with Roquefort, then rolls a strip of it around a boiled egg. "You put the ship in the bottle," he says, demonstrating. He rolls the pork-covered egg in whole wheat flour and sets it on a plate, then repeats with the others, one by one.

In the next room, the breakfast room, we fill our leather-bound flasks with cherry brandy and sloe gin for the next morning's hunt, drinks that will keep us warm in the sunless British fields. While we siphon the brandy into the containers, Fergus stirs another bowl of pork and announces in a slow British staccato, "Time to go to the pub." And so, with the flasks full and the pork mix resting, we wrap ourselves in coats and rubber shoes, and walk out into the black night, among the shadows of the great trees again until we get to the end of the driveway where the wrought-iron spikes line the row of glowing brick houses. We make a left onto silent country blacktop, and a few hundred yards down, across a wooden footbridge, we come to a pub named the White Fox.

It is lively beyond the creaking door. A small fire burns at the end of a small stucco room that seems to contain the entire population of Ellington. Men stand grinning broadly, their chins raised slightly. They wear wool sweaters and corduroy and leather boots laced above their ankles. An old man with sunken lips talks about cricket, and I am told that he plays it better than anyone ever has before. Eyes twinkle and the laughter reverberates as the room gets warmer and people drink on, save for the bursts of cold air that enter with each new patron. The rule is that villagers buy a pitcher of beer in the order in which they enter the pub, and so pitchers of room-temperature British ales are passed about, and ciders, too, and the room is filled with the movement of fluttering eyelids and blond heads, and a pretty girl floats from side to side behind the sticky, lacquered bar.

Tom the gamekeeper sits beside the fire drinking a Pink Lady, cider with a dash of port, a drink from the 1930s that is said to have rendered the French worthless when they drank it during wartime. People talk about the next morning's hunt, whether the fog and wind will behave and whether anyone will catch a woodcock or the mystical, rare white-headed pheasant they call the Christopher Reeves, which once chased Fergus as he drove across the field in his green John Deere Gator. The villagers laugh and tell other stories about one another, because the community is, in truth, an extended family all dwelling side by side in the glowing brick houses of Ellington. And when they are done with their stories and their laughter, and the last pitcher has been emptied of its last drop of foam, people begin to trickle out, and we do, too, walking out under the lanterns laced with cobwebs, where the air smells like fish and chips lingering from the pub kitchen, back over the wooden footbridge, back along the silent country blacktop, to the doorstep of Ellington Estate.

At eight o'clock the next morning, the muted light leaks through the yellow taffeta curtains of my room, and I can hear a tinkling sound crescendo as Magdalen brings a tray of Earl Grey up the stairs and to the door. She knocks and sets down the tray, snaps on the lightbulb under the fluted lampshade with its ruffled edges, and pours my tea, the milk, as always, first. I sip it until it is gone, and eat a chocolate biscuit laced with orange marmalade, and when I return from the bathroom an invisible butler has already removed the tray.

Downstairs in the breakfast room are chocolate croissants and grapefruit and a chorus of jams. Soon I can hear the villagers come in the front door and head to the drawing room, where Fergus is already pouring cherry brandy into small crystal cups. The people are as cheery as they were the night before, but now instead of wearing corduroy and wool sweaters, they are wearing tweeds, and knee socks with tassels, and some are wearing rubber Wellingtons and olive-colored newsboy caps, and almost all of the men are wearing ties. One is even wearing a Mexican ammo belt, a ring of golden shot shells clinging to the circumference of his belly.

The room fills and when everyone has arrived, the chatter subsides and Tom the gamekeeper passes out the peg cards to the eight guns, which assigns their shooting station, and explains the rules and the choreography of the day ahead. Fergus announces a ten-pound bonus to the shooters if they get a white-headed Christopher Reeves pheasant and a five-pound fine if they don't, and the room lets out a roar of laughter.

The tradition of this kind of driven shoot in England began with nobility and is rooted in the class system. It is almost always held on estates and is almost always an elaborate affair, if not quite as elaborate today as it once was. It is shooting, more than hunting, and I have even heard it called grocery shopping by my serious Texas hunter friends, because most of the work is done by those *not* shooting the guns. But if this is grocery shopping, then it is a formal and elegant form of it, one that British of noble descent practiced for centuries at home and in colonies, and a form that has now been adopted in part by the Texans and others in the United States.

A shoot requires advance planning on the part of the estate. Birds are placed in the fields weeks before the season begins so they can orient themselves to their surroundings and so the gamekeeper can ensure their health. The birds are encouraged to stay in the shooting area through the good animal husbandry of the gamekeeper, who makes sure the habitat and environment is appealing to them.

On the day of the hunt, the shooters, called guns, are placed in assigned positions with assistants to help load their shotguns. When in position, a team of beaters, led by the gamekeeper, move through the areas of cover, swinging sticks or white flags to drive the game out. These events are called drives, because the birds are driven over a line where the guns wait patiently in their predetermined places, spaced twenty to fifty yards apart, bellies full of cherry brandy and chocolate croissants.

In the drawing room, we guns now select our violet peg cards, then walk down the stone steps of the estate onto the gravel drive. We walk up the ramp into the back of a horse cart lined with wooden benches on either side, and pile in with our leather gun slings, puffing clouds of brandy-laden breath into the bitter air.

When we step out onto the first field, the ground is sodden and sucks against my rubber boots. A mythical scene of the English moors unfolds, the colors and the fog painted in beige and cream and gray. In the distance, an old, white-bearded man with a walking stick emerges from the mist, making his way along the bushes with his white flag, keeping a distance from the other beaters so his wobbly legs aren't lost in the thorns. As he approaches the guns, he looks like a sorcerer emerging from the pages of a book of legends, the tangled wires of his beard swaying as he waves his flag.

Traditionally, it was less prestigious to be a beater. It was the aristocracy who held the guns while the servants beat the bushes, managed the dogs, and carried the equipment. Today, in most cases, it is still about money; people usually pay several thousand dollars to be a gun in places that make a business out of this kind of hunting. But here at the Ellington shoot, it is more about preference. I am the only woman standing in a line of men, in their caps and tweeds, holding guns in the field. In front of me in the distance are the rest of the men and all of the women and city girls, giggling and chattering through the woods in their pink and olive-colored Wellies.

The blow of Tom's high-pitched horn pierces the picture as the first drive begins, and from far off I hear the pitter-pattering of more white flags slapping against the brush, as the beaters push the birds toward a flushing point. Sometimes the birds begin to flock in large numbers; sometimes they are partridge, sometimes pheasant, sometimes wood ducks. Sometimes the birds are smart and scurry ahead along the edge of the woods, rather than take to the sky.

The drives are twenty-five to fifty minutes long. They begin when Tom blows his horn and the beaters begin beating the bushes, and they end when the beaters reach the end of the wooded area and Tom blows his horn a second time. Each gun fires against the strip of sky in front and behind, and always above the tree line. Depending on the position they occupy and where the birds are breaking, the guns will get many or few birds, and so the guns rotate pegs at each drive to ensure they all get a shot.

The shots ring out in the misty air, the guns pausing only to reload—ancient, double-barreled over-unders and side-by-sides, some no doubt worth upward of $100,000. It feels a bit as I imagine wars used to be in ancient times; people lining up in an orderly fashion and simply shooting; waiting to see how the chips fall when it is all over. In my case, when it is all over, there is a colorful pheasant at my feet, but not the Christopher Reeves.

Once the second horn sounds, the dog handlers and their anxious dogs begin the task of retrieving all of the birds that have dropped. The birds are loaded on to the game cart and the beaters reassemble to prepare for the next drive, as the guns walk up the ramp into the horse cart and ride the bumpy ride to their next peg.

It is all extremely civilized. There are moments when I feel ashamed of how civilized I appear in my houndstooth coat and rubber Wellies, as birds drop from the air in an accelerating arch across the sky. But what I do like is that I touch the birds. I collect each one and carry it by its feet to the game cart. I inspect it, feel its weight in my hands, and internalize the moment. I can almost taste curried pigeon and smell roasted pheasant smothered in apples and cream. I conjure in my imagination sherry sauce to drizzle on roasted woodcock, something I have never tasted but always dreamed of. I anticipate the moment when Annabelle and I will stand in the cold basement and pluck pigeon to take back to London for Thanksgiving dinner, and how I will have to hang my pheasants from a London fire escape for four days to age it well enough to eat. I don't think I ever aged a bird from my Manhattan fire escape. Nor did I pluck and gut one an hour before I served it, while my dinner guests looked on in horror. This is all new and strangely invigorating.

There are six drives altogether, some in the morning and some in the afternoon, with a break for elevenses—a snack break an hour before noon. Our elevenses takes place in the conservatory, after we have hung the birds in the larder in pairs of two. Tom, Fergus, and I tie a loop around each bird's neck and pull it snugly, then place one bird on either side of a wooden rafter so that they balance each other out. "You hang them by their head, not their feet; it's the natural flow of food," Tom says, contrary to French and American instructions I have seen for this.

The guns and the beaters file into the conservatory, and food follows them on silver platters—crisp cups filled with prawns and mayonnaise, mugs of steaming mushroom soup, sausage rolls, and Fergus's Scotch eggs fried and cut in half, yolks oozing. There are Fergus's famous Slogasms, sloe gin mixed with champagne, and more cherry brandy, too, which he uses to spike the mushroom soup.

Beyond the fogged windows of the conservatory, the dogs and their handlers run the span of green grass, while inside, silver cups pass from hand to hand, full of bubbles and pink liquid. I wonder how good people's shots will be after this, then let the thought drift past, joining once again in the revelry and accepting another Slogasm.

The beaters and the guns are standing under the orange vines that lace the ceiling of the greenhouse. They pat one another on the back, laugh at the thorns and the mud on their tweeds, and exclaim, "Good show!" and "Well done!" And then at last, their bellies full, people set out on the next drive, and I follow, a hundred-year-old double-trigger side-by-side balanced on my shoulder.

No two drives are exactly the same on these hunts—different locations, weather, wind, direction of light, and the birds make every time new. And each community makes it different. The hunt in itself becomes a kind of cultural litmus test as it varies from region to region. This Ellington hunt plays on the "us and them" quality of the English shoot. But in the same way I played house as a child, there is an air of make-believe, as if I were stepping into a game of Clue or a Brontë novel. There is even the requisite bit of drama from time to time, such as when a muntjac, a beast that is best described as a kind of small deer with horns, spears the side of a terrier, and in the distance we hear commotion among the beaters, and the whole hunt stops as a dog is hauled off to the vet for stitches. There is still also that subtle hierarchy—this is the great estate and Fergus is the beloved patriarch of this domain. Despite all of this, though, there is an underlying sense of equality and respect between the villagers and him—they can be overheard saying that they like how inclusive he is with them, and he can be overheard saying, "If I were immersed in people just like me, I'd be pretty unbearable." And so this ancient game of "the guns and the beaters," continues until we reach the last field, strategically chosen because it is adjacent to the pub.

According to the villagers, there is a place on the Devon coast, a wonderful dreamy sort of place, where the birds can be seen flying off cliffs 120 feet high, and all you can do is stand in the moorlands and watch them in awe and forget to shoot. As I stand in the meadow now, I see a bird that I have never seen before, but I know what it is simply by how I feel when I see it.

"Wow, look at that!" I say, watching it fly by.

"It's a dodgy woodcock," Fergus says, observing through a puff of smoke from his green Gator.

The woodcock is small, with a needle for a beak and a thirty-mile-per-hour speed. I have heard stories about its delectable dark meat and have wanted to taste it, but all I can do is watch the moment fly by, quick as a flash, as I stand mesmerized by its acrobatic flight.

By the end, I have bagged several ducks and several pheasant, and there are pigeon and partridge in the larder as well, from other people's shots. But the truth is, no one really knows which birds are precisely whose, and that is decidedly not the point of this hunt. It may be the most social hunt I have ever experienced.

The whole village walks back to the estate for three o'clock lunch that soon drifts into six o'clock. The beaters and the guns eat in separate rooms, another mark in the game of "us and them." But after several courses have been served and consumed, the beaters enter the dining room where the guns sit, and line up around the table. They praise the guns for their great skill and their success and their general standing as superior citizens of the world. And after everyone has nodded and clapped, they file back to their room and we all continue to eat course after course of lamb and potatoes. Everywhere there is cut crystal and silver cups; and the sound of wine splashing, soon followed by crimson port; candlelight that twinkles over shakers of cinnamon and salt; and the gurgling of laughter that fills the room and echoes in time from the room that holds the beaters. We eat cheese and biscuits and I begin to hear the cigar cutters snipping and the ring of the cigar lighter popping on, and the flavors of cigars and Camembert mix with the smell of clementine on my fingers.

When the guns have had enough wine and food to make them generous, they file into the beaters' dining room and line up in front of the granite mantle all the way to the end of the table. Someone leads the way in, saying, "We saw your work and it was impressive. We saw your dogs and they were fierce. And you looked nice doing it." The room erupts in laughter. Someone else lifts a glass to Fergus for hosting the shoot, and carafes of cut crystal are passed quickly to fill the glasses for the toast. "May I drink with you?" Fergus asks, as the glasses are raised and tapped together.

The rest of the evening is an everlasting medley of food and drink and chatter and smoke. "Put a breeze behind the white wine," someone says. "Good luck to you," Fergus says as people begin to leave. "Love to Sue. Cheerio, then."

Fergus turns to a young man next to him. "Why don't you propose to her, for fuck's sake?" He takes a thoughtful puff on his pipe and then, "If you're going to make the girl move out there, at least do the proper thing. I'll give you a month and check up on you. Get off the pot, for chrissake. You can't keep these girls on the line for year after year after year."

Around the room, chunks of ash fall and flake on the marble ash-trays, and I begin to feel a bit dizzy. My throat begins to sting from the cigar, when all I can do is wash it down with port, and just when the revelers begin to seem generally pickled, Fergus announces it is time to go to the pub again.

A crowd of young people, still in their Wellies, step out onto the gravel driveway and begin to head to the pub. Drowsy and finished with the bone-chilling cold, I join Fergus in his antique navy blue Bentley. He snaps on the radio while we wait for Magdalen, and loud orchestra music begins to roar. Cymbals clash and trombones bellow and vibrate in the crevices of the old leather-smelling interior, and soon we are driving away from the stone pillars, through the colon-nade of conifers, over the clicking of the cattle guard, stopping to pick up one of the villagers who was the "top gun" of the day. "Is His Lord-ship still sleeping?" Fergus says over his cell phone. "Give him a kick and tell him I'm outside your front door." And just like the story of the Hare and the Turtle, the young people walk by making clouds with their steaming breath, while we wait for the villager who stumbles out of bed, still in his clothes, and skips out the door, into the Bentley.

Inside the pub again, the silver mugs dangle from the bar hooks, glittering, and the room smells of fried fish again, and of roasting nuts. Pickled herring on toast is the special of the night, but the villagers are here for pints. They stand in the twilight of their drinking, some look-ing weary, some invigorated with each successive sip.

The gamekeeper's wife, Emma, the expert wild game cook in the village, sits besides the fireplace and I listen to her talk of curried pheasant kebabs smothered in yogurt, and layers of pheasant breast and cream cheese wrapped in bacon, and pheasant stir-fry. Her paint-ings of springer spaniels peer down at us from above the mantle, as her husband, Tom, leans in to give me notes on the dogs—that springers die half-trained, and Labs are born half-trained. We talk about the birds and how we will age them, whether the tradition of this hunt will include aging the birds until their skin is green as used to be done. "They used to hang them until their heads popped off," Tom says, smiling. But for him it isn't necessary. "People don't like food high these days," he says; "just put it in the chiller for three to four days."

The villagers stand in a cluster in the pub, the beaters with grass stains on their knees, the guns with mud caked to their heels. They hold their pints high to their chests, and through an amber liquid crowd, I see the face of Fergus, sitting on a stool at the end of the bar, the long tendrils of his eyebrows in disarray, a hint of amusement in his azure eyes. The villagers buzz around him, and they talk about the strangeness of American politics, and the Oxford University Beagles and Hounds—a university hunting club. Shooting clubs are common in British schools, in the same way debate club or sailing is—it is considered one of those essential life skills that make you a well-rounded person. They ask why we don't have shooting clubs in American schools.

It all brings me back to a very similar conversation I had in a place so very far off from here, the place my new British friends call "Ar-Kansas." Guns are one of the great American debates, one of the most singularly divisive topics. Once in Arkansas, sitting on a tree stump around a campfire, the Commish told me that he taught his daughter how to use a shotgun when she was ten. He wanted to demystify it, to teach her responsibility, to help her understand it was a tool to be respected and understood. But in America, guns are not associated with class, but with those who are less evolved—more "backwoods." Here in the "backwoods" of England, however, shotguns and rifles are a symbol of class and sophistication. They are desirable and viewed as useful, tools with a purpose. To know how to shoot them well is to demonstrate that you are, in fact, *evolved*. Somehow that notion was lost on the journey across the Atlantic. Hunting in the United States became associated with some sort of white, middle-aged mancation—guys going out into the woods together to drink gallons of beer, tell dirty jokes, and occasionally shoot at something. But in truth, just like Texas Hill Country, this kind of hunting at Ellington is once-in-a-life-time hunting—it isn't easily accessible for an everyday omnivore.

I think about all of this as I walk slowly along the wet path back to the estate, listening to the conversation turn to another meal to come. It seems impossible that one could consume any more food and drink on this day, but there is the important matter of supper, which includes a bowl of drunken berries. Fergus is already making plans for the full English "brekkie" the next morning. But as is expected with the fragile human body, people begin to fall in and out of sleep on the couch in the library, leaning their heads on each other's shoulders, breathing softly and sometimes heavily. Fergus sits with a girl's head on his shoulder, puffing his pipe, wearing a faint look of amusement.

"Sleep, sleep, sleep," he says, "Sleep, sleep, sleep mode. And when you awake, if you're so inclined, you can have a light pastor dinner." And we do. With cheeks ruddy and bellies full, we all fall asleep.

Curried Pigeon

The day of the British estate shoot, my college friend Annabelle invited me to help her "curry the pigeons." I had never done this before. She told me that curry was recently voted England's national dish. We unhooked two pigeons from the larder, brought them down to the stone cellar, and plucked and breasted them. She had always just removed the breast meat, but I suggested we pluck the breasts and leave the skin on, to improve the moisture. The results were worth that bit of extra work.

    2 teaspoons salt
    4 cloves garlic, sliced thinly
    2 tablespoons hot curry powder
    1 teaspoon cumin seeds
    2 tablespoons olive oil
    4 pigeon breasts, skin on or off, bone in

1. In a small bowl, combine the salt, garlic, curry powder, cumin seeds, and olive oil and rub the mixture into the pigeon breasts.
2. Place in a container and cover. Marinate in the refrigerator overnight or up to 3 days.
3. Preheat the oven to 450°F. Remove the meat from the refrigerator.
4. Place the pigeon in a baking dish and roast for 10 minutes. Remove and serve each breast on a bed of watercress, or slice the meat thinly off the breastbone and serve it on toast points with chutney as an hors d'oeuvres.

Also try: brant, coot, duck, gallinule, goose, grouse, prairie chicken, partridge, pheasant, pigeon, ptarmigan, quail, rail, snipe

Browned Woodcock with
Sherry Sauce

Serves 2 to 4 as an appetizer

Woodcock should be cooked simply so that you can revel in the meat, which is so hard to obtain. I like to simply brown them and use a simple sauce based on the pan juices, for a little extra flavor. American restaurants and food stores are not allowed to serve hunted game, but in England woodcock is sold at all kinds of farmers' markets and butcher shops. Sometimes they will even tell you exactly which woods it was hunted in.

> 4 woodcock, bodies plucked and insides removed, heads and beaks still attached
> Salt and pepper
> 2 tablespoons all-purpose flour
> 1 tablespoon butter
> 1/2 cup sweet sherry
> 1/2 cup game bird stock (page 212)
> Pinch of cayenne
> 1 teaspoon freshly squeezed lemon juice

1. Preheat the oven to 400°F. Season the woodcock inside and out with salt and pepper. Dust it on all sides with 1 tablespoon of the flour. Secure the beaks between the two legs by tucking each long beak under a toothpick, which is speared through the thighs (this is the most traditional presentation, because it features the impressive beak).
2. Melt the butter in a sauté pan and brown the woodcock on all sides, 2 to 3 minutes. Transfer the pan to the oven and roast for 15 to 20 minutes.
3. Remove the woodcock from the pan and set it aside. Place the pan on the stove top. Deglaze the pan with sherry and bird stock; let simmer and reduce for 2 minutes. Whisk in the remaining tablespoon of flour, until there are no lumps and the flour begins to bubble, 1 minute. Season with a pinch of cayenne and a dash of lemon juice. Let simmer and reduce for 2 to 3 minutes.
4. Pour the sauce over the woodcock while it is hot and serve immediately.

Also try: brant, coot, duck, gallinule, goose, grouse, prairie chicken, partridge, pheasant, pigeon, ptarmigan, quail, rail, snipe

Duck with
Cherry Sauce

Serves 2 to 4, depending on the type of duck

When cooking a whole duck, it is important to consider the variety. A shallow water duck (e.g., mallard, teal, pintail, gadwall, black duck, wood duck) is ideal, one that has been feeding in grain fields, versus one (e.g., canvasback, redhead, scaup, and ring-necked duck) that has been deep-diving for fish. Any duck that is being cooked whole will also benefit from a brine (page 219), so that the breast meat and leg meat cook a bit more evenly.

> 1 whole shallow water duck, skin on
> Salt and pepper
> 3 tablespoons butter
> 3 shallots, minced
> 1 cup frozen or fresh cherries, pitted
> 1/4 cup vermouth
> 1 cup duck stock (page 212)
> 2 sprigs fresh thyme

1. Preheat the oven to 450°F. Season the duck with salt and pepper inside and out. Cut 1 tablespoon of butter into pieces, slip them under the skin, and massage them throughout the skin.
2. Truss the duck with kitchen twine. Brown it on all sides in 1 tablespoon of the butter in a heavy-bottomed pan. Remove the duck from the pan and set it aside.
3. Add the remaining 2 tablespoons of butter to the pan. Sweat the shallots and add the cherries. Deglaze with the vermouth and simmer for 2 to 3 minutes, then add the stock and thyme and simmer for 5 minutes.
4. Place the duck in the bottom of the pan on top of the cherry sauce. Put the pan in the oven and immediately lower the temperature to 425°F for 20 to 25 minutes, until the internal temperature is about 135°F. Remove from the oven and cover in tinfoil for 10 minutes, to help the juices retract into the meat. Then untruss the bird, carve it into joints, and serve with the sauce from the pan.

Also try: brant, coot, duck, gallinule, goose, grouse, prairie chicken, partridge, pheasant, pigeon, ptarmigan, quail, rail, snipe

Pheasant with Roasted Apples

Serves 4

There is something about pheasant and apples. They are simply meant to be together. The meat itself is a bit sweet and blends together with the muted sweetness of the apples and cream. It is a classic combination.

     2 whole pheasant, skin off or on
     Salt and pepper
     6 pieces bacon or pork fat, cut into 1/8-inch-thick strips
     2 tablespoons butter
     2 large apples, cored and sliced into 1/4-inch wedges
     1 tablespoon Calvados
     7 tablespoons heavy cream

1. Preheat the oven to 450°F. Season the pheasant with salt and pepper inside and out. Lay the bacon over the pheasant and secure it with kitchen twine or toothpicks.
2. In a heavy-bottomed ovenproof pan, melt 1 tablespoon of the butter and brown the pheasants on all sides, 5 to 10 minutes.
3. Remove from the pan and set aside. Add the remaining tablespoon of butter to the pan and fry the apples quickly in the butter. Place the pheasants on top of the apples. Cover with tinfoil or a lid and place in the oven. Immediately lower the temperature to 425°F for 30 minutes. Five minutes before removing from the oven, pour the Calvados and heavy cream over the pheasant. Remove from the oven, untruss the pheasant, carve into joints, and serve very hot with the apples and sauce.

Also try: brant, coot, duck, gallinule, goose, grouse, prairie chicken, partridge, pheasant, pigeon, ptarmigan, quail, rail, snipe

Pheasant Tagine

I first learned a version of this recipe while cooking in the south of France, where the cuisine is so heavily influenced by the Mediterranean. The combination of spices is wonderfully aromatic and lends itself well to any combination of vegetables and protein. In true Mediterranean fashion, the dish itself is light and tangy, using only olive oil, not butter, and a good dose of lemon in two forms. You will need to pre-serve the lemon in advance or buy it from a specialty spice shop. A tagine is actu-ally a clay pot with a deep cone-shaped lid, which is designed to keep the moisture within the dish. Once the cover is removed, the base can be used to serve from at the table. I tend to use a skillet, though, instead of a traditional tagine, because it browns the meat and vegetables better and can also be served tableside. It is also easier to use around the campfire.

8 pheasant legs, or 4 legs and 4 breasts, bone in
4 medium-size carrots, peeled, halved lengthwise, and cut into 3-inch pieces
4 medium-size zucchini, halved lengthwise and cut into 3-inch pieces
2 large red bell peppers, seeded and cut into 3-inch-long thick pieces
1 whole preserved lemon (page 236), rinsed well, pulp and pith removed, sliced
  into strips or diced
2 tablespoons grated fresh ginger
1 tablespoon ground coriander
1 tablespoon ground cumin
1 teaspoon cumin seeds (optional)
2 cloves garlic, minced
Juice of 1 lemon
1/2 cup olive oil, plus extra for browning
1/2 teaspoon sea salt
Freshly ground black pepper

1. Combine all of the ingredients in a bowl and let marinate for 20 to 30 minutes.
2. Heat a tagine, large skillet, or heavy-bottomed casserole dish until very hot. Brown the pheasant parts in a bit of olive oil until browned on both sides, about 5 minutes.
3. Add the vegetables and sauté with the pheasant.
4. Deglaze the pan with the marinade from the bowl and then lower the heat. Cook, covered, over low heat or in the oven at 350°F for 45 minutes.

Also try: brant, coot, duck, gallinule, goose, grouse, prairie chicken, partridge, pheasant, pigeon, ptarmigan, quail, rail, snipe

*The whole secret of the study of nature lies
in learning how to use one's eyes.*

—GEORGE SAND

8

Waiting for Pâté in the Floatant

The morning of my very first turkey hunt in the Village, in the days when high heels and martinis were much more familiar to me than camo and turkey callers, I saw a group of young wild hogs running across our taillights as the Commish and I drove to the woods before sunrise. I was blurry eyed still, sucking in hot coffee when I saw them and blurted out, "Those look *good*." It was an instinct, a voice that came out and spoke without my help. The Commish laughed and I did, too. In the dark morning, those small hogs didn't look like hairy four-legged creatures to me; rather, like running sausages. For as long as I have been alive, my memories have been defined by what I ate during those experiences. I couldn't always tell you the name of the person I was with during that particular moment, but could describe in precise detail the Niçoise salad I had in 1995. I have a friend my age that may be the only person I know who also hunts with visions of running hams in his mind. Like me, Peter Pagoni found hunting not at birth but a bit later in life, while visiting all of his relatives in the Village. He is a lawyer and a professor by day, but in the wee hours of the morning, when it is still dark, he is a Louisiana duck hunter, as sincere as the rest, but a little more thoughtful and philosophical, a little more self-deprecating about the uncertainty of it all. I decide to go hunting with Peter next, in his beloved New Orleans.

On Bourbon Street, a shiny, smooth-skinned girl beckons to me from her door with two scarlet nails, dollars attached to her hips, her voice sweet and oily. The air is filled with competing music, some from the room of the girl, and some from other doors and windows, the notes collide, mixed into a cocktail of music that somehow makes sense, but only here.

Inside, against the sounds, are the sincere faces of the singers making them. Past that, through a miniature doorway, under a golden fleur-de-lis, is a man with a stiff underbite and a tall, black cap and shiny, tasseled shoes, who catches shrimp by day, and by night plays the drums as they have never been played before. Whiskers protrude from under his polished nose and his face reflects the orange light of the room crowded with strangers, all tapping their feet on the old wooden floor.

Out on the street, the blacktop shimmers and sweats in the lamplight and reflects the houses above, their facades studded with Romeo catchers and balconies that sag like rotting lace. The narrow shotgun houses wear peeling shutters with holes punched through and weeping ivy that slips its way in and out of the slats.

At Café du Monde, a man sits on a fire hydrant humming into his tuba, and inside, powdered sugar floats in a cloud across the room as people exhale into their beignets, and it drifts down again, into the pores of the place, soaking into the blue slate ground to be pecked by waiting pigeons.

Here in New Orleans, everyone is named Baby. It is one of the only places I know of where you can indulge in watching the girl with the two scarlet nails and sweet oily voice and have access to good duck hunting a few hours later, at five a.m. on Bayou Terra Buff.

At four a.m., Peter and I drive the road through Saint Bernard Parish and a series of bays that interconnect, until we arrive at a concrete boat launch. At the launch, a freshly dead coyote is being casually ignored, and surly-looking men in faded jeans look as though they haven't left the site for many weeks. It is possible that they haven't; duck hunting season for some is a religious institution.

To remind us, a pickup truck comes roaring from behind and screeches to a halt. Two boys jump out in full camouflage, their pirogue (*pea-row*), a narrow metal boat, decked out in fake straw cover.

"How has the hunting been?" Peter asks, to break the ice.

"Ah terrible!" the boy replies, rapidly setting up his boat to back into the water. "Five, four, one and seven," he says, listing their kill for the past week. We let them go ahead; we can see in their eyes that they need to do it.

Once in the water, I slip down into our pirogue and sit on a netted pile of duck decoys. Peter's golden Lab Marly jumps in after me and we slink into the shallow waters of the marsh, kicking up black mud with our propeller engine as we move farther away from land.

"Seven sounds like a lot to me," I say to Peter, watching the boys disappear into the bayou.

"For some people, if you haven't bagged your limit, then it's a bad hunt," he says. "Not everyone is as enlightened as we are," he chuckles.

More than anything, it is the thought of a crisply roasted duck that wakes Peter at three a.m. on a Saturday morning. It is the thought of the sweet and salty tang of thinly sliced duck prosciutto that makes those early dark mornings worthwhile. A true academic at heart, he will study and research for hours how best to treat his kill; he will experiment in earnest and tell you all about his findings. He is a walking encyclopedia of well-researched thoughts and conclusions. He is the kind of person you want to be hunting with when your ultimate destination is the dinner table.

Bayou Terra Buff that we propel through is a naturally occurring swampy inlet that was once solid earth. The name came about because there were once many bison here, on the rare, firmer ground that could support such large animals. Now it has a shallow layer of water that moves like black hills of oil behind us, as smooth and uniform as mercury, with only a sliver of a moon to reflect on its motion.

On Bayou Terra Buff, it all seems a bit like an alternative world: water higher than earth, pelicans rising diagonally in a rope of pearls in the tall smartweed ahead. We are at sea level, higher than the city of New Orleans in the distance. As our boat sends ripples through the marsh, speckled coot, looking like a cross between seagulls and ducks, begin to walk on water in groups, their thick legs a blur of frenzied motion.

Peter banks the pirogue into the mud and I step out in my waders. I try to keep from sinking deeper and deeper into the marsh, which dances the line between stable ground and quicksand. Marly dives in, too, as Peter throws plastic duck decoys into the water, one by one, where they bob, peering down at their flawless reflections in the pink morning water. These decoys will hopefully signal to the real ducks that there is food here and they should come pay a visit.

There is a whole upside-down world in the reflection, even prettier than the one swimming right side up. The sky is a spectrum of color that repeats itself from up high to deep in the water, while the leafy green vegetation called floatant quakes, lights up green and incandescent on the surface.

The killdeer and snipe begin to streak low just where the upsidedown world becomes right side up, and a single great blue heron lifts and beats its enormous paper wings.

So much of hunting is waiting. It is that waiting that makes the fleeting, action-packed moments so thrilling. Those uncomfortable moments among the elements, those feelings of despair, the slight adrenaline flush that comes and goes in an instant, are what make hunting feel like hunting. It is when the discomfort no longer feels like discomfort, as you learn to adapt and become more integrated with your surroundings, that you begin to feel like a hunter. As we wait, the cold pushes us to hunch down on a stool to store warmth. I can see my breath in the cottony air as the ducks come in waves, high in the sky and far in the distance; sometimes they flirt with our decoys, but never close enough. There are green-winged teal and blue-winged teal and a cinnamon teal from time to time. Once there is even a pintail. Their silhouettes against the quiet panorama are impressive. There is nothing but glowing violet sky and water and the green incandescent floatant, simmering above the shoreline.

In southern Louisiana, there are two predominant species of ducks—teal and gadwall. There are some pintails, too. The mallards spend their time in Arkansas, unless it is very cold, then they are forced south. The first ducks to arrive from Canada are blue-winged teal. They begin their journey in the middle of August. They are the first to migrate and the last to go back, which means they are especially averse to cold. In some areas in the South, there is a special early season to hunt them.

The federal government gives each state a window to set a sixty-day duck-hunting period. It is often scheduled in two segments, with a break between. In years when the duck populations become too low, there is a forty-five day season, though it has been over a decade since that has happened.

What determines duck populations more than anything are the conditions in Canada, and in North and South Dakota, called the pothole region, because the landscape is full of gouges—1- and 2-acre holes. These potholes are determined by the rainfall in Canada and the Dakotas. The more rain and snow, the more potholes that provide good nesting and breeding grounds, and the better the duck population. When there are fewer potholes, the ducks are more concentrated, which means in turn that the population is more vulnerable to predators, which means the ducks have a lower rate of nesting success.

In dry years, the potholes begin to fill in, and farmers that have been farming around them can suddenly farm across them. When this happens, the nesting grounds, with their good, tall, grass cover, disappear.

Blended into the marshland that connects with Bayou Leary, Peter lets out a hail call, the mating call of a female, then he lets out a feed call. "That's our signal to the other hunters that we aren't seeing anything," Peter laughs, letting the sentence die. There is an art to calling ducks—the high-pitched *preep-preep* of the male teal; the soft, rasping *kreep* of the male mallard. In true scholarly fashion, Peter listens to duck-calling CDs in his car as he drives.

After the calls, the tinkle of dripping water is the only sound as we hover behind our blind of straw grass, fastened to two poles to break up our silhouettes. This is a meager attempt to compete against one of the duck's strongest senses—their sight. They can detect our slightest movement from high in the sky.

The ducks fly by in different patterns, depending on their breed; the lead at the point trades off from time to time, once it tires of being a windbreak for the others. The wind is helpful to the duck hunter. When it is very windy, the ducks don't want to expend their energy being out in open water, so they come into the marsh. On windless days, they go out far from the hunter's shotgun, where no one will bother them.

The Commish, who is Peter's second cousin, once put it to me very simply while sitting in a deer stand. "Every animal wakes up every morning thinking about one thing," he said. "Survival. What they're going to eat. So that dictates their movements."

That instinct dictates their daily movements and also their migratory patterns. "If everything freezes up here, then they can't get to the food, so they'll go a little farther south," he said. "They'll follow the freeze line. This is my theory, but I think there are certain

ducks imprinted to certain areas; there are ducks that will only migrate to Chicot County. But then, there's a bigger concentration that
are just coming as far south as they have to. Mallards usually show
up in numbers in Arkansas at the end of December, when it freezes
up in Missouri."

The truth is, we don't really know why ducks or any animals do
what they do. And that is a beautiful thing. People make a career out
of trying to understand the behaviors and patterns of nature. The best
outdoorsmen will tell you that it is endlessly satisfying to them—the
great mystery of nature and animal behavior.

Peeling clementines and watching the glow of the marsh and the
occasional darting cloud of birds, Peter and I sit and talk about what
is endlessly satisfying to us—the place in the world where the outdoors and food collide. You will often hear such phrases as "a gaggle
of geese" or "a brace of duck"—Peter refers to coot as a "pâté of coot"
because their livers and gizzards are so big. They aren't really in the
duck family and are virtually impossible to pluck, with hairlike fibers
in the skin, but their livers are luscious. "Canvasback are the best eating duck," Peter declares, feeding Marly a piece of clementine. We
talk about how to make New Orleans duck taste better, because it has
a fishier taste than ducks do in Arkansas.

The beauty of cooking wild animals is that it doesn't just start with
you and the cutting board; it is the whole cycle of life that you have to
consider: What did this duck eat? And what did the thing it ate, eat?
All of this affects how it tastes, how you prepare it, and what exactly
you eat from it and with it. Maybe the duck is brined to remove the
fishiness from the skin; maybe the skin is removed and the meat cured
in salt. At the very least, it is always eaten rare.

The water hyacinth are flourishing in our patch of shaky ground. This
means that the salt water that drifts in hasn't overrun the plant life
this year. One of Peter's other passions is environmental law, and while

we talk about duck terrines and pâtés, he also talks about the erosion of the land he calls home. He says that the levees prevent the silt from rebuilding the erosion. He talks about the bodies of water as if they are his children, of the arteries named Delacroix and Reggio; and the mouth of the Mississippi named Venice; and the series of bays that interconnect; and Lake Bourne, the lake that released the huge wall of water, like a tidal wave, onto New Orleans during Hurricane Katrina. "Katrina punctuated a lot of environmental problems that were already here," he says.

Just then, three ducks fly low toward our decoys, and we both spring up from the blind, clementine peels flying from our laps and shots ringing into the air. All three of the ducks drop from the sky and make a dent in the water, sending up a splash with their limp bodies. Marly begins a running dive toward them paddling with gusto. She brings them back one by one, small and wet, in the soft pink padding of her jowls. Then just as quickly things are quiet again, and we sit and wait, clementines once again in our laps. Yes, it is beginning to feel like hunting.

By ten o'clock we have collected four green-winged teal. It is not enough for a terrine or a pâté or a confit or a large dinner party. So we decide to hunt coot. Coot are considered by many to be a "garbage" bird, not quite duck status. But they have hearty legs nice for a confit, and their gizzards are large enough to fill a terrine with ease. We drive the pirogue through the shallow water, past decoys and litter stranded in the marsh, past fishermen casting. The coot are on the move, tapping their feet against the surface of the water and letting up a splash. Hunting coot that are walking in shallow water turns out to be just as difficult as shooting a duck high in the sky. But in the end we have enough bird for some experimental cooking.

We pluck on the dock, and the pelicans sit and observe us, their necks bent in S-shaped curves, inquiring about some fish scraps. But all we have are duck feathers, which fly up and out onto the water, flickering green and purple. Ducks are easiest to pluck when they are freshly killed, and some ducks give their feathers up more easily than others. It is a commitment to pluck one, but the duck you pluck will taste so much better than the one you don't.

So will the food you eat for lunch after a morning hunt like this. In New Orleans, that is often a potato that has been sitting in a boiling pot of shellfish with whole vegetables, lemons, peppers, and whole cloves of garlic, soaking it all into its pores until steaming and ripe to eat. That is what we drive toward, through the tired towns of Saint Bernard Parish, the littered streets, the roads anchored into Cypress Swamp, and the waist-high line of gray on the buildings—the scar of Katrina.

We pass it all, en route to ripe boiled potatoes and po'boys, anticipating the duck preparation, and perhaps once more the girl with two scarlet nails, and the man with shiny-tasseled shoes. In New Orleans it is all part of the same beautiful, rambling meal.

Apple Roast Gadwall

Serves 4

I don't usually roast wild ducks whole because the legs can be muscular and are best braised, and the breast meat is always best rare. But sometimes, a roasted whole bird is called for, because there is nothing more picturesque at the dinner table. The bird to use is one that has fed more in grain fields, and less on fish. So in addition to considering the size of the duck (smaller is usually more tender), consider where it was harvested. And if you aren't sure, cut off a piece of the skin and render the fat to determine whether it is fishy. This will signal whether it is worth keeping the skin on and roasting the duck whole. And as with any whole roasted bird, it is best to brine it first. Be sure to save the carcass for duck stock (see page 212)!

> 1 (2-pound) gadwall, brined (page 219)
> 1 apple, cored and sliced
> 2 sprigs fresh rosemary
> 1 tablespoon olive oil
> Salt and pepper
> Vermouth or white wine (optional), for deglazing
> 1 tablespoon all-purpose flour (optional), for gravy
> 1 cup duck stock (page 212) (optional), for gravy

1. Preheat the oven to 450°F. Inspect the duck to see if there are any remaining pinfeathers; if so, remove them. Rinse the duck with water. Thoroughly pat dry with paper towels. Lightly stuff the duck with the sprigs of rosemary and the apple slices.
2. Slather the duck inside and out with the olive oil. Generously sprinkle all sides of the duck with salt and pepper. Lay, breast up, on a roast rack in a roasting pan. Place on the middle rack of the oven. Immediately lower the heat to 425°F. Roast for 30 minutes (see Note), or until the internal temperature reads 135°F on an instant thermometer. The juices will run red, and the meat will be quite red. You want the meat to be rare, not raw. The more the meat is cooked beyond the rare stage, the more gamey it will taste.
3. Remove the duck from the oven and place it on a separate plate or cutting board, breast side down, to rest for 10 to 15 minutes. Cover it with tinfoil while it rests.
4. If there are any juices left in the bottom of the roasting pan, place the pan on a stove-top burner and deglaze with vermouth or white wine, scraping up any brown bits on the bottom of the roasting pan. Let simmer for about 2 minutes, then spoon it over the carved duck before serving. If you want to make the deglazed juices into a full gravy, whisk in 1 tablespoon of flour until it bubbles, 1 minute, then add 1 cup of duck stock and let it reduce to the desired consistency.

Note: The cooking time will vary, depending on the size and variety of duck. Teal, for example, will only require about 15 minutes. See the temperature guide on page 238.

Duck Cassoulet

My favorite thing about this dish is that the meal is cooked and served in the same skillet. It is a baked stew of sorts, in the French style, and makes use of all of the duck parts. The recipe suggests duck leg confit, but the gizzards, hearts, and other offal can be confited and used here as well. Be sure not to add much if any salt to this recipe, as the confit already has plenty of salt from the cure.

1 head garlic
6 tablespoons olive oil
2 cups cipollini or pearl onions
Salt and pepper
1/2 cup diced bacon
1 cup diced shallots
2 heaping cups kale that has been cut into bite-size pieces
4 cups duck stock (page 212)
1 1/2 cups cooked white cannellini beans, or 1 (15-ounce) can, drained and rinsed
3 cups duck confit, leg and skin pulled from bone (page 136)
2 cups panko or other plain bread crumbs
1 teaspoon finely chopped fresh rosemary
1/2 teaspoon red pepper flakes

1. Preheat the oven to 350°F. Drizzle the head of garlic with 1 tablespoon of the olive oil, then wrap it in tinfoil. Roast until the cloves are soft, about 1 hour. Remove from the oven and squeeze the cloves from the garlic skin. Mash with a spoon on a cutting board and set aside.

2. In a skillet or ovenproof pan, heat 1 tablespoon of the olive oil and brown the onions, about 3 minutes. Season them with salt and pepper, turn them, and place the pan in the oven. Cook until browned and tender, about 30 minutes, tossing frequently, then remove from the oven. If using cipollini, cut them into quarters; if using pearl onions, leave them whole. Set aside.

3. In a 10-inch skillet (see Note), render the bacon over medium-low heat until just crispy. (A smaller skillet will not be large enough to hold the entire contents of the recipe.)

4. Add the shallots and let sweat.

5. Add the kale and let wilt.

6. Add stock and simmer for 10 minutes.

7. Add garlic puree, beans, and cipollini and simmer for 15 minutes.

8. Add the duck meat and simmer for 30 minutes.

9. In a separate sauté pan, heat the remaining 4 tablespoons of olive oil. Brown the bread crumbs, stirring constantly. Add the rosemary, and red pepper flakes.

Remove the bread crumbs from the heat and continue to stir for a few minutes until the pan cools down.

10. Garnish the cassoulet with the bread crumbs and place the whole thing in the 350°F oven. Bake for 10 minutes.

11. Remove from the oven and serve immediately at tableside from the skillet.

Tip for peeling onions: Soak them in a bowl of warm water. When you're ready to peel, use a small knife and cut a slit down the side, then peel the skin back around the onion in one layer.

Note: This dish can be cooked in a casserole or other pan that can be transferred to the stove. A skillet works best, however, because the flavors aren't lost in the transfer and it can be served at tableside from the skillet.

Coot Legs in Sherry   Serves 4

This recipe was introduced to me by the queen of cuisine in the Village, and every-one's favorite great-aunt. She pointed out a version to me one afternoon, in a thin pink church cookbook on her kitchen shelves that are home to hundreds of cook-books, many from Southern churches. This is a good recipe for tough bird legs. I like to use coot legs, rather than some of the smaller duck legs, because there is a substantial amount of meat on them. The key is to keep the liquid level low so that you are braising the legs, not submerging and boiling them.

12 to 16 coot legs
Salt and pepper
1 tablespoon olive oil
1 large onion, diced
6 cloves garlic, roughly chopped
2 sprigs fresh thyme
1 cup Amontillado sherry, or other sweet to medium-sweet variety
2 cups duck stock (page 212)
1 teaspoon Worcestershire sauce
1/2 teaspoon Tabasco or other hot sauce
3 cups sliced shiitake mushrooms

1. Preheat the oven to 250°F. Season both sides of the legs with salt and pepper. Heat the olive oil in a Dutch oven or heavy-bottomed, ovenproof pot over high heat. Brown the duck legs in the olive oil, about 1 minute per side.
2. Remove the duck legs from the pot and set on a plate. Add the onion and gar-lic to the pot and let brown. Add the thyme and deglaze with the sherry.
3. Return the duck legs to the pot and let the sherry reduce by half.
4. Add the duck stock, Worcestershire sauce, and Tabasco. Add the mushrooms and stir.
5. Cover the mixture with parchment paper or tinfoil and then with a lid.
6. Transfer to the oven and roast for about 2 hours, or until the meat falls off the bone. Serve with wild rice, Israeli couscous, or pasta.

Also try: other small game bird legs

Duck, Coot, or Goose Confit

Serves 4

Confit is traditionally a salt cure for a piece of meat, usually goose or duck, followed by poaching it in its own fat. Once cured, cooked, and cooled, the meat can be removed from the bone and stored in a glass jar in the fat for up to six months. It is ideal to confit legs with the skin on, but with wild ducks you can't always be picky. If you don't have skin, simply use extra fat during cooking and turn the meat more often. You can keep it simple or play with flavorings, as long as you have the fat and the salt. Either way, the meat shreds from the bone in a buttery kind of way.

> 4 mallard or speckled goose legs (about 1 pound), or the equivalent in smaller duck legs, or gizzards, hearts, and necks
> 4 cloves garlic, crushed
> 1 tablespoon kosher salt
> Zest of 1 orange
> Zest of 1 lemon
> 1 sprig fresh rosemary, leaves removed and stem discarded
> 2 sprigs fresh thyme, leaves removed and stem discarded
> 1 teaspoon cracked black peppercorns
> 1/2 teaspoon fennel seeds (optional)
> 1 piece star anise, crushed (optional)
> 1 teaspoon juniper berries (optional)
> 6 tablespoons duck fat

1. Rinse the duck and pat dry. If using a leg, expose the leg bone with a paring knife
2. Make the confit salt by roughly chopping the herbs and combining all of the ingredients, except the duck and duck fat, in a small bowl.
3. Place in a baking dish or ovenproof skillet and rub on all sides with the salt mixture. Cover and refrigerate overnight.
4. Preheat the oven to 300°F and remove the duck from the refrigerator.
5. Rinse the legs or duck parts very well under running water for several minutes. Wipe out the baking dish and return the duck legs to it.
6. Scoop the duck fat into the baking dish and cover with tinfoil.
7. Place in the oven and roast for 2 to 3 hours. If there is skin on the legs, remove the foil for the last 30 minutes; if not, turn the meat over halfway through cooking. It is ready when the meat is very tender and has a shredded quality when pulled with a fork.
8. Remove the baking dish from the oven and let rest for 10 minutes. Serve the meat hot or eat cold over a salad. It is also excellent in a terrine or a cassoulet.

Duck Terrine

About 12 servings

A terrine is a piece of architecture that takes several days of work and a bit of pre-cooking. It requires a rectangular ceramic terrine mold and consists of layers of ingredients pressed and held together with cold fat. It may seem daunting, but it is worth every bit of work, and is an impressive appetizer, not just in how it tastes, but how it looks. If you want to start simply, you can leave out the inlay and add a bit more confit to the recipe to fill out the terrine. You can also experiment with the inlay—try a medley of pickled vegetables or rehydrated dried morels.

Inlay:

- 3 tablespoons Armagnac
- 1 tablespoon Earl Grey tea leaves steeped in 2 cups water until strong but not bitter
- 1/4 teaspoon kosher salt
- 1/2 cup dried figs (about 16), stems and base cut off so that both ends are flat
- 8 to 10 thin slices pancetta

Filling:

- 1 cup duck offal confit, including necks, gizzards, hearts, and livers (page 136), at room temperature
- 2 cups duck leg confit (page 136), at room temperature
- 1 cup braised hog belly, picked apart (page 176)
- 1/2 cup small-diced bacon
- 1/2 cup toasted and salted Sicilian pistachios
- 1 cup warm duck fat
- 1 teaspoon finely ground allspice
- 1/2 teaspoon coarsely ground black peppercorns
- 1/2 nutmeg seed, grated

For the Inlay:

1. Preheat the oven to 300°F.
2. Combine the tea, Armagnac, and salt. Add the dried figs and let sit overnight.
3. Lay out the pancetta in a line on a sheet of plastic wrap. The slices should overlap.
4. Drain the figs and arrange in a layer on top of the pancetta, so that the flat sides are snugly aligned.
5. Roll into a long rod, sealing the pancetta around the figs, using the plastic to help keep it tight. The pancetta fat will stay together most easily if it is at room temperature.

For the Filling:

1. Combine the two duck confits with the hog belly and bacon in a large bowl. Add the pistachios, duck fat, allspice, pepper, and nutmeg. Mix well with a wooden spoon or by hand.
2. Pour a few drops of water into the bottom of the terrine mold. Line it lengthwise with plastic wrap so the plastic drapes over both ends of the mold. Fill the mold with water to help press the plastic into the contours of the mold, and press with your fingers. Pour out the water and pat the inside dry with a paper towel.
3. Press half the meat mixture into the mold.
4. Unroll the inlay and press gently along the center of the terrine. You may have to trim the inlay to fit the mold.
5. Gently place more of the meat mixture on each side of the inlay, making sure the inlay does not shift off-center. Add more meat on top and press down gently until the top of the meat is covered and smooth and compact.
6. Cover the terrine and place in a larger pan. Pour water into the pan halfway up the sides of the mold. Bake at 300°F for about 2 hours.
7. Remove the terrine from the hot water bath and let it cool slightly. Press down the terrine. If possible, weight it down with a box of kosher salt wrapped in plastic and tied with more plastic to the terrine. Or use a similar heavy object that will fit into the opening of the mold. Chill overnight in refrigerator.
8. When ready to serve, and while it is still very cold, use a serrated knife and gently cut the terrine into slices 1/2 inch thick. Lay the slices out on a cutting board and let come to room temperature. Garnish with micro greens, and sea salt if needed, and serve with crusty bread.

Goose or Duck Prosciutto

Serves 8 to 10

Curing meat was widespread among historical civilizations because it prevented food waste and guaranteed a food supply in the case of a poor harvest. The French and Italians were the first to raise this skill to an art form. Local craftsmen formed guilds and produced a range of cooked or salted dried meats, which varied from region to region. The only raw product they were allowed to sell was unrendered lard. These preservation methods ensured that meats would have a longer shelf life, and this is done even in more modern times. Goose and duck prosciutto is simple to make at home, and is a perfect way to store the meat when you don't have time to cook it and you just can't fit another thing in your freezer. All that it requires is salt, cheesecloth, and some twine, plus a cool room with good relative humidity. The flavor is gamier and richer than hog prosciutto, and the color is a deeper red. But it still has that signature chewy, delicate, salty flavor. It is better to use larger breasts, because the smaller ones will cure and dry too intensely to have a delicate flavor and texture. You can keep the skin on and play with the seasonings—add rosemary, thyme, or garlic to make it more interesting. Store it in the refrigerator for one month or more and serve it sliced thinly with pears, crackers, cheese, or just by itself.

> 2 cups kosher salt
> 2 speckled goose or duck breasts, skin on or off (about 1 pound)
> 1/2 teaspoon freshly ground pepper

1. Pour half of the salt into a nonreactive container that will hold the breasts snugly without their touching. Place the breasts on the salt, skin side up if the skin is still on. Pour the remaining salt on top and pack it well into the container with your hands.
2. Cover the container with plastic wrap and chill it in the refrigerator for 24 hours.
3. Remove the breasts from the salt, rinse them well under running water, and pat them dry. They should be a deeper red and feel firm to the touch.
4. Dust the breasts with pepper and wrap them individually in cheesecloth. Tie one end with a piece of string, which you can use to hang the breasts.
5. Hang in a relatively humid (60 to 80 percent humidity), cool (45° to 65°F) place for 5 to 7 days (sometimes longer for larger breasts), until the flesh is stiff but not hard throughout. Remove from the cheesecloth and slice thinly to serve. These will keep refrigerated for about 1 month or so, well wrapped to prevent drying.

One does not hunt in order to kill, on the contrary,
one kills in order to have hunted.

—JOSÉ ORTEGA Y GASSET

9

All of the Jewels That
Go Unnoticed in the World

The next morning, Peter and I ride through Cajun country on
the same highways anchored in the Cypress Swamps, and into
southeast Arkansas, back to the Village, where his old Lebanese
Aunt Evvy is sure to be making kibbe or stretching Arabic bread and
laying it on a griddle to bubble and crisp; and it is the place where
his Lebanese uncle Roger Mancini is sure to be saying something
wise or profound while whittling something in front of the fire at
the deer camp.

The road to southeast Arkansas is full of curious names. As we
drive the contours of Cajun country and enter into deep Delta country, we pass places called Darlove, Hollandale, Tallulah, Silver City,
and Midnight. There is Pigalicious Barbecue, which only serves ham-
burgers; and Belzoni—a town in Mississippi with a museum devoted
to catfish. On narrow roads with narrow houses, men rake leaves into
mountains and hawks balance on telephone lines. Old and slow

Crown Victorias squat in the right lane, and we pass a painted bus celebrating the anniversary of the 1955 Montgomery bus boycott.

As we cross the Yazoo River, the fields of brilliant green winter wheat begin, and for hundreds of acres there is only pitch-black alluvial soil with royal green cover, and the deep shadowy trenches of irrigation.

The road through Arcola has a number. It might be seventeen, I don't know. But on that road, the first Roger Mancini Co. sign appears, the only sign of thriving commerce for 100 miles. There is the same Weico chain broiler for sale, on the same homemade sign I saw two years ago; and a hedged-off Dow AgroScience testing facility, with warning signs not to touch anything.

And at the very end of it all, after a long ride on the levee of the Mississippi River, through a metal gate, past hundreds of cottonwood trees, we arrive at a large campfire, where Roger Mancini is roasting peanuts from his pocket on the end of a shovel.

He drops them in my palm, the shells scorched. I pop them open and they taste like hot, salty peanut butter.

"What's on these that tastes so good?" I ask.

"It's the paint off the shovel," he replies.

He sticks tongs into the fire, brings out a burning ember, and lights his cigar with it.

"Cuz . . . this is a delicious cigar," he says to the Commish, who is sitting and puffing to his left. "Get me two boxes of these." Then to me, winking, "He's my cigar broker."

Peter and I begin to roast venison sausage on the fire as a prelude to dinner, and Roger breads deer cutlets, sliced from the backstrap of a deer hanging in his vast walk-in cooler. "If you cook it out of the cooler rather than the freezer, it tastes better," he says, heating an inch of oil in a cast-iron skillet over the fire.

"How is business?" Peter asks. Roger looks to the sky, gives a thumbs-up, and smiles.

Roger Mancini has found opportunity all his life. He once bought the inventory of a pawnshop, then went into the jewelry business, then opened a series of stores that appeal to the Southern Woman. He is an artisan and an explorer with an eye for interesting things, which he gathers wherever he goes throughout the world.

He has a workshop where he builds furniture made from the siding of abandoned homes—those antebellum homes that have been left behind, romantic and melancholy; homes that cost pennies to buy and millions to fix. Roger gives them a new life. He makes their old wood clapboard into beautiful handmade furniture, and builds new walls with them, too.

And in his workshop he collects other things, like many hundreds of old bee homes that he turns into shelves; and church windows and pews, antique bicycles, and ballpark benches, deer antlers, and lots of nice wood. All of the jewels that go unnoticed in the world, Roger notices.

The deer cutlets fry in the skillet, the hot oil bubbling in the smoky light. And we eat it with a good wine and Roger's homemade bread and an elegant salad bejeweled with pecans.

It is the peak of the deer rut, the first two weeks of December, when you expect to see deer in daylight. In the words of the Commish, "They have one thing on their mind: acting stupid."

It is a moonless night in Arkansas. The nature preserve is silent except for the inside of the deer camp, which is lit with a deer-antler chandelier and golden lamps, and filled with Roger Mancini's words of wisdom.

"Hunting is at its zenith," he says from his end of the dinner table, still wearing his hunting hat with the ear flaps tied up. "It's never been like this before. The highlight of my weekend was two blue jays standing around my stand." The heads lining the table nod to the sound of crunching lettuce and the tapping of forks against paper plates.

Roger continues, "The best woodsmen are those who view nature as a sanctuary where they are a guest. They don't try to control it; they try to blend in and they view it as a privilege to be there. That is the posture that they take." He turns to me. "That's the kind of outdoors-man I want to be."

Roger wasn't born owning a gun, the way the Commish was. His father didn't hunt.

"How did you know what to do?" I ask.

"I didn't. I just went," he says.

"How did you pay for it?"

"I mowed yards. I bought my first gun on time. A man sold me that gun for five dollars a month on no interest. It was eighty-five dollars and I paid it out. It was a twelve-gauge Remington and I still have it."

The next afternoon, Roger and I drive together on his golf cart toward the deer stand. There is a cooler of Diet Cokes and beers, in his pocket are peanuts, and candy, too; and in a small white bucket he carries an dog-eared copy of Faulkner's *Big Woods*. He began leasing these 3,000 acres in 1989, then bought them in 1995. In the years that he has owned the land, he has only killed three trophy bucks. This isn't because he hasn't had the opportunity; it is because he is selective and patient. There isn't the same thrill in it for him at his age, as there would be for some-one starting out, so he saves it for those who will get the most out of it.

There also are rules that govern which bucks a hunter can shoot, depending on its age and the number of points on its antlers. The rules at Roger's camp are even stricter than Arkansas's rules. He man-ages the genetics of his deer population like an artisan, patiently whit-tling it into the best possible form. In the golf cart he begins to tutor me on the ways of his deer camp.

"If you're gonna shoot a cull buck [one considered to have inferior genetics], then you're gonna shoot him with my big gun. And you have to make sure your eye is away from the scope. 'Cause that hurts like hell. Kinda firm against your shoulder. And still you gotta squeeze it. It's gonna kick the shit out of you, but you won't even notice when you're shooting at a deer."

"If you're gonna shoot a doe, then you're gonna use the small gun. If you feel confident with the small gun on the doe, I'd shoot 'em in the head. It's instant death with them and I like that. If you feel confident, you do that. Try to pick out a hair on the deer. And then squeeze that trigger where you don't ever know when it's going to go off. It's just a gradual pull."

We stop to peer at a doe and fawn through binoculars.

"Can you see 'em?" he asks, inspecting the inventory with a faint pride. "I'm gonna have to scare 'em away."

We drive along for a time, with only the electric sound of the golf cart in our ears and the cold breeze off the Mississippi in our faces.

"We're gonna try to ease up in there," he finally says. "I have the door propped open. Sometimes it's possible to sneak up in that stand without them seeing you."

Then we are silent again, save for the sipping of Diet Cokes and the bumps on the road and the whistle of the wind through the cottonwood trees destined for the paper mill.

"I keep a stick inside of my stand," he says again. "And I use it as a shooting guide. And what I'll do is, when I'm getting ready to shoot, I'll aim it where I think I'm shooting at and then I'll put it under my arm and put the gun up here and it'll give me an anchor back here and I'm able to hold it perfectly still. If you wanna kind of try it on when you first get in the stand, you can, and see if you like it that way."

I follow his footsteps to the deer stand, the one he calls the Chad stand, placing my foot on the forest floor where he has, and feel it crackle under my feet. We climb the ladder up to the stand and open the door, which is watermarked from the Mississippi floods.

We settle into two metal folding chairs, and position our guns and feel the wind with our fingers to know which direction is downwind, for if we know which way the wind is blowing, we know where the deer are most likely to appear—upwind from human scent. Then, once settled, he leans back with a book of crossword puzzles, and there is silence, and soon, the sound of sleep.

I watch the ladybugs march in single file along the windowsill of the stand, and past them I can see the string of cobwebs that link the great woods and twinkle in the late afternoon light. In the silence is the machine-gun chirping of a bird and then a distinctive sound. Is it rain or just dried leaves cackling in the wind?

A barge floats along the Mississippi and I spy on the captain through the binoculars. And I can hear the barking of bucks in the distance and the clash of their antlers as they fight.

Bucks travel in bachelor groups of the same age, except during the rut, when they disperse and fight wherever they cross paths. They begin this at two years of age. Before that, they are yearling spikes and aren't very smart. They have been cast out of the family by the head doe. It's always a doe that is in charge of the family; if she gives birth to a doe, it becomes a dominant member of the clan; if she has a buck, then she runs him out of her domain. It is nature's way of preventing inbreeding.

During the rut, the bucks spread their scent. They have scent glands on either side of their nose near the eye, which they rub against trees. With their hoofs, they scrape a patch of ground and urinate in it, then assume a certain posture and urinate on their legs, too. Does are receptive to different scents; it is like an ID system; or in the words of the Commish, "It's like their business card."

The cold moist air rises through my nostrils as I sit and hear the bucks clash in the distance and watch the ladybugs march along and the squirrels and the blue jays flutter through their chores.

Roger wakes and gives me peanuts from his pocket. "There's a spike, can you see him?" he asks. That is the mark of a seasoned hunter, someone who can see animal life in an instant where everyone else just sees trees. We peer through the binoculars and watch the yearling wandering through the woods without a sense of caution. Soon a two-year-old buck with a chipped horn emerges from the fight in the distance. He nibbles his way through the woods, too, with only slightly more caution.

"If a doe comes out, they are a lot more careful than a buck or a hog," Roger says in a whisper. "They do a lot more watching than they do eating. Don't make any moves until she's got her head down. If there's a group of them, they all gotta have their head down. Don't do anything; I mean, don't even blink your eye. Especially if they're in this lane because the sun is shining, it's like having a spotlight on you."

We can't shoot this two-year-old buck or the yearling. In Arkansas, aside from a few exceptions, the general rule is that a buck must have three or more points that are at least one inch long on one side of his rack, or both antlers must be shorter than two inches (a button buck) to be legal to harvest. There is no age requirement for a doe. Identifying which buck is legal to harvest can sometimes be difficult and requires experience.

"How can you tell how old it is?" I whisper.

"Just imagine a thirty-year-old guy you know is akin to a three-year-old buck," Roger whispers. "But think how he looked when he graduated high school. He could very easily wear the same clothes, the same jeans, but he'd be filled out more in the shoulder and chest now. He's starting to begin his maturity as a man. A four-year-old would be like when he's forty."

Roger's camp is DMAP (Deer Management Assistance Program)–designated, which means he works with a wildlife biologist to manage the health and genetics of the deer population and the habitat. It requires him to collect data from the deer that are harvested, from their weight to their antler size, as well as extract a jawbone from each deer. After each hunt, all hunters fill out an observation form, listing how many deer and other types of wildlife they saw during the hunt. Based on the deer population, a biologist and Roger decide on what constitutes a cull buck—that is, one that has poor genetics based on its age relative to its antler size. At Roger's camp, a cull buck must be four and a half years old to receive that designation. A noncull buck must have at least four points on one antler to be harvested.

If the deer aren't hunted, their life span is about ten years, under ideal conditions; a doe will live slightly longer than a buck. But in these parts, five years is a lot, due to insect pressure, parasites, and fighting. And in some parts of the country there is severe overpopulation, which causes disease and starvation. That is when the deer become suburban road kill.

Roger snaps open a can of PBR beer and sucks in a sip. "None taste like that very first one," he whispers, gulping. We shell more peanuts and watch a raccoon waddle over in the path and feed on a pile of corn that has been left for the deer. We wait and watch the two young bucks wander off, and in time the 'coon waddles off, too, a little bit slower. "That coon ate so much he can't hardly walk," Roger says, looking up from his crossword puzzles.

We wait as the sun descends and begins to bleed through the trees. Roger begins to sharpen his knife. The sound of the blade scrapes against the diamond steel, sharp, abrupt, it scrapes, scrapes. It goes in double time and sometimes in short scrapes but it keeps going like a tin engine.

Roger tells me the deer are bigger now than they have ever been, and that today there is something different in the barometric pressure. He tells me a buck will shed its antlers within three days of the same day every year, and that a lot of mystery goes on out there that we don't understand, and that they act differently every day. And he says modern hunting technology has taken over and removed some of the mystery, and it won't be long before we can Google up a deer.

Then he tells me that sometimes when you don't see any deer, it is because there are hogs in the area. And as if to prove his point, a large female feral hog, with five smaller hogs, enters into the path and begins to feed. Hogs are Roger's nemeses and the enemy of all who tend the land. They are destructive for crops and farmland, so much so that people are paid to hunt them around the country. The hogs are always pregnant or breeding and their population can double in six months. The term *boar* actually refers to the adult male of several mammal species, including the beaver, the raccoon, the guinea pig, or the domestic pig. But for wild boar, it applies to the whole species, including adult females (sows) and piglets. In America, in addition to wild hogs and razorbacks, we have Eurasian boars, a species not indigenous to the United States, introduced in 1539 as a food source by the Spanish explorer Hernando de Soto. Today, what you see running through the hills in so many rural and semirural sections of the country is often a mix of domestic pig and Eurasian boar. Farmers discovered long ago that, rather than fence in a domestic pig and feed it, they could let the animal range freely to fatten itself on acorns, grasses, roots, grubs, eggs, rodents, and fruit—and rendezvous with one another in the woods. When the farmer wanted his pig for food, he would head out with a rifle and bring home the bacon.

Along with coyotes, the wild boar is about the smartest wild animal there is, able to smell and hear from remarkable distances and stay alive and thrive under almost any circumstance they face. More so than any other wild animal, they learn quickly. Hogs easily learn to root under and break down fencing. They quickly become "snare smart" and learn to avoid traps of all kinds. They are among the most destructive animals because when they dig up the ground for roots, they kill native plants, particularly near water sources, and this often causes serious soil erosion. They destroy valuable crops and devour the eggs and young of small native animals and endangered species, while consuming much of the food source of those native populations. They are genetically programmed to be aggressive toward wolves, a natural predator, which means they are equally aggressive toward domestic dogs. Their population is so large in the United States today that their activities are no longer limited to rural areas. They are now arriving in people's backyards and living rooms from Fort Worth to Cleveland to Abbeville, Georgia, because nature can't support them in such large numbers. Even when unprovoked, they are always fast and aggressive, and sometimes fatal.

And so I am faced with six hogs in my path, instead of deer. This is what happens sometimes. You go out with one meal in mind, and come home with something else all together. It adds to the magic and mystery of it all.

I peer through the scope of the small gun and rest my elbow on the anchor stick. I squint and place the crosshairs of the scope at the base of the big hog's head. The golden foggy light spreads horizontally through the trees and floods into the scope, so that all I can see is a silhouette.

"Be patient now, be patient," Roger says, his voice a touch unsteady. He is clearly unsure about how this is going to unfold. He has never seen me hold a gun before and my appearance doesn't instill the same confidence as his typical deer-stand companion.

I don't say much as I lean forward and look at the big hog. I lose her silhouette in the scope as the sun shifts again to shoot into my eyes. I pull away from the pain and readjust. I tightly squeeze my left eye shut and try with my right eye only, holding my breath to minimize the shaking. Through the golden mist I find her again and place the crosshairs again at the base of her head. I pull the rifle toward me and add pressure to the trigger, clenching the gun into the pocket of my shoulder. With my right eye peering through the scope and barely steady, I pull the trigger and watch her fall in her place.

The other pigs run squealing into the woods.

"You are bad!" Roger says, howling in surprise and delight. "That is the biggest hog I have ever seen here."

"Then that one will be for bacon," I whisper, smiling.

We sit in silence as the big hog lies in the golden streaks of sun and the breeze of the Mississippi gets colder and stronger.

"I'd be surprised if the other ones don't come back," Roger says. "They ain't got nothing better to do."

To my surprise, they do. They all return and eat in the same place as before, working around the big dead hog. I place the crosshairs of the scope on the head of the next biggest pig, small and black, and see only its silhouette again. As the sun drops lower, the haze shoots even more sharply through my scope and into my eyes. I fix the crosshairs on the still silhouette and then lose it again. The image begins to shake as I squint; perhaps it is the haze, or my hand, or my breathing. When I find the silhouette again, I hold my breath and squeeze and watch it drop.

"Two," I say. Roger begins to howl with pride. The remaining four hogs run off squealing. "Isn't that a sweet little gun?" he asks.

"Beautiful," I say, envisioning sausage. There is a silencer on the gun that makes me sound like a sniper. It adds an air of mystique.

The hogs all come back again. And again after that. And they eat around those that lie in their way.

"Three," I say hitting a third hog. Roger smiles.

And then a fourth. Roger chuckles in surprise.

"Five." Roger just shakes his head and grins. But the fifth one gets up after it falls and runs a few yards to the left, out of sight.

We wait. Roger peers through his binoculars. "I don't think it went far, unless the coyotes got him," Roger says.

The worst moment in hunting is an imperfect shot. It is hard to prepare for the moment you are responsible for suffering. Rather, it is hard to prepare for the moment you *know* you are responsible for suffering. It is all in the knowing.

Grabbing a couple of chicken breasts from the meat aisle of the grocery store so I could put together a quick stir-fry after twelve hours in a cubicle, I wasn't forced to internalize the suffering the animal had gone through in a factory farm, which I was now endorsing with my wallet. There weren't pictures of the bird whose breasts were bred to be so big that it couldn't walk but only drag its chest, along with the thousands of others sitting in a dark, confined space.

Similarly, there were no images of a cow with bloodshot eyes on my Styrofoam-packaged filet mignon, to help with the *knowing*. There wasn't the big, bold warning sign that they put on cigarette packages. Sure, I had options of all-natural, whatever that means, and organic, which means something more in theory. But it never meant the animals roamed freely through the wild, exercised their muscles as much as they pleased, ate whatever they pleased, and had the natural life that nature intended. I like to think that the animals I eat now never suffer, because I watch them die. It sounds callous but I have come to believe it is actually more humane this way. Except the rare moments like this: They're hard when it isn't an instant death. When my shot is imperfect. But even here, I am paying the full karmic price of the meal. I will *know* while I eat. I will know how it all went down. And I still think that is better. Because it makes me a more conscious chef, a more careful hunter, and a more awake human being.

We wait for a short while, but the sixth hog doesn't return and I have to find the fifth one that I shot imperfectly. The air is rapidly becoming gray and murky as we climb down from the deer stand. I search the woods while Roger guts the rest one at a time like an expert surgeon, using their blood to clean the meat as he goes. He finishes all four in under fifteen minutes, then uses a pulley and a tree and a push of his golf cart's gas pedal to string them up on the back of the cart while I continue to look for my last hog or a trail of blood. Then I hear the hysterics of a pack of coyotes, screaming like banshees only yards away. They have found my last hog first. As the cycle of life goes, they will kill one less animal tonight.

We leave the entrails of the hogs on the forest floor for the coyotes as well, and drive away into the muddy night, the four hogs hanging behind us on the golf cart. We speed along the dirt road of the preserve, and the cottonwood trees become a fine lace against the purple sky.

When we return to camp, Peter is skinning another hog and the Commish is smoking, and the electric hook goes up, creaking as it goes, a pig attached, and one by one we skin them all with knives, starting at the hooves and peeling down toward the head like removing a latex glove. We power wash the stomach cavities and the spray hose splatters and drips pink, and soon we roll the hogs into the cooler to lower the temperature of the meat before I begin to butcher them for sausage, and roasted whole hog, and braised belly. The largest hog is so big that her hind legs hang down and settle on the concrete floor. I cut out the thick slabs of belly, its thick layers of fat unusual for a wild hog, and massage it with pink salt and sugar and herbs. The massive hams I debone and place in the freezer so they will be easier to grind into sausage. The backstrap is so thick and long that we stop to admire it, pastel pink and thick enough for elegant round medallions.

In the evening, Roger and I talk about classic literature on the way to Walmart, the only place within 50 miles to get dinner ingredients. "Read *The Brothers Karamazov*, then read *East of Eden*," Roger tells me. "See if you don't see any similarities. Steinbeck was heavily influenced by Dostoyevsky."

Inside Walmart, the woman cleaning the floors is giving a church sermon, while we select from a pile of Pink Lady apples for our whole roasted pig. "A'right, I wanna bare my soul to you for a second," Roger continues, inspecting the apples. "Astronomy. The speed of light is one hundred and eighty-six thousand miles per second. A light year is how far you can go at that speed in a year. Now, how many seconds are there in a year, I don't know, but you multiply that times one hundred and eighty-six thousand and that's one light year. Okay. The edge of our galaxy is two point two million light years. So if you consider something that vast, isn't it a bit silly to take things too seriously in life?"

I smile and nod, turning a Pink Lady in my hand and dropping it in the bag.

"I'm baring my soul to you now! That's what I think about."

We drive back to camp in the moonless night, where the fire is high, the hog is roasting, and venison is braising. At the dinner table again are the sound of lips smacking and the high flavor of roasting meats dripping their juice from a well-used cutting board. The cousin they call "the Dream" dines with us now, wearing an orange bobble hat knitted by their Aunt Evvy. He has been hunting for a week at Island 86, the hunting club started by his father, many years ago.

"I'm hunting ghosts now," he says. "It's just as fun to hunt them as it is to hunt the real thing." And here, one hundred years later, Spanish philosopher José Ortega y Gasset's words seem never more fitting.

This is where we fit into the universe, as a very small part of a vast 2.2 million light year galaxy: soaking up the juices of roasted meats, at a long table of friends, under the warm light of an antler chandelier, on a moonless December night, somewhere deep inside the Mississippi Delta. That part of being human will always be inside of us.

Braised Venison Shoulder

The venison shoulder also lends itself well to braising. It is high in muscle tissue and will benefit from slow cooking at a low temperature in a bit of liquid and aromatics. Over time, the cooking breaks down the muscle tissue further than if you were to simply age it; and as the collagen melts, it gives it a buttery texture. Before cooking any venison dish, however, it is best to age the meat, which will drastically improve the flavor and texture. See the aging chart on page 242.

Marinade:

    4 tablespoons olive oil
    1 carrot, peeled and chopped
    1 onion, chopped
    1 celery stalk, chopped
    1 (750 ml) bottle dry red wine
    2/3 cup red wine vinegar
    1 clove garlic, crushed
    2 whole cloves
    2 bay leaves
    1 sprig fresh thyme
    1 bunch fresh parsley sprigs
    8 peppercorns
    4 small or 2 large venison shoulders

Braise:

    4 tablespoons olive oil
    1 cup diced onions
    1 cup diced carrots
    4 garlic cloves, crushed
    1/2 cup diced celery
    2 sprigs fresh thyme
    2 bay leaves
    2 whole cloves
    1 1/2 cups red wine
    3 cups antlered game stock (page 213)
    1 cup diced ripe tomatoes
    Salt and pepper

For the Marinade:

1. Heat the oil in a heavy pan and sweat the vegetables over medium heat. Add the wine and vinegar and remaining aromatic ingredients and simmer slowly for 30 minutes.

2. Let cool thoroughly at room temperature and pour over the venison. Let it soak for several hours.

For the Braise:
1. Remove the shoulders from the marinade and pat them dry.
2. Heat a roasting pan over medium heat and add the olive oil. Add the venison shoulders and sauté on all sides until nicely browned. Remove and set aside.
3. Add the onions, carrots, garlic, and celery to the pan and cook until well browned. Pour off any grease and add the thyme, bay leaf, and cloves.
4. Add the wine and deglaze the little caramelized brown bits at the bottom of the pan, scraping them with a wooden spoon. Add the stock and tomatoes and a little salt and pepper. Return the venison shoulders to the liquid.
5. Tightly cover the roasting pan with tinfoil and place in a 300°–325°F oven to braise for about 2 1/2 hours.
6. When the shoulders are tender, remove the roasting pan from the oven. Remove the foil and let the shoulders rest for 10 minutes.
7. Carefully degrease the cooking liquid by skimming the fat off the top with a ladle.
8. Remove the shoulders from the pot and set aside in a warm place, covered. Strain the braising liquid through a fine-mesh sieve. You can reduce some of this liquid in a separate saucepan until it is thick, and pour it over your venison to serve.

Also try: hog, bear, all antlered game

Liver Mousse   Makes 3 cups

Many people are reviled by liver, but I call it God's pudding. It is slightly sweet and very rich and I could eat it endlessly. It serves as the basis for all kinds of internationally popular and unpopular foods—depending on whom you ask. Foie gras, for example, beloved in France, was for a time banned in Chicago. Then there's liver and onions in Britain, *Leberwurst* in Germany, fish liver sashimi in Japan, and the Jewish dish turned idiom, chopped liver.

I like it not just because it tastes good, but also because it is a way to turn an often overlooked part of the animal into something delicious. Some people avoid liver because they think it stores toxins, but the liver doesn't store toxins, it neutralizes them. It does store important vitamins, minerals, and other nutrients, though. I would also argue that the liver from a hunted animal has probably processed far fewer toxins than that of a domestic one, so it is better for you.

When harvesting a liver, take a good look at it first to make sure it looks healthy. It should be free of spots, and not enlarged or discolored. The underlying sweetness in liver lends itself well to other subtly sweet foods, such as shallots and onions, or red wine and port. And a dash of vinegar balances it to prevent it from becoming too cloying.

    4 tablespoons grape seed oil, plus more as needed
    1 deer liver, sliced into 1/8-inch pieces, or 1 1/2 to 2 cups other liver
    Salt and pepper
    2 cups thinly sliced shallots
    4 cloves garlic, roughly chopped
    1/2 cup red or white wine
    1/4 cup port
    1 tablespoon half-and-half or cream
    4 tablespoons cold butter, cubed
    Balsamic vinegar
    Cider vinegar

1. Heat the oil in a wide, heavy-bottomed sauté pan over medium-high heat. Pat the liver dry and season it with salt and pepper on both sides. Sear the slices on both sides just until browned (about 1 minute per side), then transfer to a plate to rest.
2. Add the shallots and garlic to the pan and caramelize. Season with salt and pepper to help release the juices. Add more oil as necessary so they don't dry out and burn.
3. Add the liver back to the pan, then add the wine and port. Cover partially with a lid and simmer until the liquid has reduced by two-thirds.
4. Let cool for a few minutes, but not completely, then puree in a blender with the half-and-half and butter. Season with salt and pepper and transfer to a bowl.

5. Here you can pass the liver mixture through a fine-mesh strainer if you want it especially silky.
6. Season with balsamic vinegar and cider vinegar to taste.
7. Chill in the refrigerator for at least 1 hour before serving. Cover well with plastic wrap to prevent the surface from oxidizing.

Also try: duck, game birds, other antlered game (if the liver is large, cut on the bias into 1/2-inch slices before searing)

Pan-Seared Deer Liver   Serves 4 to 6

This is a second way to prepare liver, a bit more traditional, how your grandmother or the women of the pioneer era would have made it when food thrift was essential. It goes like this:

1 deer liver
Salt and pepper
4 tablespoons grape seed oil
1 white onion, sliced thinly
2 cups sliced button mushrooms (one standard package, whole; or you can really use any mushrooms, even the more exotic ones)
1/2 cup vermouth
1/2 cup whiskey
1/2 cup cream

1. Soak the liver in well-salted water for 30 to 60 minutes. Remove from the water, rinse under running water, and pat dry.
2. Cut the liver on the bias into slices. Lay them on a plate and season with salt and pepper.
3. Heat 2 tablespoons of the oil in a skillet over medium-high heat until you can see the heat coming off it. Sear the liver slices on both sides, about 1 minute per side. You want them medium rare; you are going to cook them again in a minute. If your pan is too small to fit all the liver in one batch, cook it in batches so you don't crowd the pan. You want a good sear.
4. Transfer all the liver slices to a plate, add the remaining 2 tablespoons of oil to the skillet, and sauté the onions and mushrooms until they are soft. Season with salt and pepper as you go.
5. Return the liver slices to the pan, add the vermouth, and simmer for a few minutes. Then add the whiskey. Light it on fire (flambé) with a match and stand back. Once the alcohol has cooked off and the flames have subsided, add the cream. Cook for a few more minutes, taste, and adjust the seasoning. Serve immediately.

Also try: duck, game birds, other antlered game (if liver is large, cut on the bias into 1/2-inch slices before searing)

Balsamic Deer Heart

Serves 4 as an appetizer

Native Americans used to eat the warm heart of their prey to inherit the animal's spirit. It was also a way to honor the animal and use every part of it. The texture of the heart is unique and unlike any other, chewy and dense like a muscle, but far more easy to masticate than any tough cut of meat. This recipe is the most delicious way to "go native" in your culinary pursuits, and is often something even the most seasoned hunters overlook.

    1 deer heart
    1/2 cup balsamic vinegar
    1/2 cup olive oil
    2 sprigs rosemary
    Salt and pepper
    1 tablespoon grape seed oil

1. Clean the heart under cold running water until the water runs clear. Cut the heart in half lengthwise so that you have two squares. Trim off the outer white membrane.
2. Cut the squares into 1/2-inch strips and the strips into 1/2-inch squares.
3. Marinate the squares in the balsamic vinegar, oil, rosemary, and salt and pepper, covered with plastic wrap, for at least 1 hour in the fridge.
4. Heat the grape seed oil in a pan and quickly sear the heart squares, about 1 minute per side. You want them to be no more than medium rare. Serve immediately!

Also try: duck, game birds, other antlered game (smaller hearts can be simply cut in half and trimmed of excess membrane)

Fireplace Venison Tenderloin

The deer tenderloin is arguably the most sought-after cut of deer meat. It is akin to the filet mignon of a cow, but far more flavorful. It is also very lean, which means it must be eaten rare, or else it will turn gray and chewy. It is one of the few cuts of deer meat that doesn't require significant aging before it can be consumed; in fact, you can enjoy it the day that you harvest it. There are several ways to cook it. My favorite is in a wire grill basket that you often see used for cooking whole fish or other delicate foods on the grill. You hold the basket by its handle over an open fire and let the tenderloins sear and absorb the wood smoke. If you don't have a campfire, an indoor fireplace works well. And if you don't have an indoor fireplace, cooking in a skillet works, too; you will just miss out on a bit of the ambient smoke flavor in the meat.

> 2 venison tenderloins, trimmed of excess tissue and silverskin
> 1 cup balsamic vinegar
> 1 cup olive oil
> 1/2 cup freshly squeezed orange juice
> 1 tablespoon chopped fresh rosemary
> Salt and pepper

1. Rinse the tenderloins and pat them dry. Place them in a nonreactive bowl and cover with the rest of the other ingredients. Cover with plastic wrap, pressing the plastic against the meat to keep out the air. Place in the refrigerator for 2 to 3 hours.
2. Remove from the bowl, shake away the excess moisture, and place in a wire grill basket.
3. Hold the basket over the fire for about 4 minutes per side. Remove from the basket and let rest for a few minutes, then slice and serve immediately.

Also try: other antlered game (Keep in mind that the size of the animal will determine the size of the tenderloin, which means cooking times may vary. See the temperature guide on page 240.)

Fried Venison Backstrap

Serves 8

I also call this recipe Campfire Fried Deer. It is a simple fried cutlet that is crispy on the outside and tender on the inside, and can be prepared easily in the outdoors with simply a skillet and a few ingredients.

> 1 venison backstrap, cut on the bias into thin slices and pounded between two layers of plastic wrap
> Salt and pepper
> 1 cup all-purpose flour
> 1 cup bread crumbs (panko or seasoned work well)
> 1 cup grape seed oil, plus more as needed
> Cranberry Relish (page 228) or your favorite chutney, to serve

1. Sprinkle the cutlets with salt and pepper. In a bowl, stir together the flour and bread crumbs, adding 1 teaspoon each of salt and pepper.
2. Pour the vegetable oil into a skillet to about 1-inch depth and heat over an open fire or stove top.
3. Brush the cutlets with a bit of oil on both sides and dip them into the crumb mixture until covered. Set aside on a plate.
4. Test the temperature of the oil by adding a cutlet and seeing if the oil begins to bubble assertively. If it doesn't, remove the cutlet and let the oil become hotter. If it does, continue adding more cutlets. Cook until one side is golden brown, then flip and cook until the other side is golden.
5. Transfer to a plate covered in paper towels or a wire rack and sprinkle with a bit more salt to keep them crispy. Serve immediately with a Cranberry Relish or your favorite chutney.

Venison Sausage   Makes 5 pounds

Sausages are one of the oldest prepared foods. Traditionally, sausages made use of the less desirable animal parts and scraps that could be cured in salt and put in the cleaned, inside-out intestines of an animal. Today, things aren't done much differently than they were in 589 BC. Sausage is simply a combination of meat, fat, salt, and spices, stuffed into natural animal casing. The combinations of flavors are endless and it is a chance to experiment with your favorite ingredients. Salt and pink curing salt are the two most important ingredients. As you experiment, write down the amounts of each ingredient that you use so you can go back and adjust.

> 3 1/2 pounds venison shoulder or haunch, cubed
> 3/4 pound hog shoulder butt, cubed
> 3/4 pound hog or domestic pig fat, cubed
> 2 tablespoons sugar
> 3 tablespoons kosher salt
> 1 tablespoon onion powder
> 1 teaspoon freshly ground white pepper
> 2 teaspoons paprika
> 1 teaspoon pink curing salt #1 (see Note)
> 1/2 teaspoon ground allspice
> 1/2 teaspoon grated nutmeg
> 1 teaspoon freshly ground black pepper
> 1/2 teaspoon garlic powder
> 1 cup ice water
> 4 tablespoons grape seed oil
> Natural pork casings, soaked in a bowl of saltwater

1. Before you are ready to grind the meat, put it in the freezer for about 1 hour, until the meat is firm but not frozen.
2. Grind the meat and fat through a medium die, taking care to alternate pieces of meat and fat.
3. Place the meat in the bowl of a stand mixer and add everything but the water. Mix well with the paddle attachment for about 1 minute, or with your hands for longer.
4. Add half of the ice water and continue mixing until the meat and fat are emulsified. The meat will develop a uniform, sticky appearance.
5. Work the meat through your fingers, squeezing it against the sides of the bowl.
6. Continue adding water until the meat is loose but not watery.
7. Heat 1 tablespoon of the oil in a small skillet. Cook 1 tablespoon of the mixture in the oil to taste the seasoning and adjust as necessary.

8. With a sausage stuffer, stuff the mixture into pork casings 6 to 8 inches long, pricking the casings with a sterilized needle as you go, to prevent air bubbles. Twist off the casing into links and let sit overnight in the refrigerator.

9. To cook, heat the remaining 3 tablespoons of oil in a skillet and sear over medium-low heat for about 15 minutes, turning often. The internal temperature should be 160°F.

Note: Also referred to as Prague powder, tinted cure mix, or Insta Cure #1, pink curing salt #1 (a mixture of salt and nitrite) is used in many types of cured meat products that are made and then cooked or eaten fairly quickly. The nitrite keeps the meat safe for a short period of time, and maintains the meat's red color as well as gives it that "cured" taste. Its main purpose it to prevent botulism poisoning.

Pink salt #2 is also known as Insta Cure #2 and Prague powder. It is a mixture of salt, sodium nitrate, and sodium nitrite, and used on meats that are dry cured over an extended period of time. The sodium nitrate breaks down over time to sodium nitrite, which then breaks down to nitric oxide, an oxidizing agent that keeps the meat safe from botulism.

Both mixtures can be purchased from many places on the Internet.

Smoked Venison Kielbasa

Kielbasa is the descendent of an Eastern European sausage. The texture is different from a regular sausage in that it is emulsified, making it most similar to a large, smoked hot dog. This emulsification is done with the aid of ice and milk powder. It is important that this meat mixture be particularly cold before it is pushed through the sausage grinder, because it will be ground more finely than a typical sausage.

> 3 pounds venison shoulder or haunch, cubed
> 1 pound hog butt, cubed
> 1 pound hog or domestic pig fat, cubed
> 1/2 cup diced bacon
> 1/4 cup kosher salt
> 1 teaspoon pink salt #1 (see Note, page 164)
> 1/2 tablespoon sugar
> 1/8 cup finely ground white peppercorns
> 1/8 cup mustard powder
> 1 teaspoon garlic powder
> 2 1/2 cups crushed ice
> 1/3 cup milk powder
> Natural pork casings, soaked in a bowl of saltwater
> Homemade Mustard, for serving (page 235)
> Homemade Sauerkraut, for serving (page 234)

1. In a large nonreactive bowl, combine the venison, pork, fat, bacon, salt, pink salt, sugar, white pepper, mustard powder, and garlic powder. Let sit overnight, if possible in the fridge.
2. Before you are ready to grind the meat, put it in the freezer for about 1 hour, until the meat is firm but not frozen.
3. Grind the meat, fat, and bacon through a medium die, taking care to alternate pieces of each of them.
4. Return the meat to the freezer for at least 30 minutes.
5. Grind the meat again, this time through a small die, while gradually adding crushed ice. Grind very small amounts of meat at a time. As the meat grinds, it should be cold enough to extrude on its own, without pressure.
6. Place the mixture in the bowl of stand mixer with a paddle attachment, and mix on the lowest speed for 2 to 3 minutes, stopping to clear the paddle as needed.
7. Add the milk powder and continue to paddle the mixture for 1 to 2 minutes on the lowest speed. Take care not to overmix, as it could result in a rubbery texture. (You may need to add some ice water to facilitate mixing—no more than 1 cup.)

8. Poach about 1 tablespoon of sausage in boiling water to test for seasoning and texture, adjusting as necessary.
9. Stuff the mixture into pork casings 6 to 8 inches long, pricking the casings with a sterilized needle as you go, to prevent air bubbles. Twist off the casing into links and let sit overnight in the refrigerator.
10. Hot smoke the sausages at 250°F for 45 minutes to 1 hour in a single layer until they are nicely red on all sides and firm. As they smoke, flip the sausages as frequently as possible.
11. Before serving, sear the sausages in a skillet until golden brown and warmed through. Serve with homemade mustard and homemade sauerkraut.

Axis Venison Loaf

Serves 6 to 8

My grandmother Frances Pellegrini is a home cook extraordinaire. Whenever she invited me to dinner growing up, I always requested her meat loaf. This is her recipe, taken from a family recipe book, as best as it can be put into words. She never was one to take measurements; it was always about whim and intuition. And there is something in her kitchen air that made this meat loaf turn out a special way that I have never been able to duplicate. This recipe uses venison, in this case axis venison, which is very lean, a little sweet, and a very beautiful color.

1 carrot
1 large onion
1 celery stalk
2 cups button mushrooms (one standard package)
2 tablespoons olive oil
1 teaspoon sea salt
2 1/2 pounds ground axis venison
1 egg, beaten
2 tablespoons Marsala
1/2 cup bread crumbs
1/3 cup tomato puree
1/2 cup parsley
1/2 cup finely chopped fresh basil
1 teaspoon grated nutmeg
1 teaspoon freshly ground black pepper

1. Blend the carrot, onion, celery, and mushrooms in a food processor until fine but not pureed.
2. Heat the oil in a skillet and sauté the mixture until softened, about 10 minutes. Sprinkle with salt along the way to help release the juices.
3. Preheat the oven to 450°F. In a large bowl, combine the vegetables with the rest of the ingredients.
4. Form the mixture into a loaf and place in a baking dish. You could also use a loaf pan. Bake for 10 minutes, then reduce the temperature to 350°F. Bake for 30 minutes more. Let cool slightly, then cut into thick slices and serve.

Also try: other antlered game, turkey

A dog in a kennel barks at his fleas;
a dog hunting does not notice them.

—PROVERB

10

NASCAR Hog Hunting

There are, of course, limits within each of us, no matter our instincts. In part, those limits are inherent to our makeup, unique
to our very fiber as a human. But some, I am starting to believe, are
also conditioned. It is the age-old question of nature versus nurture.
Could my urbanite girlfriends hunt their food if they had to? Would
they have walked up that hill toward the turkeys at the command of a
scary chef? Probably. But then there is the question of the word *hunt*.
How far would they be able to take the act?

Much of the hunting I do today is very different from what my cave-
man ancestors did. I have never stolen from a cheetah in the trees; I
have never outsmarted a lion; I have never chased and killed an animal
with a sharp object. The day I killed my first turkey for a restaurant
was the closest I had really come to holding an animal as it made the
transition from life to death. Perhaps that is why it awakened a dormant part of me. There was something that I recognized that had been
stored deep in my marrow. It was something that was now active and

pulsing, something that made sense. A gun is a tool, useful and efficient when used properly. But it is also a bit of a cop-out. It is a modern luxury. It is how we manage to not expend more calories hunting
our food than we get from eating it. Using bows and arrows would
make it a slightly greater challenge, but today even they have been so
improved by technology as to be virtually unrecognizable to those of
our ancestors. But what about hunting in its most primitive form?

The next early morning brings the first sprinkling of Arkansas snow,
the kind that melts into your eyelashes, leaving your face gleaming
and wet. The Commish and I climb into his white pickup, the back-
seat filled with waterproof clothing and gloves, the front seat appointed with two McDonald's coffees. We drive along the Mississippi
levee in any lane we please, skidding on the loose pebbles and listening to the sounds of country music, then take a steep right into 1,700
acres called the Lakewood Hunting Club. We are here to meet two
landowners named Lonny Carson and Jack Bates. Lonny and Jack are
serious hog hunters, the kind that own a menagerie of dogs trained
and suited just for hog hunting—brave dogs with scars and the remnants of stitches in their chests. There are two kinds of dogs in this
menagerie—dogs that trail the hogs and dogs that bring them down.
They are combinations of blackmouth cur and mountain cur, with
clear blue eyes or fierce black ones.

They sit in beige plastic kennels at the base of the hunting camp,
peering out from a patchwork of metal doors, their nostrils wet and
brimming with experience and anticipation. Lonny and Jack pull up in
a set of four-wheelers. All at once they release the doors of the kennels
and watch the dogs erupt from inside, their muscles twitching under
their thin, tight skin. They are bred in rural areas as an all-purpose
hunting dog; not recognized as a breed but as a type, leaving their appearance for Mother Nature to decide. A tan one hops to the back of
the four-wheeler and sits. The only female dog Lonny has ever owned,

she is chained to the seat behind him; he revs up the jackhammer sound of his motor, and takes off with her as if she is his girlfriend.

I climb into a two-person ATV with the Commish, as the snow begins to spatter on the windshield.

"Aw, hayell," he says, looking down under his hand. The gear shift of the four-wheeler has been upholstered with a tanned deer scrotum.

We follow Jack and Lonny through the woods of Lakewood Hunting Club, down narrow bumpy roads, and stop along the way to collar the dogs. Once long ago, hunters used to walk their dogs in pursuit of the hog. Then, in time, they rode horses. Years later they began to use four-wheelers with a marginal antenna system to help monitor the location of the dogs as they dashed through the woods. Now the dogs are fitted with collars that track them through a modern GPS system, which will tell the hunter how fast a dog is traveling and how many feet north or south it is from the tracking device. Jack and Lonny enter the names of the dogs into their locators and, one by one, attach collars to their necks. Once fitted, the dogs jump off, their necks blinking.

"You can practically see what they're thinking on this," Lonny says. "Soon they'll be using video."

"Hell, y'all need an IT person with y'all," the Commish says as we wait for them to tinker.

"Look at 'em. He knows they're hogs out there," Jack says, fitting a gray spotted cur.

"What's his name?" the Commish asks.

"He got a bunch of names," Jack says.

"What's his name today?"

"Uh . . . Bobby."

"He's Bobby 'til he messes up, then he's Sonofabitch."

The last dog jumps from the kennel more slowly. He has piercing blue eyes and the round head of a cur. He has a mess of fresh stitches on his chest. He is the oldest and the wisest of the menagerie. He has seen things.

"If the other dogs can't find one, you turn Beau loose and he'll make one," Lonny says. Beau jogs off slowly, ready to go to work, unamused, his neck blinking.

The low pressure and the moist, snowy air improve the dogs' sense of smell. This morning they are fervent with the burning perfume of hog in their throats. We follow them until all we can do is watch them as blinking red dots on a screen, as they disappear into the woods. We stop to listen from time to time. Lonny bites into a McDonald's biscuit as the Commish sips coffee, and tucks his cup next to the deer scrotum. I sit smelling the wet air, feeling the snowflakes settle onto my lips. The light glints off the long knife holstered against Lonny's hip, attached to a chain dangling in a loop from his leather belt. We sit and wait with the motors turned off, the snow in our faces, and the fumes of McDonald's biscuit in the air.

Then a distinctive howling sound fills the woods. In a few swift movements, biscuits are gulped, engines roar, and the four-wheelers are hiccuping and jerking through the woods toward the baying dogs. "This is NASCAR hog hunting," the Commish yells above the thundering engine.

You don't know what you will find when you arrive at a standoff between hysterical dogs and a 300-pound boar with needle-sharp tusks. Sometimes you will find an injured dog and a boar running away through the woods; sometimes you will find a dog with its jaws on the neck of the beast; sometimes you will find them face to face, working each other into a lather; sometimes it will be a dance of all three possibilities, changing and transforming by the second.

When we arrive, three dogs surround an angry boar. One dog has a firm grasp on his neck, and the others jump forward and back, yelping and seeming a touch unsure about what to do next. More dogs emerge from the woods now, attracted to the noise, and Beau comes forward and looks on at the scene, coolly impervious to all the fuss.

Lonny and Jack thrash through the woods toward them all and begin to yelp, too, and as they do, the boar tears loose and runs for the brush. The dogs follow until we see that they are under a dense patchwork of branches fallen over a ditch and overgrown enough to serve as a stable floor. I climb onto the floor of branches, walk toward the center, and look down through the cracks. In between the space in the branches is a mess of flesh and growling and stench. Lonny draws his long, glinting Rambo knife that makes a whistle as he pulls, kneels down on the floor, and thrusts his hands between the cracks to try to stab the boar. When he pulls his knife out, it is dressed in a thin layer of blood.

"I don't know if that was a dog or the boar I just got," he says.

As I stand on the floor, the grumbling in the cracks below me becomes more violent, sticks snap, and the Commish and old wise Beau look on stoically. Jack holds a pistol without purpose.

The boar suddenly breaks away, tearing through the floor, which shakes beneath me. Snorting and wheezing, he runs through the tall grass, but the dogs overtake him once more. Jack and Lonny stumble and run after them until they can reach the dogs to pull them off. When the Commish and I catch up, the dogs are beside themselves with excitement, and Jack and Lonny are sitting on a prostrate hog. I stand looking down at him, big and long haired, with a tubular snout and miniature tusks. He emits steam into the air in small bursts and chortles. I hear the ring of the Rambo knife coming back out of its holster and someone say my name. When I look up I see the red-stained knife in the air and a look of curiosity on Lonny's face. "Do you want to do it?"

It is true that in addition to guns, four-wheelers and GPS systems are also luxuries not afforded to our ancestors. But there is also the matter of practicality. Today's Western humans are more starved for time than for food. There isn't time to put on a suit in the morning and hunt by foot with a knife in the afternoon. And so there are two shortcuts that we can choose from—the meat section of the grocery store; or the gun, the GPS system, and the deer stand. How often do humans in this age use a knife and their bare hands to bring home their food from the woods? But more so, how often do humans become this entangled with nature? Hunting, after all was a physical endeavor for our ancestors; it was about bringing home food but also living close to the land. There is no doubt that some hunters are attracted to it for that reason, for the physicality of it. But, in a sense, this most primitive act brings our role in the cycle of life back to its most basic level: We eat animals, animals eat animals and plants, plants feed from the dirt, and we turn to dirt. The opportunity to participate so honestly and physically is rarely offered to us anymore.

I reach out my hand and take Lonny's red-stained knife and kneel on the grass beside the boar. I grasp the bone handle tightly in my leather glove until I can feel the blood in my hand pulsing. I look down at the skin above the heart and point the tip of the knife toward it. And with all of the weight and strength of my body I push the knife in, and feel Lonny grab my wrist and pull me forward, too, my body moving forward with it all, until I am draped over the boar. When I pull back, and watch the river of blood come with me, it is quite simply all over. I have, for the first time, channeled the primitive woman, and for a few fleeting moments recognized what it was once like to be a human—I recognize the casual way in which nature treats life and death.

When I stand and step back, Lonny and Jack begin to field dress the boar on the forest floor, removing all of the insides until he is much less heavy, yet still too heavy to carry. We tie a rope from the four-wheeler to his front hooves and pull him out of the woods. After skinning and power washing, the large boar becomes a pièce de résistance, marinated and smoked whole for a day, dripping in molasses, oozing in crisp fat. If I were living thousands of years ago, my status within the community would have been greatly improved with this wild hog. Although even now, as I watch a table of people lick molasses from their fingers, I think perhaps it still has.

Boar Loin in Sherry Marinade   Serves 4 to 6

The loin is also referred to as the backstrap and is the long, thick portion of bone-less, tender meat that runs on either side of the spine on the exterior of the rib cage. The tenderloin is the most tender part of the animal and is smaller. It is located on either side of the spine on the interior of the rib cage. These cuts of meat are extremely lean, and are best eaten rare in the case of antlered game. But in the case of wild boar, they must be cooked through to 160°F, which means they will benefit from a marinade or brine first, to retain moisture.

1 1/2 sticks (12 tablespoons) butter, melted
1 tablespoon lightly crushed juniper berries
2 teaspoons coarsely cracked pepper
2 teaspoons kosher salt
6 whole cloves
3 cups Amontillado or other sweet sherry, cooked for several minutes to burn off
  the alcohol, then cooled
2 wild boar tenderloins or backstraps (see Note)

1. Combine all the ingredients and pour over the tenderloins in a roasting pan. Cover and let sit covered in a cool place for 4 to 6 hours, turning over periodically so it marinates evenly.
2. Preheat the oven to 475°F.
3. Tie the tenderloins with kitchen twine, the way you would a roast. Place the roasting pan in the oven and roast for 10 minutes. Lower the temperature to 350°F and continue to roast for about 10 minutes more, or until the internal temperature on a meat thermometer reads 160°F. Turn the meat over several times to help it cook evenly. The sherry will begin to caramelize onto the meat and separate from the butter.
4. Remove the pan from the oven, place the tenderloins on a cutting board, and cover loosely with tinfoil. Let the tenderloins rest for 20 minutes before serving so that the juices retreat back into the meat.
5. Remove the string and serve thinly sliced, drizzled with some of the flavored pan butter.

Also try: javelina, antlered game, bear, upland game birds

Note: Sometimes you'll hear the term *boar taint* in discussions about wild boar. Most people don't cook the male wild boar because they have high testosterone levels, which can give the meat an unappealing flavor. Some hunters will go so far as to trap the boar, castrate it and release it, then hunt it a year later. If given a choice, female Eurasian boar or feral hogs tend to taste better, but I'm of the mind-set that a male can be made to taste good with a clean shot, impeccable field dressing, and a good brine prior to cooking.

Braised Hog Belly   Serves 8

If you are fortunate enough to come upon a very large hog, this is the recipe I recommend for the belly. Wild hogs don't have thick bellies the way domestic farm
pigs do, but a large hog will come close enough to make this recipe worthwhile. It
is tender and wonderful and any extra fat can be skimmed, trimmed, and saved to
render (see page 187). If you are on a quest for a large hog, they are best found at
night. The oldest and largest are also the smartest, and stick to their nocturnal rou-
tine more carefully than the rest.

> 1 hog belly (3 to 5 pounds)
> 1 (750 ml) bottle white wine
> 6 cups hog stock (page 213)
> Zest of 2 oranges, sliced into thin strips
> 6 whole jarred jalapeños
> 4 sprigs fresh thyme
> 2 bay leaves
> 1 stalk lemongrass, bruised with the back of a knife and cut into 4-inch pieces
> 1 tablespoon black peppercorns
> 1/4 cup salt

1. Preheat the oven to 325°F.
2. Trim the belly for neat edges and remove any glands or damaged parts.
3. In a saucepan, bring the wine to a simmer and cook out the alcohol for 5
   minutes.
4. In a separate saucepan, bring the stock to a boil and add the rest of the ingredients, including the wine, which all becomes the braising liquid.
5. Place the belly in a shallow, flat, ovenproof pot and cover with the braising
   liquid. Cover with tinfoil or a lid and place in the oven. Braise for 3 hours, until
   very tender.
6. Remove the belly from the liquid and slice into small, square portions. Serve
   with a bit of braising liquid in a shallow bowl.
7. Alternatively, heat grape seed or vegetable oil in a skillet and sear the fat side of
   the belly until it crisps. Serve it with leafy green vegetables such as bok choy or
   kale, steamed or sautéed.

Cotechino Sausage   Makes 5 pounds

The fresh spices in this recipe make it stand out. It is best to grind each freshly with a spice grinder, rather than use preground spices. In any recipe, drying your own herbs creates the greatest flavor and potency. This sausage is typically served poached rather than grilled. Because the meat of a wild boar has more muscle tissue, this makes it important to grind the meat finely to avoid a dense or chewy sausage, qualities that become more prominent when the sausage is poached. Having the meat and equipment very cold before putting the meat through the grinder will help achieve a fine grind.

3 pounds hog butt, cubed
2 pounds hog or domestic pig fat, cubed
3 1/2 tablespoons kosher salt
1/2 teaspoon pink curing salt (see Note, page 164)
1 1/2 tablespoons finely ground black peppercorns
1/4 teaspoon finely ground cloves
1/2 tablespoon grated nutmeg
1/2 teaspoon ground cinnamon
1/2 teaspoon cayenne
4 garlic cloves, minced
1/4 cup ice water
Natural pork casings
20 cups hog stock (page 213)
2 sprigs fresh thyme (optional)
2 bay leaves (optional)
2 whole garlic cloves (optional)

1. In a nonreactive bowl, combine the pork, fat, salt, pink salt, black pepper, cloves, nutmeg, cinnamon, and cayenne. Cover and let sit overnight in the refrigerator, if possible.
2. Before you are ready to grind the meat, put it in the freezer for about 1 hour, until the meat is firm but not frozen.
3. Grind the meat and fat through a 1/8-inch die, taking care to alternate pieces of meat and fat. Gradually add the minced garlic while grinding.
4. In a mixer fitted with a paddle attachment, mix the meat for about 1 minute, until it is cohesive when smeared. Gradually add ice water to make the mixture uniform. You can also use your hands here, but it will take longer to get a cohesive mixture.
5. Mix until the meat pulls away from the sides of the bowl and the sausage feels somewhat tight.
6. Put the sausage casings in a bowl of warm water for at least 30 minutes, then drain out the water. Carefully run water through each casing and look for water

that comes out of any holes. Cut out any portions of the casings that have holes.

7. Bring the stock and optional thyme, bay leaf, and whole garlic to a simmer in a small saucepan and poach about 1 tablespoon of sausage to test for seasoning and texture. Adjust as necessary.

8. Stuff the mixture into the pork casings 6 to 8 inches long, pricking with a sterilized needle as you go, to prevent air bubbles. Twist off the casing into links and let sit overnight in the refrigerator.

9. When ready to cook, preheat the oven to 170°F and pour the stock in a roasting pan, baking dish, or pot wide enough to hold the sausages in one layer. Pour the stock over the sausages and bake in the oven for about 30 minutes, until the internal temperature reaches 160°F on a meat thermometer.

10. Take the sausage out of the liquid immediately to let cool and so that it stops cooking in the hot liquid. Let the poaching liquid cool separately to room temperature. Then, once it is room temperature, store the sausage in the poaching liquid in the refrigerator and reheat in small amounts as needed.

Chorizo Sausage

Makes 5 pounds

This chorizo can take multiple forms, and this is a good one to make if you don't have natural pork casings to make these into fresh sausages. Chorizo can be broken up into pieces as part of a casserole or chili, or it can also be made into a patty and seared with eggs for breakfast. Chorizo can also be dried until it loses 40 to 50 percent of its weight, when it is eaten like charcuterie. But I always start with a batch of this as fresh sausage, then turn any extra meat mixture into other forms.

3 pounds hog butt, cubed
2 pounds hog or domestic pig fat, cubed
1/8 cup kosher salt
1/2 teaspoon pink curing salt #1 if cooking while fresh, or pink curing salt #2 if allowing to air dry (see Note, page 164)
1/8 cup sweet paprika
1/8 cup ancho chile powder
1 teaspoon coarsely ground black peppercorns
1 teaspoon coarsely ground cumin
1 1/2 teaspoons cayenne
2 garlic cloves, minced
1/4 cup chilled red wine
1/4 cup chilled tequila
Natural pork casings
1 tablespoon grape seed oil

1. Combine the pork, fat, salt, paprika, chile powder, black pepper, cumin, and cayenne. Let sit overnight, if possible.
2. Before you are ready to grind the meat, put it in the freezer for about 1 hour, until the meat is firm but not frozen.
3. Grind the meat and fat through a 1/8-inch die, taking care to alternate pieces of meat and fat. Gradually add the minced garlic while grinding.
4. In a mixer fitted with a paddle attachment, mix the meat for about 1 minute, until it is cohesive when smeared. Gradually add the wine and tequila to make the mixture uniform. You can also use your hands here, but it will take longer to get a cohesive mixture.
5. Mix until the meat pulls away from the sides of the bowl and the sausage feels somewhat tight.
6. Put the sausage casings in a bowl of warm water for at least 30 minutes, then drain out the water. Carefully run water through each casing and look for water that comes out of any holes. Cut out any portions of the casings that have holes.
7. Sauté about 1 tablespoon of sausage in the oil to test for seasoning and texture. Adjust as necessary.
8. Stuff the mixture into the pork casings, pricking with a sterilized needle as you go, to prevent air bubbles. Twist off the casing into links 6 to 8 inches long, and let sit overnight in the refrigerator, after which point you can freeze them or store in the refrigerator for 3 to 5 days.

Hog Backstrap, Chops, or Tenderloin   Serves 6 to 8

This recipe is really an ode to how simply prepared game meat can be, when treated with a good brine. The leanest cuts—chops, backstraps, and tenderloins— are best seared with my favorite hog brine and finished with my silky beurre blanc (page 228). It can also be served with homemade applesauce (page 233) or mint vinaigrette (page 227). This recipe can be done at home or on a campfire with a hot skillet.

> 2 to 3 pounds hog backstrap, chops, tenderloin, brined (page 219)
> 2 to 4 tablespoons grape seed oil

1. For the tenderloin and backstrap, truss them as you would a roast before cooking. The chops can also be tied around the meat and secured at the bone to maintain a uniform chop when sliced.
2. Preheat the oven to 350°F. Sear the meat in a skillet in some oil until browned on all sides. Transfer to the oven and cook for about 30 minutes, or until the internal temperature reaches 160°F. Remove and let rest for 10 to 15 minutes, covered in tinfoil, then serve.

Also try: javelina, antlered game (cooked rare)

Smoked Whole Hog

Serves 15 to 40

One of the questions I get most often is, "What is your favorite wild game dish?" I always describe this one. From the first moment I tasted it, it earned itself a special place in the crevices of my mind. This whole wild hog is marinated for days and then smoked for many hours. Bacon and apples and molasses are also involved. It is essential in this recipe how the animal was killed, where it was shot, how it was dressed and cleaned. All of that needs to be done in an impeccable way. Cleanliness can be helped with a good marinade that includes a lot of acid in the form of vinegar, olive oil, lemon juice, and orange juice, in any combination. The size of your hog will vary, and so you have to rely on intuition when it comes to how much marinade to use. You can marinate the hog for one to eight days, and the acid will clean it and also impart flavor. You can marinate it in an ice chest if your hog is up to about 80 pounds on the hoof or 45 pounds cleaned. Or you could even use a garbage bag.

The smoking time varies, depending on the size of your hog as well. It could be six hours, it could be twelve. The temperature should never go above 250°F in your smoker, and it is best to heat the coals to a uniform temperature before you put in the hog, to create an even, radiant heat. What smoker should you use? There are many large barrel smokers on the market, or if you want to be particularly traditional, you can dig a pit in the ground and smoke the hog there, in the Italian fashion.

Although you can heat with charcoal, pecan wood is best if you have it in your region of the woods, or you can use a tree indigenous to your area. In the Southwest it is mesquite, in Washington State it is apple wood, and in the Midwest it is hickory. The following instructions are guidelines more than an exact recipe. You must go with your intuition and your hog to determine the right amounts of the ingredients.

Marinade:

    1 whole hog, dressed, skinned, head and hooves removed
    1 to 2 cups Worcestershire sauce
    1/4 to 1/2 cup Cajun salt seasoning
    3 to 4 onions, peeled and cut in half
    10 to 20 garlic cloves, peeled and crushed
    5 to 8 sprigs fresh rosemary
    1 to 2 cups white vinegar
    1 to 2 cups freshly squeezed lemon juice
    4 to 6 cups freshly squeezed orange juice

To Smoke:

    6 to 10 Granny Smith apples, cored and cut in half
    1 tablespoon ground cinnamon

20 to 30 bacon strips

3 to 4 cups molasses

For the Marinade:

1. Combine all the marinade ingredients with the hog in a large cooler or new garbage bag and let sit for 1 to 8 days, turning the hog every 12 hours so it evenly marinates. A hog that is 80 pounds on the hoof, 45 pounds cleaned, will fit well in a standard cooler. The acid cleans it. Cleanliness is important.

To Smoke:

1. When ready to smoke, bring your wood coals of choice to no more than 250°F in a large smoker. Let the coals become nice and uniform so that you have an even, radiant heat.
2. Smoke the hog for 6 to 12 hours, depending on its size. Once the densest part of the hog reaches 140°F, add a pan of apples to the bottom of the smoker, sprinkle with the cinnamon, and let them steam up under the hog.
3. At this point, also blanket the back of the hog with bacon and pour on 3 to 4 cups of molasses. Be generous with it and pour most of it in the area where it will drip down into the pan of apples.
4. The hog is ready to serve when the densest, deepest part is 160°F; under the front shoulder is usually the coolest part to test. Serve immediately tableside as your pièce de résistance.

Sweet Porchetta Sausage

Makes 5 pounds

This is most like a traditional Italian-flavored sausage, thanks to the fennel seeds and hint of sweetness. It would go well with roasted red peppers and onions, or sliced thinly, with some coarse mustard. Like all sausage, it should be cooked at a low temperature for a long period of time so that the casing doesn't burst and it is cooked through.

    4 pounds hog butt, diced into 1-inch pieces
    1 pound hog or domestic pork belly fat, diced into 1-inch pieces
    3 tablespoons kosher salt
    1/2 teaspoon pink curing salt #1 (see Note, page 164)
    2 teaspoons sugar
    2 teaspoons minced garlic
    2 tablespoons fennel seeds, toasted
    2 teaspoons ground black pepper
    2 tablespoons sweet paprika
    3/4 cup ice water
    1/4 cup chilled red wine vinegar
    Natural pork casings

1. In a nonreactive bowl, combine all the ingredients except the water, vinegar, and casings, and toss to distribute the seasonings. Chill until ready to grind.
2. Grind the mixture through a small die into a mixing bowl set on ice.
3. Add the water and vinegar to the meat mixture and mix with the paddle attachment or your hands until the liquids are incorporated and the mixture has developed a uniform, sticky appearance, about 1 minute on medium speed in a mixer, longer with your hands.
4. Put the sausage casings in a bowl of warm water for at least 30 minutes, then drain out the water. Carefully run water through each casing and look for water that comes out of any holes. Cut out any portions of the casings that have holes.
5. Sauté a small portion of the sausage, taste, and adjust the seasoning if necessary.
6. With a sausage stuffer, stuff the mixture into the pork casings, pricking with a sterilized needle as you go, to prevent air bubbles. Twist off the casing into links 6 to 8 inches long and let sit overnight in the refrigerator.
7. To cook, heat some oil in a skillet and sear over medium-low heat for about 15 minutes, turning often. The internal temperature should be 160°F.

Hog Croquettes

Serves 6 to 8 (about 14 patties)

This recipe is a great way to use extra scraps of meat left over from a braise or a soup. It is also an excellent way to make the most of the tougher cuts of meat, by breaking them down over a long cooking time and then adding flavorings of your choosing. You can experiment with your favorite herbs, add chopped jalapeño or pickle, or even add a little cayenne for an extra kick.

Croquette Meat:

> 5 pounds hog meat (shoulder or haunch is best)
> 6 to 10 cups hog stock (or enough to cover three-quarters of the meat) (page 213)
> 3 bay leaves
> 3 tablespoons kosher salt
> 1 teaspoon black peppercorns
> 3/4 cup minced shallots
> 1 cup equal parts finely chopped fresh parsley, tarragon, and dill
> 2 tablespoons whole-grain mustard
> 2 teaspoons ground white pepper
> 1 teaspoon sea salt
> 2 teaspoons grated nutmeg

Breading:

> 2 cups all-purpose flour
> 6 large eggs, beaten
> 3 cups panko
> 1/2 cup grape seed oil, plus more as needed

For the Croquettes:

1. In a pot, cook the hog meat in the hog stock with the bay leaves, kosher salt, and peppercorns. Simmer, covered, over a low flame for 3 hours, or until the meat is fork tender and comes apart easily.
2. Let cool until just warm. Chop the meat into smaller chunks and then place in a food processor. Blend to a fine consistency. You will need to do this in three or four batches to get an even blend.
3. Transfer the mixture to a bowl and mix with the shallots, herbs, mustard, pepper, sea salt, and nutmeg. Taste and add more salt as needed. Form the mixture into 4-ounce patties.

For the Breading:

1. Place the flour, eggs, and panko in three separate bowls.
2. Dip the patties one at a time, first in the flour, shaking off any excess; next, in the

egg (remove with a fork or slotted spoon to let any excess drip down); then in the panko, coating them evenly on both sides.

3. Panfry the patties in the oil for about 2 minutes on each side, until golden brown, then tip them on their side and quickly rotate so that the edges are browned slightly.

4. Transfer them to paper towel or wire rack and sprinkle with salt to help retain the crispiness at the table. Serve immediately.

Also try: javelina, antlered game

Hog Ragout

Serves 8

This recipe dances the perfect line between a stew and sauce. For a lighter meal, eat it as is in shallow bowls, with a bit of bread to soak up the juices. For something heartier, or for a larger crowd, serve it over fresh pasta or add large croutons to the bottom of the bowl as a kind of bread soup.

2 tablespoons olive oil
1/2 cup peeled and diced carrots
1/2 cup diced celery
1 cup diced onion
Salt
1/2 cup peeled and minced shallots
4 cloves garlic, peeled and minced
1 tablespoon Pimentón pepper
1/4 cup white wine vinegar
4 cups crushed tomatoes
3 cups braised hog meat, shredded (page 176)
1 cup canned chickpeas
1 teaspoon red pepper flakes
1/2 cup chopped basil
1/4 cup chopped fresh parsley leaves

1. Sweat the carrots, onion, and celery in the olive oil. Add a sprinkle of salt to help release their juices.
2. Add the shallots and garlic and cook until translucent.
3. Add the Pimentón and mix until well combined.
4. Add the vinegar and let simmer for 5 minutes.
5. Add the tomatoes and cook for 1 hour at a very low simmer, stirring occasionally.
6. Add the shredded pork meat, chickpeas, and red pepper flakes and simmer for 30 minutes.
7. Finish with the basil and parsley and serve in shallow bowls.

Also try: javelina, antlered game

How to Render Fat

1 pound fat = 1 cup rendered fat

Rendered hog fat makes the best, flakiest piecrusts (page 99), and duck fat is a nice alternative to butter. A meat's distinctive meat flavors reside in the fat, and so with wild animals, it is important to think about what they have been eating, and the environment that they came from. Ducks that have had a strong diet of fish, for example, do not produce good-tasting skin, whereas hogs that have been feasting on a forest of acorns will be slightly sweet and nutty. The best way to find out about an animal's fat qualities is to render a piece of its fat slowly in a pan and then taste the fat. Simply trim off the fat of any animal you don't like the taste of and the meat will always be good. The fat is what carries the flavor. The fat of wild animals is less saturated than that of domestic animals because their diet is varied; you can tell by how quickly wild animal fat becomes liquid at slightly warm temperatures. It is also full of vitamins A and E, and in some cases omega-3 fatty acids. There is rarely a lot of fat on a wild animal, but what you find should often be preserved.

1 pound hog or duck fat, cut into 2-inch pieces
Water

1. Place the fat in a skillet or pot.
2. Add enough water to come about halfway up the sides of the fat.
3. Put the burner on its lowest setting and let the liquid simmer for 60 to 90 minutes, turning the fat pieces every so often.
4. When it starts to look as though the simmer is dying down, watch the fat carefully. It should be a warm golden color, with smaller bubbles. As the water evaporates, those bubbles will come closer to a boil and the remaining liquid will turn a darker golden. Eventually, the boiling bubbles will suddenly become much smaller, just back to a bare simmer, which means all the water is gone.
5. Remove the pan from the heat immediately and pour the fat through a fine-mesh strainer into a glass bowl. Placing a layer of cheesecloth in the strainer first is even better. Let the fat cool to room temperature, transfer to a glass jar, and place in the refrigerator. The rendered fat will keep for 1 month in the refrigerator or in the freezer for 6 months.

Apple Juice Smoked Ribs   Serves 6 to 8

My friends in the Village taught me that the secret to good ribs is maintaining the temperature of the grill between 225° and 275°F, and cooking with indirect heat. A rotisserie cooker with a fire box in the back works well. And placing a chunk of mesquite in the box adds good flavor.

> 2 hog racks
> 2 batches Everyday Dry Rub (page 222), or 1 cup of your favorite rub
> 2 cups apple juice
> Barbecue sauce (page 227) (optional)

1. Remove the skin from the bone side of the slab, leaving a bit of fat.
2. Season with the dry rub all over, rubbing it in. Wearing latex gloves as you do; this will help the mixture adhere best.
3. Place the ribs, bone side up, on the grill and cook for 2 hours, maintaining the heat at 250°F. You may need to add more wood coals along the way.
4. Remove the ribs from the grill and place them on a sheet of tinfoil with the sides turned up to prevent the juices from escaping.
5. Pour 1 cup of apple juice over each rack and seal the foil tightly. Let the racks rest for an hour or two before serving. Serve with barbecue sauce or simply as they are.

Like a small grey
coffee-pot,
sits the squirrel
—HUMBERT WOLFE

11

Seeing the Forest for the Squirrel

It was summer at our home in the Hudson Valley when my grand-mother told me about Squirrel Brunswick. She stood above the stone steps, in the skewed rectangle of her kitchen doorway, her gnarled toes jutting out from her cotton skirt. It was an old-fashioned stew, and she remembered her mother making it in this same house after they purchased it from the Smith family. My great-grandmother used a coal stove, and made supper by kerosene light when the days grew dark, until finally giving in to the modern adventure of electric-ity in 1949, twenty years after everyone else in the neighborhood had. She was a steadfast Puritan and the fact that her kitchen flooded with sunlight in the daylight hours seemed enough.

Eating what was available was a given. So she stirred a pot of Squirrel Brunswick from time to time, while my great-grandfather wrote books in the upstairs study on a Remington typewriter and an old wooden desk—books on the marvels of science, and articles on things like the great underground cable that served as the artery of communication once upon a time, between Chicago and London. If working at night, of course, he did all of this by kerosene light.

The Smith family had kept a refuse dump on this land that my great-grandfather named Tulipwood. Once, after a windstorm knocked down several tulip trees like dominoes, I found the remains of the old Smith family dump in the roots of an old tree trunk. There were glass medicine bottles in every color, the kind of thick blown glass children covet on beaches, and broken china, and once in a while even a single unbroken piece. When I brought a pile of dump materials to my grandmother's door, her eyes widened almost as widely as her mouth, and that is when she told me about the Smith family and their dump.

The reason I mention the dump is that I am sitting now in the snow-covered woods of Upstate New York, an hour north of Tulipwood, against a young conifer, next to a mint green toilet. As it turns out, it is still common practice to have a refuse dump on your land. I don't know precisely whose land this is, or whose mint green toilet this was. But I am sitting near it; sitting covered in a white bedsheet, my seat damp from the snow I am trying to blend into. My friend Wyatt, who got permission to hunt this land, is stalking rabbits 40 yards away, just beyond a pile of rubber tires. I feel the chemical pebbles of the feet warmers in my shoes begin to cool inside their cotton casing, the left one more than the right. I can feel my biggest left toe begin to tingle and grow numb. I wiggle it while I wait for squirrels.

The fields beyond are covered in knee-high snow. There is a crust of ice on the top, and fault lines that cut through it all and branch off like the stencil of a tree—sometimes, thanks to the ice crust, you can walk on the surface of the snow. Sometimes you sink suddenly and the snow tips over the top of your rubber boots and soaks into your socks.

Squirrel nests speckle the sky high underneath a veil of gray branches. There is a hawk up there, too, waiting for the same thing we are. He plans to use his talons; I plan to use a number six load from my over-under. But we are here for the same thing, this hawk and Wyatt and I, except I imagine I have a more interesting recipe in mind than does the raptor.

The air is broken by the explosion of a semi blowing from the highway and through the conifers, and the tinkling sound of snow melting into the thickening stream. But mostly, things are still. I wait for the squirrels to come out and cavort in the drizzle, and feel the chemical pellets in my right shoe begin to extinguish. Soon my right toe begins to tingle and the left toe graduates to a gentle throb. I adjust my position against the base of the young conifer and slide down farther underneath my white sheet. I unzip my green sack and rustle for snacks inside.

More than any other kind of hunting, squirrel hunting says something about a person. It may seem from the outside that there isn't much to a squirrel. But in pursuit of a squirrel, you learn things, such as how to follow the patterns of the woods just as you do with a deer.

Some consider squirrel to be the best meat in the woods, and while squirrel is a desirable little beast, time spent in the woods may lead to other animals as well. You meet raccoons while pursuing squirrel, and sometimes you see a hare or a cottontail. All are legal to hunt, and the end of a squirrel hunt may leave you with a mixed bag and to dishes you thought impossible but turn out to be enchanting.

Once, while I prepared squirrel in the Village, Betty the housekeeper was cleaning in the same kitchen. She stopped and watched and told me how she prepares 'coon, her lips tucked into her mouth as she talked. She pushed her hands into her armpits and inside of her leg to show me where she takes out the 'coon glands, and described how she parboils it and then bakes it with sweet potatoes until it is all golden. Then she sat down to watch me; her back was hurting, she said. Ten children and a lifetime of chopping cotton can do that to a woman.

That day she sat humming while I chopped onions and told me about gar gravy made from the flesh of a fish, and about Mr. Mancini's fried venison. "I don't have teeth, but he make it so tender that you can eat it with your tongue," she said, continuing to hum. As my eyes wept from the onions, she said, "If you put a toothpick in your mouth, you won't feel nothin'." And I did, and soon felt nothing in my eyes, save for the pure romance of cooking squirrel to the sound of Betty humming through tucked lips.

My seat grows ever more damp against the young conifer as I fetch peanuts from my green sack. There is a haze at the lip of the horizon and there are buzzards orbiting around us—me and the young conifer—eyeing our flesh.

The phrase, "You are what you eat," befits a squirrel as it does a Spanish acorn-fed pig. Squirrels are hoarders, and after having feasted on a grove of pecans or acorns, their meat is nutty and sweet, buttery and tender. A fat, nut-fed squirrel is better tasting than any meat in the woods, perhaps better tasting than that Spanish pig that sells for seventy euros per kilo. But if you were to tell that to a group of my stiletto-heeled pals on a warm Manhattan evening—which I have done—you would be met with textbook female gasps and sideways glances. Those *squirrels* linger around the soot-covered fire escapes of their studio apartments. Aren't they really tree rats?

No. The squirrels I speak of have never been anywhere near a studio apartment. The best-tasting squirrel is the one you find in the woods—the kind of woods I sit in now, beside a mint green toilet and a thickening stream. It has been a long journey to know such a thing, to appreciate squirrel.

Squirrel hunting is more American than apple pie, than Babe Ruth, than a twenty-dollar Manhattan. Whole traditions have formed around these squirrels; guns have been crafted in their honor. Few things are more intertwined with American history and tradition. Squirrel is one of the most popular game animals in the eastern United States.

This surprises me still, perhaps because I have never understood squirrel, or have never cared to until now. But there are towns, tucked away, linked by the spines of narrow roads, where microwaved catfish sandwiches are eaten on porches, where undiscovered men make guitar music, tapping their hands on the strings until the notes swell and glow like fireflies. Towns where children skip school on the opening day of squirrel season.

The night after I made squirrel with Betty one year ago, a man named Toomey came over. He was driving his truck home along the levee when Roger Mancini called and asked him to teach a girl how to make a real putach. Toomey paused at first. He doesn't let many people be his friend. But Roger Mancini was his friend, and he figured if he couldn't do that for Roger Mancini, then he couldn't call him a friend. So Toomey showed me how to make a true putach. I watched his small, fat hands move like magic among the pots and silver bowls, the vinegars and the squirrel meat. I smelled the fumes of rosemary vapors rise from the pot, and watched his round leather eyes glitter.

In the Village, the Italian immigrants go squirrel hunting together after the pecan trees drop. This was a bad year because there was no pecan crop. The squirrels that Toomey and I cooked were from the dwindling supply of one of the Italians who, with his squirrel dogs, normally gathered seven hundred squirrels in a single year. He loved the squirrel dogs; it was probably them that drove him to hunt squirrels. But Toomey had the best hunting dog, a dog named Bear, which was perhaps the best in all of Arkansas.

But now I sit far away from there, against the young conifer, my over-under split open, the primer of my shells glinting in the breach like the tips of golden knitting needles. I remember a trick I once read about to help call in squirrels and decide to try it. I feel around the bottom of my green sack and pull out two quarters. I rub the edge of one against the side of the other and emulate the chatter of a squirrel. And sure enough, after some time, the squirrels come and cavort in the drizzle at last, just two. They start and stop across the brown leaves. Sometimes they sit, just like a small gray coffeepot. I close my split-open shotgun and hold it against my shoulder, trembling just slightly under the white bedsheet, and squint into the woods where a squirrel sits. When I pull the trigger, the woods reverberates and the hawk flies closer. But then things are silent again. I walk over and retrieve my gray squirrel in the brown leaves and think about that Brunswick.

Then I hear two more shots fire in the distance, and not long after my friend Wyatt appears with two cottontail rabbits dangling from his left hand. For some reason, America has never been a land of rabbit eaters the way that we have been squirrel eaters—or chicken and beef eaters. We leave that to China, Italy, Spain, and France, and are instead content with our squirrel. There is something about the squirrel that resonates with us, that propels us to craft special guns and seek keen dogs. Once, in the early 1700s, gunsmiths in Pennsylvania developed the superbly accurate Kentucky long rifle, which soon earned the name *squirrel rifle* by early pioneers. The gun made today just for a squirrel hunter is the combination .22/.410 or .22/20 gauge, an over-and-under combo with a selector button giving said hunter a choice of rifle or shotgun barrel. We go into detail for squirrel.

A squirrel lives for six to seven years, whereas a cottontail lives for only one. The texture of squirrel meat is denser, the color grayer, and the flavor more complex because of this. Squirrels are wanderers, sometimes ground dwelling and social, living in well-developed colonies; or sometimes tree dwelling and solitary. Squirrels persevere, hoard, and make dietary sacrifices to survive. Maybe the early pioneers saw a bit of themselves in squirrels. Or maybe these animals just tasted better. Either way, this meat has somehow never reached our elite dinner tables. It has never gained favor with the palates of kings abroad, the way it has here among certain Americans.

I think I have crossed over and become one of those Americans. It is true I have spent evenings sipping *nouveau* martinis, but as I sit and close my eyes, I recall the sound of lips smacking, and remember my dabbing with crusty bread at the rosemary vapors of squirrel putach, that night one year ago in the Village. I can hear the rumble of distant thunder past the lake, and smell the whiskey steaming from the ice, and recall the sight of men tapping tenderly on the pearl notes of a five-string, clenching their teeth and grimacing into their music making. Yes, I have crossed over.

Squirrel Brunswick Stew with Acorns
Serves 8 to 10

Young squirrel is good simply quartered and fried. Old squirrel is good stewed. When in doubt, it is safest to braise or stew a squirrel. Sometimes, for flavor and for whimsy, I like to add acorns to this recipe. Native Americans used to eat acorns, usually by grinding them and then boiling them. They are sometimes bitter because of their tannins, but this can be improved by grinding them and running them under cold water. Acorns from the white oak, the chestnut oak, the swamp white oak, and the Garry oak are all ideal.

4 squirrels, cleaned and quartered, plus rib cage and loin
1 lemon, cut in half
1 sprig fresh rosemary
1 bay leaf
1 teaspoon cayenne
Sea salt
3 strips bacon, diced
1 medium-size onion, chopped
6 garlic cloves
1 cup beer
3 cups crushed tomatoes
2 cups red potatoes, skin on, which have been cut into bite-size pieces
2 cups okra that has been cut into bite-size pieces
1 cup canned chickpeas
1 cup corn, fresh or frozen
1/2 cup shelled and minced acorns
1 tablespoon Worcestershire sauce
Salt and pepper

1. Place the squirrel parts in a pot and cover with water. Add the lemon halves, rosemary, bay leaf, cayenne, and about a tablespoon of sea salt and bring to a boil, then lower the heat to a simmer. Cook until the meat is tender, about 1 hour, skimming the foam from the surface as it forms. Once the meat is tender, turn off the heat and let the liquid cool.

2. In a separate pot, render the bacon. Add the onion and garlic and cook until softened. Deglaze the pot with the beer, scraping up the brown bits at the bottom of the pot with a spatula. Add the tomatoes, potatoes, okra, chickpeas, corn, and acorns and stir.

3. Add 2 cups of the squirrel cooking liquid and stir in. Add the squirrel and Worcestershire sauce and simmer for 1 hour. Season with salt and pepper to taste. With this stew, as with most, it is best to let it sit for several hours before serving.

Also try: rabbit, dove, turkey, upland game birds

Squirrel Dumplings   Serves 6

These dumplings are vaguely like dim sum. They have a very tender texture and are versatile—they can be flavored with your other favorite herbs and used with any meat. They are good alone with a dipping sauce or also nice on the same plate as a Brunswick stew or other tomato sauce. They also reheat well for several days afterward.

    1 squirrel, whole or cut into portions
    1 bay leaf
    1 teaspoon cayenne
    1 tablespoon + 1/2 teaspoon kosher salt
    1 egg
    2 cups all-purpose flour
    3 tablespoons minced fresh flat-leaf parsley
    1 teaspoon garlic powder

1. Place the squirrel in a pot and cover with water. Add the bay leaf, cayenne, and the tablespoon of salt and bring to a boil, then lower the heat to a simmer. Cook until the meat is tender, about 1 hour, skimming the foam from the surface as it forms. Once tender, turn off the heat, transfer the squirrel to a plate, and let the liquid cool.

2. In a medium-size bowl, beat the egg. Whisk in the flour, parsley, remaining 1/2 teaspoon of salt, and the garlic powder. Whisk in 3/4 cup of the squirrel cooking broth until well incorporated, then stir in the squirrel.

3. Bring the squirrel poaching liquid to a simmer. Take walnut-size spoonfuls of the squirrel mixture and drop them into the simmering water. Simmer for 10 to 15 minutes, turning every so often. Remove with a slotted spoon or drain them in a colander, and place in a serving bowl. Serve with a dipping sauce, in a tomato sauce, or with a stew.

Also try: any other meat you please

Traditional Squirrel Putach

Serves 4 to 6

Unlike Dove Putach (page 38), which is my more elaborate version, this is a true putach in all of its simplicity, as taught to me by one of the experts in the Village. The secret is the vinegar, which can be increased or decreased to your tastes. Remember that the putach cooks down over several hours, so it is good to be generous with the vinegar in the beginning.

1/4 cup olive oil
1 large onion, roughly chopped
Salt
6 squirrels, quartered, plus rib cage and loin
5 garlic cloves, skin on
Freshly ground black pepper
A mixture of 2 parts white wine vinegar and 1 part water (I start with 2/3 cup of vinegar to 1/3 cup of water)
2 sprigs fresh rosemary

1. In a heavy-bottomed pot, heat the oil and add the onion. Season with salt. Sweat the onion slowly over low heat until soft and translucent, about 15 minutes.
2. Add the squirrel and garlic cloves, and brown slowly for about 10 minutes. Season liberally with salt and pepper.
3. Add the vinegar mixture as well as the rosemary. Cover with tinfoil and cook slowly over low heat for about 2 hours, or until the meat falls off the bone. Add more salt and pepper to taste and serve with crusty bread or rice.

Also try: rabbit, dove, turkey, upland game birds

Buttermilk Fried Rabbit   Serves 4

Introduced in France in the Middle Ages as a game animal, rabbit became pervasive and overtook crops, providing more incentive to hunt them. King Louis XVIII became such a connoisseur of rabbit that he could tell which region of the country a rabbit was killed in, simply by smelling its flesh. You are what you eat, after all, and Provence was flush with sage. Young rabbits are best fried, because they are so tender. The best way to check a rabbit's age is to tear one of its ears lengthwise; if it tears easily, the animal is young. Also look for very white teeth. Before cooking a rabbit or a squirrel, I also typically soak it in saltwater for several hours, if not overnight. This helps extract impurities and retain its moisture during cooking.

> 1 young cottontail rabbit, cut into serving pieces
> 2 cups buttermilk
> 1 medium-size onion, sliced
> 3 garlic cloves, diced
> 1 teaspoon dried oregano
> 1 teaspoon dried thyme
> 1 teaspoon dried tarragon, or 1 teaspoon each of your three favorite dried herbs
> 1 teaspoon smoked paprika
> 1 tablespoon cayenne
> 2 cups all-purpose flour
> 1 teaspoon garlic powder
> 1 teaspoon onion powder
> Salt and pepper
> 2 to 3 cups grape seed or vegetable oil

1. Soak the rabbit overnight in the buttermilk, along with the onion, garlic, herbs, paprika, and 1 teaspoon of the cayenne.
2. Drain in a colander, leaving some herbs on the rabbit. In a large resealable plastic bag or in a large bowl, mix the flour with the garlic and onion powder and remaining 2 teaspoons of cayenne, as well as a pinch of salt and pepper. Meanwhile, heat the oil in a large, heavy-bottomed skillet over medium-high heat until a pinch of flour starts to sizzle when dropped in the hot oil, but not so hot as for the oil to be smoking.
3. Place the rabbit pieces in the bag with the flour mixture and shake until thoroughly coated. Do this in small batches, dredging just enough rabbit to fit in the pan at one time.
4. Add the rabbit to the skillet and fry on one side for about 10 minutes, until golden brown, then use tongs to turn the pieces over and fry for another 10 minutes, again until golden brown. Be careful to keep the oil hot enough to fry the rabbit, but not so hot that it burns.
5. Remove the rabbit from the skillet and place it on a wire rack over paper towels. Season immediately with salt and pepper to taste, to help preserve the crispiness for the table. This is good served immediately or also good cold for lunch the next day.

Also try: squirrel, dove, turkey, upland game birds, or any other young game meat

Jugged Hare

Serves 6 to 8

Then there is the hare, not to be confused with the rabbit. Red fleshed like venison, not white fleshed like rabbit, hare live longer, run faster, and have sharper wits. In the days of the Roman Empire, hare meat was believed to preserve beauty, while its blood possessed medicinal qualities. Hare are mostly known in America as jackrabbit, or in some cases snowshoe hare. Because they are older and can run as fast as 45 miles per hour, this means that their meat is flavorful but also tough, and needs to be cooked slowly for a long time. Jugged hare is an ancient dish in which a whole hare was typically marinated and cooked in red wine and juniper berries in a tall jug that stands in a pan of water. It was traditionally served with the hare's blood, which thickened the sauce. The liver can also be seared and pureed with a bit of cream to thicken the sauce, and should definitely be saved from any hare you hunt, if possible. Make sure the liver is healthy looking, and free of any white spots. And of course, if hare blood and liver are not at your fingertips, this recipe works well without them.

To Marinate:

- 1/4 cup brandy
- 1 (750 ml) bottle red wine
- 2 carrots
- 2 celery stalks
- 1 large onion
- 2 cups button or other mushrooms
- 3 bay leaves
- 1 tablespoon fresh thyme
- 1 tablespoon chopped fresh rosemary
- 8 juniper berries
- 4 garlic cloves
- 1 hare, 2 swamp rabbits, or 3 cottontail rabbits, cut into serving pieces

To Stew:

- 1 stick (8 tablespoons) butter or lard
- 6 to 8 strips bacon or pancetta, diced
- Salt and black pepper
- All-purpose flour, for dusting
- 2 cups pearl onions, soaked in warm water, then peeled
- 1/2 cup dried mushrooms (e.g., porcini or chanterelle), soaked in brandy until reconstituted (optional)
- 1/4 cup port wine
- 1/2 teaspoon ground cloves
- 1/2 teaspoon grated nutmeg

1/2 teaspoon freshly ground black pepper

1/2 teaspoon ginger powder

2 cups game bird stock (page 212) or turkey stock (page 214)

2 tablespoons crème fraîche or sour cream

1/2 teaspoon chili paste

2 tablespoons minced fresh parsley

To Marinate:

1. Bring the brandy and wine to a boil for 3 minutes to burn off the alcohol. Turn off the heat and let cool to room temperature.
2. Meanwhile, combine the carrot, celery, onion, and mushrooms in a food processor and blend until minced. You may have to do it in batches to get an even blend.
3. Add the minced vegetables, bay leaves, thyme, rosemary, juniper berries, and garlic to the wine while it cools.
4. Trim the hare parts of any excess tissue or hair and place in a nonreactive bowl. Pour the liquid over the hare once it comes to room temperature, and cover. Chill in the refrigerator overnight.

To Stew:

1. Remove the hare from the marinade and set aside on a plate. Strain the liquid through a fine-mesh sieve into a small saucepot. Reserve the marinade ingredients and bring the liquid to a simmer. A foam raft will form as the liquid bubbles. Skim this off with a ladle and let it continue to bubble until the foam no longer forms and the liquid is fully clarified. Turn off the heat and let the liquid sit.
2. Heat two separate skillets or large sauté pans on the stove top. Place 4 tablespoons of the butter in one and heat until it begins to bubble. Place the bacon in the other and let it render slowly. As the butter bubbles in the first sauté pan, sprinkle the hare parts with salt, pepper, and flour and place them in the skillet. You may need to do this in batches so as not to crowd the pan, and you can add the remaining 4 tablespoons of butter as you brown the hare and the pan dries out. Brown the parts on both sides and transfer them to a clean plate once they are well browned. Leave the skillet on the stove top and turn off the heat.
3. Preheat the oven to 300°F. As the bacon renders in the second skillet, add the pearl onions and let them brown. Once the bacon is crispy and the onions well browned, add the minced vegetable mixture from the marinade. Sauté the vegetables and let them cook and render their juices. Sprinkle with a bit of salt and pepper.

4. Place the rabbit parts back into their skillet and add the vegetables, bacon, and pearl onions from the other skillet so they are distributed evenly. Add the mushrooms here, if using, along with the port, cloves, nutmeg, ground pepper, and ginger. Pour in the clarified marinade and add additional stock as necessary until the liquid comes almost to the top of the meat. Cover with tinfoil and place in the oven. Braise for 2 to 3 hours for a hare or slightly less for rabbit, until the meat falls off the bone.

5. You have the option now, once the meat cools slightly, to pick the meat off of the bones and return it to the pan. This is ideal for the texture and final eating experience and doesn't take much effort, but you can skip it if you are short on time. Either way, finish this dish by stirring in the crème fraîche, chili paste, and parsley, and serve.

Also try: duck legs, pheasant legs, squirrel

Braised Rabbit with Olives and
Preserved Lemon

Serves 4

This rabbit dish is light and tangy, with a hint of Provence and the Mediterranean. The preserved lemon needs to be made in advance, but can be skipped in a pinch and replaced with blanched lemon zest, or it can be purchased at a specialty spice store. When butchering your own rabbit or hare, whether wild or domestic, be sure to wear gloves. One in a million carries the tularemia virus, which you should avoid direct contact with.

1 whole rabbit, cut into serving pieces
1/2 large onion, cut into chunks
1 medium-size carrot, cut in half lengthwise and then into 1-inch pieces
1 celery stalk, cut into 1-inch pieces
3 cloves garlic, crushed
1 bouquet garni (see Note)
1/2 (750 ml) bottle white wine
2 tablespoons olive oil
1 tablespoon butter
Salt and pepper
1 tablespoon all-purpose flour
1 tablespoon tomato paste
2 tablespoons red wine vinegar
2 cups game bird stock (page 212) or turkey stock (page 214)
Zest of 1/2 preserved lemon (page 236), well rinsed and julienned
1/4 cup Niçoise, kalamata, or mixed olives
1 teaspoon chopped fresh parsley
1 teaspoon chopped fresh rosemary
1 teaspoon chopped fresh thyme

To Marinate:

1. Combine the first seven ingredients in a bowl and let sit at room temperature for at least 1 hour.

To Braise:

1. In a heavy-bottomed skillet over medium heat, combine the olive oil and butter. Remove the meat from the wine, pat dry, and sprinkle with salt, pepper, and flour.
2. Place the rabbit legs and loins in the skillet and cook until well browned. Turn over and brown the other side. Transfer from the pan to a clean plate.

3. Add the vegetables from the marinade to the pan, and lightly caramelize in the same fat. Sprinkle with flour, stir, and cook for a few minutes. Add the tomato paste and cook for a few minutes more. Deglaze the pan with the vinegar and reserved marinade, scraping up the brown bits on the bottom of the pan, and reduce the liquid until the sauce is thick.
4. Return the meat to the skillet. Add the stock and bouquet garni, cover, and let simmer for about 1 hour, or until the meat is tender. Turn off the heat and add the preserved lemon, olives, and chopped herbs. Stir and let sit for 15 minutes before serving.

Also try: squirrel, turkey, upland game birds

Note: To make a bouquet garni, tie in a piece of cheesecloth: 1 bay leaf, 1 sprig of fresh thyme, 1 sprig of fresh rosemary, and 1 small bunch of fresh parsley with stems.

*We arose over ten thousand centuries ago from hunters who loped,
with weapons in hand and animal flesh on their minds, across the
yellow plains, and it may be every bit as long before the need to
hunt is in any way quenched within us. When, and if, it ever is, it
will probably mean that for better or worse we are no longer
human but have become something quite different.*

—THOMAS MCINTYRE

Epilogue

To me, the great mystery of the human species is how we got to where we are—how we came out of the trees, stood on just two feet, and ended up on the trading floors of Lehman Brothers—how we got "so smart."

I believe the answer is that we joined the Great Forage—we participated in the delicate dance between predator and prey, which forced us to develop complex thinking, to premeditate, to strategize, and to know to share our prey with others for social and personal advantage. There have been scientific tomes written that support all of this. But I am not an archaeologist or sociologist. Instead I am a girl who has been sharpening her human instincts and discovered in the process how satisfying, how natural, and how inspiring it is to play an active role in my omnivorous life. For me, it is tapping into that natural human instinct for which we—as animals, too—are genetically hardwired.

There is an intense debate as to when exactly we became true omnivores, but it makes sense that we began by scavenging dead animals. It allowed us to take in more calories compared to the number of calories we expended to find the food. Our climbing ability grew as a way to steal kills stashed in trees by leopards, as did our ability to run fast. We had to know when our prey—and our competitors—slept, grazed, watered, changed locations, mated, and bore young. It all required complex thinking, observation, and growing intelligence as we learned to imitate and outwit the other lethal species. And ultimately, we had to be able to fight these other meat eaters. This required us to develop tools and weapons and plans to defend ourselves. Today still, the very act of being alive by definition requires us to also know how to survive or perish. But hunting and gathering taught us more than survival—it taught us that by bringing food back to the tribe, by feeding the community and the women especially who were then more fertile, our position in the world was elevated. Hunting and gathering not only taught us how to stay alive, it was the act that made us more human.

Where I am writing now, on a screened-in porch beside the crescent-shaped lake in the place they call the Village, I have never felt more human. It is dusk. The smell of barbecue is in the air, intermingled with the inimitable smell of old cigars and new whiskey. The weather is shifting—I hear the drips of water, the tittering of wrens; I see the melting, the fiddleheads beginning to peer above the brown leaves, their fronds tucked in like great green question marks over what is to come.

I am entirely different than the girl who came here four years ago to learn how to hunt a turkey. There are the obvious differences, such as the fact that I can shoot a deer through the heart without batting an eye, then promptly take out the innards on the forest floor with only a pocketknife and my bare hands to help me. I can skin it with the pocketknife, too, then run the knife along the contours of the muscle until it is broken down into manageable parts. Then, if I want to, I can portion the meat into those elegant pieces we see neatly wrapped up in plastic in the grocery store meat section, with no signs that it was ever a living thing. Except that for me, that will never be the case again. I will always know. I will have looked my food in the eye and made a choice; I will have felt the warm innards in my hands as I pulled them out and laid them on the forest floor for the coyotes and the mountain lions to eat.

It was a struggle to get here, mostly a mental struggle. It required a slap on the ass and a horseback-riding escapade with a poacher. It required humility, frustration, hundreds of skeptical looks, and waking up in the dark for most of the fall and winter months—all in the name of sausage, venison meat loaf, and whiskey-glazed turkey breast. It required run-ins with airport security that wanted to know why there were frozen animal parts in my suitcase, and with border patrol dogs sniffing my car wildly where the edges of Texas meet Mexico.

It was all amazing. Even the so-called bloody bits.

It was more amazing than the irreplaceable meals, the incomparable vistas, the fine cigars and scotch, the almond cakes and gourmet chocolates, because now I am more awake than I ever was when working in fast-paced four-star kitchens, or on a high-pitched trading floor. It is as if I have realized again those first pleasures I knew sitting beside my creek in the Hudson Valley, watching the orange fishing bobbin float by under the willow tree. I am a more thoughtful eater, a more thoughtful chef, and a more awake human being. I am a fuller woman and in a way, I am much more like Diana than I ever was . . . there are even days, stepping out into the morning, when I think perhaps that I could rule the forest and the moon.

Of course, many wild, edible foods are missing from this book. This was my journey, shared for the sole purpose of inspiring you to have your own. May you find a place where you can hear the foghorn on the river at night, or where you can hear the woods wake up at dawn. Most of all, may you find a place where you can discover what it is to feel the omnivore genes in you stir with the distinct vibration that makes us really human. Whatever your journey, wherever you find it, may it be a wild one.

Acknowledgments

There are days as a writer when time passes differently in the blur of travel and note-taking. When my mind gets entangled with the work there are people who have to put up with it all, who intervene on my behalf and recognize when my "fearlessness" has gone a bit too far. Without them this book would not exist. Without their support, I would probably be lost in the desert of Wyoming. Being "fearless" often requires a lot of help.

To T. Kristian Russell there aren't enough words to thank you for guiding me every millimeter of the way. You were there when I blurted out this little idea and you made it happen as much as I did. Thank you to my brother, Gordon, for giving me editorial, creative, and life perspective in equal doses. Thank you to Roger Pellegrini for teaching me to fish and love the outdoors, and for suggesting years ago that I join the ranks of women hunters; and Maureen Pellegrini for instilling in me a respect for all living things.

To my editor, Renée Sedliar, thank you for "getting" *Girl Hunter* from the beginning, and for your intuition and depth. You are by far my favorite vegetarian! Thank you to the rest of the team at Da Capo for being so flexible and receptive to my vision, and to Brettne Bloom, my agent, for bringing us together.

Thank you, Janie Fransson, for giving me a much-needed fresh perspective and invaluable advice. You were that burst of energy I needed to push me over the finish line; and Abigail Cleaves for being a continual connector and cheerleader.

I also had research assistants who helped me in various stages along the way, from recipe testing to sanity checking, Julia Becker, Athena Gee, Rachel Wegman, and Abigail Hansen were immensely helpful.

Thank you to the late Thomas Russell for the praise and support as I read you rough drafts up until the very end, and to Jimmy and Deborah Russell, Sarah Perkins, and Heather Herrington for continuing it always.

For the friendship and the wild game to finish my recipes, thank you to: Paul and Debbie Michael, Freddie Black, Mike Pappas, Worth Williams, Faith McCormick, Solonje Burnett, Kelsey Contreras, Spencer Kehe, Tamara Mendelsohn, and Emily Goldman. For being my masterful recipe-testing assistant: Courtney McLeod.

And of course, thank you to those in this book, for their true generosity, the valuable life lessons, and the wild ride.

Gravy

Stocks, Marinades, Brines, Rubs & Sauces

Stocks

Stocks are a great base for many wild game dishes. They also lend great flavor when used in the place of water for rice and grains. It is best not to season stock until you are ready to use it in a dish, as each dish will have different needs. It is also useful to freeze stock in small portions in resealable bags or in ice cube trays; this way you can use small amounts as needed and don't have to wait for a large batch to defrost. Stock is also very forgiving and provides you with a chance to flavor with whatever you have on hand. This means that if you have chicken bones instead of pheasant bones, beef bones instead of venison bones, or pork bones instead of feral hog bones, they will all work within these recipes. Even a simple vegetable stock will work. The whole purpose of stock is not to limit you, but to give you the opportunity to make use of the scraps you have on hand. Because of this, your yields will also vary based on your ingredients and heat level.

Game Bird Stock   Makes 4 to 6 cups

15 dove carcasses, or equivalent in other game bird carcasses
2 tablespoons grape seed oil
1 cup white wine
2 cups chopped celery, with leaves
1 cup peeled and chopped carrots
1 cup chopped onion
1 cup washed and chopped leeks

1. Over high heat, brown the carcasses in the oil in a large pot. Add the vegetables and brown. Pour off any grease, deglaze the caramelized brown bits at the bottom of the pot with the white wine, then cover the carcasses and vegetables with water.
2. Bring to a boil and lower the heat to a simmer. Skim off any foam that forms on the surface.
3. Simmer for 4 hours, or until the liquid is full flavored. Strain and store.

Duck Stock   Makes about 8 cups

2 duck carcasses, plus any necks
4 tablespoons grape seed oil
5 shallots, roughly chopped
4 cloves garlic, roughly chopped
2 celery stalks, chopped
2 pieces orange zest
2 pieces lemon zest
2 pieces grapefruit zest
1 bay leaf
4 sprigs fresh thyme
5 sprigs fresh parsley
1/2 teaspoon coarsely crushed star anise
1/2 teaspoon coarsely crushed fennel seeds
1/2 teaspoon coarsely crushed coriander seeds
1/2 teaspoon coarsely crushed cloves
1/2 teaspoon coarsely crushed black peppercorns

1. Preheat the oven to 375°F. Place the duck carcasses on a sheet tray, drizzle with 2 tablespoons of the oil, and roast for 30 minutes, or until golden brown.
2. Heat the remaining 2 tablespoons of oil in a stockpot, add the shallots, garlic, and celery, and sweat them.
3. Add the duck carcasses, about 16 cups of water, and the herbs and citrus zests.

4. Cover and simmer gently for 3 to 5 hours, until full flavored. Skim off any foam or fat that forms on the surface.
5. Strain and reduce the stock further until the flavor is more potent.

Hog Stock   Makes about 8 cups

10 pounds hog bones
4 tablespoons grape seed oil
1/4 cup tomato paste
3 carrots, peeled and chopped
3 celery stalks, peeled and chopped
3 onions, peeled and chopped

1. Preheat the oven to 375°F. Place the hog bones on a sheet tray, drizzle with all of the oil, and roast for 30 minutes, or until golden brown.
2. Remove the bones from the sheet tray and place in a large stockpot.
3. Cover with water and bring to a boil.
4. Add the tomato paste, carrots, celery, and onions. Simmer for 6 to 8 hours, until full flavored. Skim off any foam or fat that forms on the surface.
5. Strain and reduce by half.

Antlered Game Stock   Makes about 8 cups

10 pounds venison bones, or equivalent in other antlered game
6 tablespoons grape seed oil
6 carrots, chopped
2 large onions, chopped
1/2 cup tomato paste
6 cloves garlic, roughly chopped
1 (750 ml) bottle red wine
4 sprigs fresh thyme
2 sprigs fresh rosemary
3 bay leaves
6 to 8 sprigs fresh parsley
1 tablespoon black peppercorns

1. Preheat the oven to 400°F. Place the bones on a sheet tray, drizzle with 4 table-spoons of the oil, and roast for 30 minutes, or until golden brown.
2. Remove the bones from sheet tray and place in a large stockpot along with 2 tablespoons of oil.
3. Add the tomato paste, carrots, and onions, and let sweat for about 5 minutes, or until the onions become soft and translucent. Add more oil if necessary.

4. Pour in the red wine and simmer for 5 minutes. Add the remaining ingredients. Cover with water and bring to a boil.
5. Simmer for about 6 to 8 hours, skimming off any foam or fat that forms on the surface.
6. Cook until full flavored.
7. Strain and reduce by half.

Turkey Stock   Makes about 6 cups

2 tablespoons grape seed oil
1 turkey carcass
2 cups peeled and roughly chopped carrots
2 cups roughly chopped onions
1 cup roughly chopped celery
1 garlic clove, crushed
A few sprigs fresh thyme
2 bay leaves
1 tablespoon black peppercorns

1. Over high heat, brown the turkey carcass in the hot oil in a large pot. Add the carrots, onions, and celery and brown. Pour off any grease, deglaze the caramelized brown bits at the bottom of the pot with water, then cover the carcass and vegetables with more water.
2. Bring to a boil and lower the heat to a simmer, then add the garlic, herbs, and peppercorns.
3. Simmer for 2 to 4 hours, or until the liquid is full flavored. Skim off any foam that forms on the surface.
4. Strain and store.

Marinades

Marinades have been used since Renaissance times, when their primary purpose was to reduce spoilage and impart flavor. They are made with an acidic liquid such as vinegar, wine, citrus juice, buttermilk, or yogurt, and today serve two different functions—as a tenderizer and as a flavor enhancer. Once the meat is fully immersed, the acid breaks down the fibrous proteins and increases its ability to retain moisture. The addition of salt will allow it to retain moisture further. Meat should always be marinated in the refrigerator to prevent bacterial growth at room temperature, and all used marinade should be discarded once the meat is removed unless you are cooking with it. If you do want to serve some of the marinade with the meat, set an amount aside before bringing it in contact with the meat. A good marinade will have a balance of ingredients so that the outer surface of the meat does not become too sour from the acid. Once a piece of meat has been marinated, it is best not to freeze it, as the outer layer will become mushy. Marinades are particularly good with red meat and antlered game.

Red Wine Marinade   Good for two venison shoulders or their equivalent in meat

4 tablespoons grape seed oil
1 carrot
1 onion
1 celery stalk
1 clove garlic
1 (750 ml) bottle dry red wine
2/3 cup red wine vinegar
1 whole clove
2 bay leaves
1 sprig fresh thyme
Several sprigs fresh parsley
8 peppercorns

1. Heat the oil in a heavy-bottomed pan and sweat the carrot, onion, celery, and garlic. Add the wine and vinegar and remaining ingredients and simmer slowly for 30 minutes.
2. Let cool thoroughly and pour over the meat so that it is completely submerged. Let it soak for several hours and up to 24 hours.

Try with: antlered game, other red meats

Orange Brandy Marinade   Good for four small game birds, or an equivalent amount of meat

Zest of 1 orange
1/2 cup freshly squeezed orange juice
Juice of 1/2 lemon
1 teaspoon salt
1/4 cup brandy
1/4 teaspoon dried tarragon
1/4 teaspoon dried parsley
1/4 teaspoon dried rosemary
1/4 cup olive oil
1/8 teaspoon freshly ground pepper

1. Combine all the marinade ingredients in a nonreactive bowl and whisk together.
2. Place the meat breast side down in the mixture. Marinate for 3 to 4 hours, turning over every hour. Cook the meat in the marinade and baste with it as you cook.

Try with: small game birds

Balsamic Marinade

Good for antlered game,
particularly the heart and other offal

1 part balsamic vinegar
1 part good olive oil
Chopped garlic
Chopped fresh parsley
Salt and pepper

1. Combine your meat with these ingredients in a large resealable plastic bag (or in a bowl covered with plastic wrap) and refrigerate for up to 24 hours.

Try with: game birds, antlered game hearts, other tough cuts, offal

Sherry Marinade

Good for two wild hog tenderloins, backstraps,
or an equivalent amount of meat

1 1/2 sticks (12 tablespoons) butter, melted
2 tablespoons lightly crushed juniper berries
2 teaspoons coarse cracked pepper
6 whole cloves
3 cups sherry, cooked for several minutes to reduce the alcohol

1. Combine all the ingredients in a nonreactive bowl, then pour over the tenderloins or other meat in a nonreactive roasting pan.
2. Cover and let sit covered in the refrigerator for 4 to 6 hours before cooking.

Try with: game birds, javelina, hog, antlered game, bear, pheasant, partridge, dove

MARINADES

Brines

Brining is an old-fashioned technique that involves soaking meat or poultry in a flavorful saltwater solution to enhance its moisture and taste. The proper ratio is 2 tablespoons of salt to 4 cups of water. Brining does not break down the proteins in the meat in the way that marinating does. Instead, through osmosis, it carries salt and sugar inside the cell walls of the meat, which causes the proteins to unravel, interact with one another, and form a matrix that traps moisture inside the meat. The true purpose of brining is juiciness, whereas the true purpose of marinating is tenderization. It is a good idea to rest a piece of meat once it comes out of a brine, to allow the moisture to retreat back into the meat. This is an especially good technique for white meats, and for ducks with skin that may taste fishy.

Spicy Apple Duck Brine

1 cup apple juice
4 cups water
6 whole cloves
1 tablespoon red pepper flakes
1/4 cup kosher salt
1 tablespoon sugar

1. Bring all the ingredients to a simmer in a large pot and stir so that the sugar and salt dissolve. Let cool to room temperature. You can speed up this process by dissolving the ingredients in only 2 cups of hot water, then diluting it with the remaining 2 cups of cold.
2. Submerge the duck in the liquid and weight it with a plate or other heavy object so that it stays submerged.
3. Let sit in the brine for 4 to 6 hours.
4. Remove from the brine, pat dry, and let sit in the refrigerator, uncovered, for several hours, even overnight. Discard the brine after one use.

Try with: coot, hog, javelina, pheasant, duck

Hog Brine

Good for 2 to 3 pounds of hog backstrap, chops, or tenderloin

4 cups water
1/8 cup brown sugar
1/8 cup granulated sugar
1/2 cup kosher salt
1 teaspoon mustard seeds
2 teaspoons crushed black pepper
1 clove garlic, crushed
1 sprig fresh thyme
1 bay leaf
1/8 cup white wine vinegar

1. Combine all the ingredients in a large pot and bring to a boil. Remove from the heat and let cool.
2. Add the meat and submerge, using a plate or other weight to keep it under water.
3. The optimum soaking time for portioned chops is 5 hours. Unportioned chops still on a rack can be refrigerated in the brine for 24 hours. The meat should be patted dry and allowed to rest for several hours and up to 24 hours in the refrigerator before cooking.

Try with: javelina, hog

BRINES

Turkey Brine
Good for one (10-pound) turkey, or an equivalent amount of meat

8 cups water (add more as needed to cover a larger bird)
1 cup white wine vinegar
1 cup brown sugar
1/2 cup granulated sugar
1 cup salt
1 tablespoon mustard seeds
3 cloves garlic, crushed
2 tablespoons crushed black pepper
3 sprigs fresh thyme
1 bay leaf

1. Combine all the ingredients in a large pot and bring to a boil.
2. Remove from the heat and let cool.
3. Add the meat and submerge, covering with a weight so it stays completely submerged in liquid.
4. For a whole turkey, refrigerate in the brine for 24 hours; for breasts, refrigerate for 12.
5. Remove the turkey and pat dry. Let rest on a rack for at least 3 and up to 24 hours before cooking.

Try with: hog, javelina, game birds, turkey

BRINES

Dry Rubs

Dry rubs are meant to form a coat of flavor on the surface of the meat, as well as a caramelized crust if sugar is added. When using a rub, the dry heat method of cooking is almost always used—grilling, baking, roasting, and broiling, for example. It helps to let the meat sit covered in the rub for a period of time before cooking, to heighten the flavor. Wearing rubber gloves helps you distribute the rub most evenly, particularly with large cuts of haunch or shoulder meat.

RUBS

Everyday Dry Rub

Makes 1/2 cup

1 teaspoon white peppercorns
1 teaspoon black peppercorns
1 teaspoon cumin seeds
1 tablespoon fennel seeds
2 tablespoons coriander seeds
1 tablespoon mustard seeds
1 tablespoon kosher salt
1 teaspoon ground cardamom
1 teaspoon grated nutmeg
1 teaspoon garlic powder
1 teaspoon onion powder
1/2 teaspoon ginger powder
1 tablespoon dried marjoram
1 tablespoon smoked paprika

1. In a small sauté pan over medium heat, combine the white and black pepper-corns, cumin, fennel, coriander, and mustard seeds. Stir for 2 to 3 minutes, until fragrant. Turn off the heat.
2. Place in a spice grinder with the rest of the ingredients. Blend until fine.
3. Store in an airtight container for up to 6 months.

Try with: hog, javelina, game birds, turkey, antlered game

Pulled Shoulder Rub

Makes 1 1/2 to 2 cups
Good for two shoulders (3 to 5 pounds total)

1/2 cup molasses
1 cup kosher salt
4 cups water
1 teaspoon cumin seeds
1 teaspoon fennel seeds
1 teaspoon coriander seeds
1 tablespoon chili powder
1 tablespoon onion powder
1 tablespoon garlic powder
1 tablespoon paprika
1 teaspoon cayenne
1 teaspoon ground allspice
1 tablespoon ground oregano
1 tablespoon mustard powder

1. Combine the molasses, salt, and water in a plastic brining bag or nonreactive container. Add the shoulders and let sit in the refrigerator for 12 hours.

RUBS

2. Place cumin seeds, fennel seeds, and coriander seeds in a spice grinder and grind until fine. Transfer to a small mixing bowl and combine with the remaining ingredients.
3. Rub the mixture into the meat, until it is evenly coated.

Try with: javelina, hog

Curry Rub

Good for four small birds, two medium birds, or an equivalent amount of meat

2 teaspoons salt
4 cloves garlic, sliced thinly
2 tablespoons hot curry powder
1 teaspoon cumin seeds
2 tablespoons olive oil

1. Combine the ingredients in a small bowl and rub the mixture into the birds.
2. Let sit in the refrigerator overnight or for up to 3 days.

Try with: game birds, antlered game, hog, javelina, duck

Sauces

Many game meats, particularly the most tender cuts, are best when simply seared in a pan with salt and pepper. The addition of a sauce on the side or drizzled on the top is a wonderful accompaniment in this case. Many sauces require stock as their base, which is one more reason to save all of your bones and turn them into stock.

Juniper Sauce

Makes 1 3/4 to 2 cups

1 tablespoon grape seed oil
3 shallots, minced
Sea salt
1/2 cup vermouth
12 juniper berries, crushed (see Note)
1/2 cup gin
4 cups bird stock
Salt and pepper
1 tablespoon cold butter

1. In a sauté pan, heat the oil and sweat the shallots. Sprinkle with salt to release the moisture.
2. Add the vermouth to the pan and deglaze. Add the crushed juniper berries, gin, and bird stock. Simmer the sauce for about 1 hour, until reduced by half.
3. Whisk in the cold butter and serve.

Try with: light meat such as game birds, hog, javelina

Note: If you don't have a mortar and pestle, use the back of a frying pan to crush the juniper berries against a cutting board.

Concord Grape Sauce

Makes 1 cup

2 tablespoons grape seed oil
1 carrot, peeled and diced
1 fennel bulb, diced
1 onion, diced
2 shallots, diced
1 teaspoon black peppercorns
2 garlic cloves, crushed
Sea salt
1 cup white port
2 pounds Concord grapes, washed and picked from the stems
2 tablespoons sherry wine vinegar

1. In a heavy-bottomed sauté pan with high sides, heat the oil and sweat the carrots, fennel, onion, shallots, peppercorns, and garlic. Sprinkle with salt to release the flavor.
2. Deglaze with the white port and reduce by about half.
3. Add the grapes to the pan and cover. Let simmer for about 1 hour, or until full flavored and dark purple.

SAUCES

4. Strain the sauce and reduce until the desired consistency is achieved. Season with salt as needed.

Try with: game bird, turkey, crispy hog, dove, duck

Apple Cider Demi-Glace

Makes 1 cup

1 cup apple cider
1 tablespoon red wine vinegar
2 cups venison stock or venison braising liquid from venison shoulder (page 155)
Salt

1. Reduce the apple cider to a syrup in a saucepan.
2. Stir in the vinegar and cook for 2 to 3 minutes.
3. Add the stock, stir well, and cook until the liquid is reduced by about half (20 to 30 minutes).
4. Skim off any fat and season.

Try with: antlered game, bear, turkey, duck

Sweet-and-Sour Dipping Sauce

Makes 1 3/4 cups

1 cup cider vinegar
1/2 cup brown sugar
1 cup water
1 cup canned crushed or plum tomatoes, drained
1 cup pineapple juice
1 red bell pepper, seeded and diced
1 teaspoon Dijon mustard
2 tablespoons soy sauce

1. Combine all the ingredients in a saucepan over medium heat. Stir and bring to a simmer. Skim off any foam that forms on the surface.
2. Let it reduce, stirring often and continuing to skim the foam, for 60 to 80 minutes, until reduced by two-thirds.
3. Puree in a blender for 15 seconds. This sauce is best if left to sit for a few hours before serving. It can be stored in the refrigerator for several weeks and served cold.

Try with: any light meat game bird, hog, javelina, rabbit, squirrel

SAUCES

Barbecue Sauce

Makes 1 1/2 cups

1 tablespoon grape seed oil
1/2 cup diced onion
Sea salt
1/2 cup cider vinegar
1 tablespoon minced garlic
1/2 cup Worcestershire sauce
1 tablespoon dark brown sugar
1 tablespoon molasses
1 cup canned crushed or plum tomatoes, drained
1 tablespoon mustard powder
1 tablespoon smoked paprika
1/2 teaspoon ground cloves
1/2 teaspoon cayenne
1 teaspoon ground coriander
1/2 cup bird or hog stock

1. In a small sauté pan or saucepan, heat the oil and sauté the onions until soft and translucent, about 5 minutes. Add a sprinkle of salt to help release the juices.
2. Add the vinegar and reduce by half. Add the remaining ingredients and simmer, stirring, for 10 minutes.
3. Transfer the contents of the pan to a blender and puree for about 15 seconds, until smooth.
4. Store in the refrigerator for up to 1 week. This sauce is best if left in the refrigerator overnight before using.

Try with: hog, javelina, game birds, antlered game, squirrel, rabbit

Mint Vinaigrette

Makes 1 cup

1/2 cup rice vinegar
1/2 teaspoon sugar
1/4 teaspoon sea salt
2 teaspoons finely diced shallots
3 tablespoons washed, dried, and finely chopped fresh mint leaves
1 tablespoon freshly squeezed lemon juice
1/4 cup olive oil

1. Heat the vinegar in a small saucepan and stir in the sugar and salt until dissolved. Let cool slightly.

SAUCES

2. In a small glass bowl, combine the remaining ingredients and stir. Pour in the vinegar mixture and whisk. Let the sauce macerate for several hours in the refrigerator, and whisk again before serving.
3. This sauce is best served cold or room temperature, with room-temperature or leftover meat.

Try with: javelina, hog, light meat game birds, rabbit, turkey

Beurre Blanc Sauce   Makes 1 cup

1/2 cup champagne vinegar
1/2 cup white wine vinegar
1/4 cup white wine
1 teaspoon freshly squeezed lemon juice
1 bay leaf
2 sprigs fresh thyme
1 teaspoon coriander seeds
1 teaspoon black peppercorns
1 shallot, sliced thinly
1 teaspoon sea salt
1 1/2 sticks (12 tablespoons) cold unsalted butter, cubed

1. Place the liquids with herbs, spices, and shallots in a small saucepan and bring to a simmer. Reduce the liquids until they just coat the bottom of the pot.
2. Whisk in the cold cubes of butter, one by one. The heat of the pan and the cold of the butter will create an emulsification. There should always be one to two cubes of solid butter visible as you whisk so that the mixture doesn't become too hot and break. Once you have added the last cube of butter, turn off the heat and whisk until incorporated. Serve immediately or keep warm for serving.
3. This sauce does not reheat well, but is great when used as a flavored butter once any leftovers are refrigerated. Stir it into vegetables, omelets, and other sauces.

Try with: hog, javelina, game birds, rabbit, turkey

Cranberry Relish   Makes 2 1/2 cups

4 cups fresh cranberries, washed and picked over
1 large navel orange, peel on and washed well, cut into small wedges
1 tablespoon freshly squeezed lemon juice

1 teaspoon lemon zest
1/2 teaspoon ground cloves
1/2 teaspoon grated nutmeg
1/3 cup sugar

1. Combine all the ingredients in a food processor and pulse until combined but still coarse.
2. Refrigerate in a covered bowl or glass jar overnight before serving.
3. This will store well for several weeks and improve with age.

Try with: turkey, light meat game birds, duck, hog, javelina

Cherry Sauce

Makes 1 1/4 cup

2 tablespoons butter
1/2 cup finely diced shallots
1 cup pitted frozen or fresh cherries
2 sprigs fresh thyme
1/4 cup vermouth
1 cup bird stock
Salt and pepper

1. Place the butter in a sauté pan at medium heat and sweat the shallots until translucent.
2. Add the cherries and thyme, and let sweat for 1 minute.
3. Add the vermouth and reduce by half.
4. Add the stock and cook, partly covered, at a low simmer until reduced by half. Season with salt and pepper to taste. Keep warm for serving.

Try with: duck, coot

Sherry Sauce

Makes 1 1/4 cups

1 tablespoon butter
1/2 cup finely diced shallots
Sea salt
1/2 cup sweet sherry
2 tablespoons all-purpose flour
2 cups bird stock
Pinch of cayenne
1 teaspoon freshly squeezed lemon juice
Salt and pepper

SAUCES

1. In a sauté pan, heat the butter and sweat the shallots over low heat until soft and translucent. Sprinkle with a bit of salt to help release the juices.
2. Add the sherry and reduce to a glaze.
3. Whisk in the flour and let bubble for 1 minute.
4. Add the stock and cook, covered, on a low simmer until reduced by three-quarters or as thick as you'd like. Add the cayenne and lemon juice, and season with salt and pepper as needed. Keep warm for serving.

Try with: woodcock, hog, javelina, rabbit, turkey

Red Currant Sauce   Makes 1 cup

2 tablespoons grape seed oil
1 cup peeled and diced carrots
1 cup diced onion
2 sprigs fresh thyme
3 sprigs fresh parsley
2 bay leaves
Sea salt
1 cup red wine vinegar
1 tablespoon all-purpose flour
4 cups venison stock
1 tablespoon black peppercorns
1/3 cup currant jelly
1/2 teaspoon orange zest
1/2 cup heavy cream

1. In a sauté pan, heat the oil and sweat the vegetables, thyme, parsley, and bay leaves for about 5 minutes, until softened. Sprinkle with salt along the way to release the flavor.
2. Add the vinegar and reduce to a glaze.
3. Add the flour and stir for 1 minute.
4. Add the stock and peppercorns and cook until reduced by half, about 30 minutes. Strain the liquid into a small saucepan.
5. Whisk the currant jelly and orange zest into the strained liquid.
6. Just before serving, whisk in the heavy cream and bring to a simmer over low heat. Do not reheat the sauce once the cream has been added, otherwise it will curdle. Simply keep warm for serving.

Try with: antlered game, dark meat game birds, duck, squirrel, rabbit

Orange Brandy Sauce

Makes 1 cup

Zest of 1 orange
1/2 cup freshly squeezed orange juice
Juice of 1/2 lemon
1 teaspoon salt
1/4 cup brandy
1/4 teaspoon dried tarragon
1/4 teaspoon dried parsley
1/4 teaspoon dried rosemary
1/4 cup olive oil
1/8 teaspoon freshly ground pepper
4 tablespoons cold butter, cubed

1. Combine all the ingredients, except the butter, in a saucepan and whisk together. Simmer over medium heat until reduced by half.
2. Just before serving, whisk in the cold butter.

Try with: game birds, turkey, duck, squirrel

Red Wine Sauce

Makes 2 cups

2 tablespoons grape seed oil
1 cup shallots, diced
Sea salt
2 cups red wine
2 sprigs fresh thyme
2 bay leaves
1 tablespoon cracked black peppercorns
4 cups venison stock
2 tablespoons cold butter

1. In a sauté pan, heat the oil and sweat the shallots until soft and translucent. Sprinkle with salt to release the juices.
2. Add the wine, thyme, bay leaves, and peppercorns and reduce to a glaze.
3. Add the stock and cook, covered, at a low simmer until reduced by half, about 30 minutes. Strain and season with salt as needed.
4. Right before serving, whisk in the cold butter. Keep warm for serving but don't heat it again.

Try with: antlered game, bear, dark meat game birds

SAUCES

White Wine Dijon Sauce
Makes 1 3/4 cups

2 tablespoons grape seed oil
1 cup finely diced onions
Sea salt
1 cup white wine
2 sprigs fresh thyme
1 tablespoon tomato paste
4 cups hog or bird stock
1 tablespoon Dijon mustard

1. In a sauté pan, heat the oil and sweat the onions. Sprinkle with salt to release the juices.
2. Add the wine and thyme and reduce by half.
3. Add the tomato paste and simmer for 2 minutes.
4. Add the stock and cook for 1 hour at a low simmer, until reduced by half. Whisk in the Dijon mustard vigorously.
5. Keep warm for serving or let rest in the refrigerator overnight to improve the flavor before gently reheating.

Try with: hog, rabbit, javelina

Mushroom Sauce
Makes 1 3/4 cups

2 tablespoons butter
1 cup finely sliced shiitake mushrooms
2 sprigs fresh thyme
1/4 cup finely diced shallots
Sea salt
1 cup red port
4 cups venison stock
Freshly ground black pepper

1. In a sauté pan, heat the butter and add the mushrooms and thyme. Let them stick to the pan and become browned; don't stir until you see brown bits forming. Add the shallots and stir into the mushrooms. Sprinkle with salt to help release the juices. Let them sweat until soft and the shallots become translucent. Add more butter if the pan becomes too dry.
2. Deglaze the pan with the port, scraping up the brown bits with a wooden spoon, and reduce the liquid by half.
3. Add the stock and cook for about 30 minutes, until reduced by half.
4. Season with pepper as needed.
5. Keep warm for serving.

Try with: antlered game, bear, dark game birds, duck, turkey, squirrel, rabbit

SAUCES

Black Peppercorn Sauce

Makes 2 cups

2 tablespoons grape seed oil
1 cup peeled and diced carrots
1 cup diced onion
2 sprigs fresh thyme
3 sprigs fresh parsley
2 bay leaves
Sea salt
1 tablespoon red wine vinegar
1 cup red wine
2 tablespoons whole black peppercorns
1 tablespoon all-purpose flour
4 cups venison stock
1 tablespoon crushed black peppercorns (see Note)

1. In a sauté pan, heat the oil and sweat the vegetables, thyme, parsley, and bay leaves. Sprinkle with salt to release the flavor.
2. Add the vinegar, wine, and whole peppercorns and reduce to a glaze. Add the flour and stir, for 1 minute, until it begins to bubble.
3. Add the stock and cook until it thickens and is reduced by half, about 30 minutes. Strain, stir in the crushed peppercorns, and season with salt as needed. Keep warm for serving.

Try with: antlered game, bear

Note: If you don't have a mortar and pestle, use the back of a frying pan to crush the peppercorns against a cutting board.

Homemade Chunky Applesauce

Makes 7 cups

When using apples in any dish, you want to use a whole variety of apples: some that are going to turn soft quickly, such as McIntosh and Golden Delicious, and some that are going to hold their shape, such as Pink Lady and Rome Beauty. Heirlooms are ideal, too, and in some cases, well-aged apples taste even better than fresh ones. Variety is good because you get several flavors and textures. It keeps things interesting. Golden Delicious, Granny Smith, Jonathan, Stayman-Winesap, Cox's Orange Pippin, and Jonagold all provide a good mix of sweetness and tartness. Other sweet choices are Braeburn, Fuji, Mutsu, Pink Lady, Suncrisp, Rome Beauty, and Empire. Good tart baking apples include Idared, Macoun, Newton Pippin, and Northern Spy. Apples that turn mushy quickly are McIntosh and Cortland.

4 pounds apples, mostly peeled, cored, and cut into 1-inch pieces
1/4 to 1/3 cup raw sugar, depending on the sweetness of your apples

SAUCES

1 teaspoon ground cinnamon
1/8 teaspoon ground allspice
1/8 teaspoon ground cloves
1/8 teaspoon grated nutmeg
1/2 teaspoon apple salt or sea salt
Zest of 1 lemon
1 teaspoon cider vinegar

1. Place the apples in a large saucepan with 1 cup of water. Add the remaining ingredients and stir.
2. Bring the water to a simmer and stir again. Reduce the heat to its lowest setting.
3. Let cook and steam slowly for 20 minutes, stirring occasionally so the bottom doesn't stick.
4. Cover the saucepan with a lid and cook the apples for another 70 minutes, stirring every 10 to 15 minutes. During the last 10 minutes, use a wooden spoon to break up the large chunks of apple that haven't broken apart.
5. Serve slightly warm or cool to room temperature and store in the refrigerator in a jar. The applesauce will keep in the refrigerator for 3 to 4 weeks, or frozen for a year.

Try with: hog, javelina

Homemade Sauerkraut   Makes 1 gallon

You can use any kind of cabbage for this recipe, but if you mix red and green cabbage you will end up with a nice pink sauerkraut. You can start a new batch before the previous batch runs out by using what remains from the crock, repacking it with fresh salted cabbage, and pouring the old juices over the new. This will act as an active starter culture and give your new batch a boost. If you develop a rhythm like this you will always have sauerkraut on hand. Caraway seeds, juniper berries, or even other vegetables can be added to the cabbage for flavoring. This is your chance to experiment. To serve warm, you can heat it in equal parts brining liquid and vegetable or chicken stock for 20 to 30 minutes.

5 pounds cabbage
3 tablespoons sea salt
Caraway seeds, juniper berries, or any flavoring you want to try

1. Chop or grate the cabbage finely or coarsely, however you prefer. Put the cabbage in a large bowl, sprinkling it with the salt as you go. This draws moisture out of the cabbage and creates the brine in which the cabbage will ferment. The amount of salt does not need to be precise: In warmer temperatures you might need more; in cooler temperatures, less.

2. Add the caraway seeds or other flavorings to the cabbage and toss to combine. Pack a small amount at a time into a 1-gallon or larger ceramic crock or food-grade plastic bucket, pressing down as you go to help release the water from the cabbage. Cover the cabbage with a plate or other flat object that fits snugly in the crock. Place a jug of water or other weight on top of the place to add pressure. This will help increase the brine over time. Cover the crock with a cloth or towel to keep ambient dust and flies away.

3. Press down on the cabbage periodically over the next 24 hours, until the brine rises above the plate. Some cabbage, particularly if it is old, contains less water. If the brine does not rise above the plate after 24 hours, simply add enough saltwater (in a ratio of 1 teaspoon salt to 1 cup water, dissolved) to bring the level above the plate.

4. Let the cabbage ferment, and check it every few days to make sure the water level is still above the plate. Keeping it in a cool place will slow the fermentation and preserve the kraut longer. The volume reduces over time and a "bloom" may appear at the surface. This is simply a reaction to contact with air and can be skimmed off.

　　The kraut will become tangy after a few days and will become stronger over time. In cool temperatures it will keep improving for months. Take it from the crock to eat as needed, but leave the rest in the crock, fully submerged, to continue to develop. If you find that the brine evaporates over time, just add more saltwater.

Try with: venison kielbasa or any game sausage

Homemade Mustard　　　　　　　　　　　Makes 3/4 cup

There are a great many variations you can create with mustard. You can change up the vinegars, use various types of mustard seeds, or add a sweetness with honey and molasses or a tang with horseradish and garlic. This is a basic recipe that can be expanded on, depending on its use. Be sure to let it rest for a good 24 hours before serving so that the flavors can develop.

　　4 tablespoons mustard seeds
　　1/3 cup mustard powder
　　3 tablespoons white wine vinegar
　　1/4 cup white wine
　　1 teaspoon sea salt
　　1 teaspoon freshly squeezed lemon juice

1. In a spice grinder or with a mortar and pestle, crush the mustard seeds so they are cracked and coarse but not a powder.

SAUCES

2. Pour the seeds into a small bowl and combine with the remaining ingredients. Mix well and cover with plastic wrap.
3. Store in the refrigerator for 24 hours before using. The mustard will be soupy when it first goes into the refrigerator but will thicken with time.

Try with: any game sausage, cold leftover game meat sandwiches

Preserved Lemons

Preserved lemons are a great flavoring element to game and fish dishes. They are commonly found in Middle Eastern dishes, where the rind is removed from the pulp, rinsed, and cut up. I have used Meyer lemons often, which are the best, in my opinion, because they have a floral undertone. A small amount goes a long way, and one jar will last for many months on your shelf. Just be sure to rinse the zest very well under cold water before adding it to a dish, and reduce the amount of salt you add to your dish to compensate for the salt in the lemon.

Lemons, cut horizontally or vertically
Kosher salt
Star anise, or whatever flavoring element suits your fancy

1. Pour an inch of kosher salt into a glass jar, then begin to add the lemon halves, making sure they fit snugly and that you are alternating with a lot of salt along the way.
2. Drop your flavoring tidbits into there and continue to add salt and lemons until the jar is completely full. Bang the jar on the counter a few times to remove air and help things settle. Top with more salt. Screw on the lid and put the jar in a cabinet for at least 1 month, preferably more.
3. If the preserve becomes very liquidy, add more salt to the top of the jar. When ready to use, remove the lemons as needed, rinse in cold water, and remove the pulp. Chop the zest to use in your bird and fish recipes.

Game Bird Characteristics

People often wonder which animals can be interchanged in a recipe and where farm-raised animals fall into this mélange. The best answer is—*try it*. Game animals are unique, each different from the last, depending on their diet and environment.

With game birds you can count on a few things: pheasant, snipe, quail, wild turkey, partridge, chukar, and some grouse are all the wild cousins of chickens. They have a similar flavor and texture, though are much leaner, sometimes more nuanced, sometimes sweeter. Pheasant and quail can be purchased at many supermarkets these days, but the flavor will be milder than anything you get from the wild. Remember—every meat protein you are allowed to buy in the United States has been farm raised. If you want to substitute chicken or other store-bought birds for these wild bird recipes, you can. Because cooking times will vary, have a meat thermometer handy to check the internal temperatures.

Many of these wild bird recipes allow for the birds to be interchanged; you might like some more than others in a particular dish, but the choice is up to you and your palate in the end. The white-meat upland birds should not be served rare, but can have a blush of pink in them. The wild ones will be more muscular and will dry out more quickly, so you need to tend to them while they are cooking, basting them, poaching them, doting on them until the very last second.

Dark-meat birds, such as ducks, are smaller than their domestic cousins, with a much thinner coat of fat. Turkeys are drier at the breast and tougher at the legs, especially an ol' tom. Therefore, whereas a domestic turkey leg will make a nice drumstick, a wild turkey leg will make a nice ground turkey burger.

Because different birds cook at different rates, you can use the following table to help guide you, keeping in mind that the smaller the bird, the harder it will be to gauge the temperature accurately. I suggest a probe-style meat thermometer as it is the most accurate

Game	Dressed Weight	Ideal Internal Temp.	Meat Characteristics
Brant	4–5 pounds	135°F (rare)	Dark, rich, gamey
Chukar	1 pound	130°–150°F	White breast, dark legs
Coot	2 pounds	130°–140°F	Dark, rich, fishy skin
Dove	3/4 pounds	130°–140°F	Flavorful, tender, medium red
Duck (Mallard, Black, Pintail, Redhead, etc.)	2–2 1/2 pounds	120°F (rare), 135°F (medium-rare)	Dark, tender, fine-grained, rich, flavorful
Duck, Canvasback	2 3/4–3 pounds	130°–140°F	Rich, dark, flavorful, tender
Duck, Teal	1/2–3/4 pound	120°–135°F	Dark, fine-grained, flavorful
Gallinule	1/2 pound	130°–140°F	Rich, medium dark, aromatic
Goose (Canada, Snow)	Up to 14 pounds	130°F	Lean, dark, rich, flavorful
Grouse and Prairie Chicken	1–5 pounds	130°–145°F	Very rich, medium, dark, aromatic
Partridge	1/2 pound	130°–145°F	Medium-tender breast, dark legs
Pheasant (cock) (hen)	2 3/4–5 pounds / 1 1/2–3 pounds	130°–145°F / 130°–145°F	White breast, dark legs, fine texture, dense
Pigeon (squab)	1 1/2 pounds / 3/4 pound	130°–140°F / 130°–140°F	Medium dark, flavorful
Ptarmigan	1–1 1/2 pounds	130°–145°F	Similar flavor to grouse
Quail	1/2 pound	130°–145°F	White-medium breast, medium-dark legs
Rail	Up to 1/2 pound	130°–145°F	Medium dark, very rich, dense
Snipe	Up to 1/2 pound	130°–145°F	Medium dark, fine-textured, flavorful
Turkey	Up to 14 pounds	140°–150°F	White breast, dark legs, very lean, rich
Woodcock	1/2–3/4 pound	130°–145°F (innards should be at least 125°F)	Rich, medium dark, dense, leg meat white

for testing wild game. Other thermometers can read high, especially with smaller game. I also suggest throwing out your thermometer at the end of a year and starting anew. As you cook each bird to the right temperature, press down on the flesh with your thumb to get a sense for what the perfectly cooked bird feels like. It will eventually become intuitive and a thermometer won't be as necessary.

Game Animal Characteristics

Game animals, like game birds, are much leaner than their domestic counterparts. They exercise their muscles every day, which means the animals are smaller, the meat is denser with tougher connective tissue, the flavor is richer, and each bite is more filling. Wild boar or hog, for example, has less fat and a stronger flavor, depending on what it was eating and how it was killed. For store-bought substitutes, a large hog will be most equivalent to a heritage breed pig, not a factory-farmed one. Venison is most similar to grass-fed beef, not feedlot beef, though the meat will still be much leaner. Cottontail rabbits are half the size of the domestic ones you can buy. Unlike the consistency of domestic meat, that of each wild animal is different from the last; the best way to get an indication of the animal's flavor and its diet is to render the fat, smell it, taste it, and treat each animal as a grand culinary adventure unlike any you have had before.

Aging Game

Voltaire once said, "The bird of the Phasis is a dish for the gods." Jean Anthelme Brillat-Savarin wrote, "Above all feathered game should come the pheasant, but once again few mortal men know how to present it best. A pheasant eaten within a week after its death is more worthless than a pullet, because its real merit comes in its heightening flavor."

The beautiful taste of a well-aged animal came by virtue of necessity. Refrigeration wasn't available until the twentieth century, which meant that people learned to enjoy game birds whose breast meat was aged until green. But as my friend the British gamekeeper once pointed out, people don't like their meat "high" anymore, or rather, rotten tasting. Their taste buds are no longer suited to it since the advent of refrigeration.

Certain game birds today, however, when relatively undamaged by shot, left in their feathers with intestines intact, and aged for a period

Game	Weight	Ideal Internal Temp.	Meat Characteristics
Antelope	100–140 pounds	125°–130°F	Very lean, dark, like deer
Bear (black)	300–400 pounds	150°–160°F	Dark, sweet flavor
Bison (buffalo)	Up to 1 ton	135°–145°F	Lean, beeflike in texture, taste
Boar	300–350 pounds	150°–160°F	Porklike but richer
Caribou	200–400 pounds	130°–140°F	Like venison, but gamier
Elk	600–800 pounds	130°–140°F	Dark, beeflike, sweet
Goat (Mountain)	Up to 300 pounds	140°–150°F	Lean, like lamb or venison
Hare	6–12 pounds	135°–145°F	Rich, gamey, deep red
Moose	1,300–1,400 pounds	130°–140°F	Beeflike but leaner, darker
Muskrat	5–6 pounds	150°F	Dark, fine-grained, gamey
Opossum	Up to 10 pounds	155°–160°F	Cross between pork and hare
Peccary (Collared)	40–65 pounds	140°–150°F	Light, lean, like pork
Rabbit (Cottontail, Marsh, Swamp, Brush, etc.)	2 1/2–3 1/2 pounds 3–5 pounds	140°–145°F	Light, fine-textured
Rabbit (Snowshoe or Varying Hare)	2 pounds	140°–145°F	Very lean, dark
Rabbit (European)	Up to 5 pounds	140°–145°F	Light, darkens when cooked
Rabbit (Jack)	6–10 pounds	135°–145°F	Dark reddish-brown, gamey
Raccoon	12–25 pounds	160°F	Like pork but less rich
Sheep (Dall)	180 pounds	140°–150°F	Rich, like mutton
Squirrel (Fox)	1 1/2–3 pounds	140°–145°F	Pink to pale red, lean
Squirrel (Gray)	1 pound	140°–145°F	Pinkish, tender, sweet
Deer (Whitetail)	150 pounds	130°–140°F	Rich, grassy, tender if young
(Mule)	175–200 pounds	130°–140°F	Gamier than others, dark rich
(Blacktail)	Up to 150 pounds	130°–140°F	Rich, dark
(Axis)	Up to 250 pounds	130°–140°F	Mild and fine, dense and sweet
Woodchuck	10 pounds	160°F	Rich game flavor, dark

of time, are much better tasting than when eaten fresh. Certain game animals are better tasting, too, when aged, particularly deer. Those animals that benefit most are: upland game birds, doves, pigeons, ducks, and antlered game.

Unlike domestic animals, wild ones have that rich, variable flavor, because they are often older at death, exercise freely, and enjoy a mixed diet. The wild flavors that result from cooking these animals are often described as "gamey." In Brillat-Savarin's day, game was hung until it began to rot—a treatment they called mortification or faisandage (after the pheasant, *faisan*)—which not only tenderized the meat but heightened the wild, gamey flavor even further.

The thought of this makes today's eaters recoil. We are used to meat that is tender, and very mild (I would even suggest flavorless). This is because today's farmed animals live a very different lifestyle than their ancestors or wild counterparts—they are sedentary, eat a uniform diet, and are slaughtered before they reach sexual maturity. It is not surprising then, that it takes a slightly different approach to properly cook a wild animal, and the secret lies in proper aging.

Aging is a change in the activity of muscle enzymes. At death, the enzymes begin to deteriorate cell molecules indiscriminately. Large flavorless molecules become smaller, flavorful segments; proteins become savory amino acids; glycogen becomes sweet glucose; fats become aromatic. All of this deterioration and breakdown of the cell molecules creates intense flavor, which improves further upon cooking, particularly slow braising.

This shift in enzyme activity also tenderizes the meat by weakening the proteins that hold things in their place. The collagen in connective tissue also begins to weaken, causing it to dissolve into gelatin during cooking, and help it retain moisture.

Because any meat that is aged tastes so much better than meat that is not, it would seem logical that modern meat producers would age their meat—but they do not. It is simply a matter of lost time and economics—an unwillingness to tie up product in cold storage and lose 20 percent of the meat's original weight to evaporation, in the name of taste. The number of days between slaughter and the dinner table are very few.

The good news is that home cooks can age meat in their own kitchen. With store-bought meat, it is simply a matter of leaving it uncovered in

Animal	Aging Recommended?	Days	Technique	Notes
Boar	Optional	2–3 days of bleeding/soaking and/or 5 days of dry cooling	Soak and tenderize the meat with enough ice water to cover the meat plus 1/2 cup of vinegar and/or lemon juice. Soak large portions of the meat for 2–3 days and change the water as needed to keep the water ice cold. Soak the meat until it turns white and all the blood is leached out. You may also quarter the meat and cool dry it in the fridge for up to 5 days.	Hunting small hogs and using brines are perhaps the best path to tender wild hog meat. Otherwise, aging off the bone in the refrigerator is ideal. Tenderness increases rapidly in the first 48 hours postmortem.
Chukar	Yes	2–6	Age the meat hanging whole by the neck with the feathers and skin on and the guts intact at a temperature of 50°–55°F.	2–3 days is best for a smaller bird, 4–6 days for a larger one. If the bird is damaged, pluck and gut it and place it on a wire rack over a pan in the refrigerator, covered in a wet cloth to prevent drying.
Deer	Yes	At least 5–7 days and up to 17 days	Skin the deer right away and age the meat by hanging by the feet in a walk-in cooler at or at 32°–40°F. If the temperature is higher, age for as little as one day, to prevent bacteria from flourishing.	The smaller the deer, the less time it will need for the muscle tissue to break down.
Dove	Yes	1–4	Age the meat hanging whole by the neck with the feathers and skin on and the guts intact at a temperature of 50°–55°F.	1–2 days is best for a smaller bird, 3–4 days for a larger one. If the bird is damaged, pluck and gut it and place it on a wire rack over a pan in the refrigerator, covered in a wet cloth to prevent drying.
Duck	Yes	3–7	Hang by the neck in full feathers with the guts still inside. The guts will become milder with time. If the meat is badly damaged, pluck or skin it, cut out the damaged parts, and place it on a wire rack over a pan in the refrigerator for 3–5 days.	

Elk	Yes	7–14	Elk should be aged like deer, but at or near freezing temperature (32°F) because they are prone to bacteria.	
Grouse	Yes	2–6	Age the meat, hanging whole by the neck with the feathers and skin on and the guts intact at a temperature of 35°–50°F.	2–3 days is best for a smaller bird, 4–6 days for a larger one. If the bird is damaged, pluck and gut it and place it on a wire rack over a pan in the refrigerator, covered in a wet cloth to prevent drying.
Javelina	Optional	7–10	Tie up the meat in a water tight bag and chill it in an ice filled cooler for 7–10 days.	When removing the hide, leave the musk gland alone. It will naturally fall away from the meat with the hide. Cutting it out will cause it to taint the meat.
Partridge	Yes	2–6	Age the meat hanging whole by the neck with the feathers and skin on and the guts intact at a temperature in the range of 50°–55°F.	2–3 days is best for a smaller bird, 4–6 days for a larger one. If the bird is damaged, pluck and gut it and place it on a wire rack over a pan in the refrigerator, covered in a wet cloth to prevent drying.
Pheasant	Yes	3–7	Age the meat, hanging whole by the neck with the feathers and skin on and the guts intact at a temperature of 50°–55°F. Pheasants are best if eaten as soon as the aging is completed.	3–4 days is best for a smaller bird, 5–7 days for a larger/older one. If the bird is damaged, pluck and gut it and place it on a wire rack over a pan in the refrigerator, covered in a wet cloth to prevent drying.
Pigeon	Yes	1–5	Age the meat hanging whole by the neck with the feathers and skin on and the guts intact at a temperature of 50°–55°F.	1–3 days is best for a smaller bird, 4–5 days for a larger one. If the bird is damaged, pluck and gut it and place it on a wire rack over a pan in the refrigerator, covered in a wet cloth to prevent drying.
Quail	Yes	1–4	Age the meat hanging whole by the neck with the feathers and skin on and the guts intact at a temperature of 50°–55°F.	1–2 days is best for a smaller bird, 3–4 days for a larger one. If the bird is damaged, pluck and gut it and place it on a wire rack over a pan in the refrigerator, covered in a wet cloth to prevent drying.

(continues)

Animal	Aging Recommended?	Days	Technique	Notes
Rabbit	Optional	Maximum 2–3	Skin and gut, then chill in a cooler for 2–3 days. The meat will benefit from an overnight soak of ice-cold saltwater.	
Raccoon	No	Soak overnight	The meat will benefit from an overnight soak of ice-cold saltwater.	
Squirrel	No	Soak overnight	The meat will benefit from an overnight soak of ice-cold saltwater.	
Turkey	Yes	3–6	Age the meat, hanging whole by the feet with the feathers and skin on and the guts intact, at a temperature of 34°–37°F.	3–5 days is best for a smaller bird, 5–6 days for a larger one. If the bird is damaged, pluck and gut it and place it on a wire rack over a pan in the refrigerator, covered in a wet cloth to prevent drying.
Woodcock	Yes	1–6	Age the meat hanging whole by the neck with the feathers and skin on and the guts intact at a temperature of 50°–55°F.	1–3 days is best for a smaller bird, 4–6 days for a larger one. If the bird is damaged, pluck and gut it and place it on a wire rack over a pan in the refrigerator, covered in a wet cloth to prevent drying.

the refrigerator to allow for evaporation (in the case of roasts and other large cuts), or storing it tightly wrapped (in the case of steaks and smaller cuts). After the extra aging, all one has to do is trim off any discolored or dry spots that occurred from drying and oxidation.

Useful Equipment

Some things are useful to have in your kitchen if you are going to hunt your own meat and cook it well.

Larding needle
Kitchen shears
Basting brush
Meat thermometer
Kitchen twine
Toothpicks
Dutch oven
Cast-iron skillet
Terrine mold
Meat grinder
Sausage stuffer
Large plastic brining bags
Smoker, stovetop or outdoor
Thin boning knife
Cleaver
Meat saw
Meat mallet or heavy rolling pin
Spice grinder
Mortar and pestle
Cheesecloth
Fine-mesh strainer
Roasting pan
Vacuum sealer
Latex gloves

METRIC CONVERSION CHART

- The recipes in this book have not been tested with metric measurements, so some variations might occur.
- Remember that the weight of dry ingredients varies according to the volume or density factor: 1 cup of flour weighs far less than 1 cup of sugar, and 1 tablespoon doesn't necessarily hold 3 teaspoons.

General Formulas for Metric Conversion

Ounces to grams	$\Rightarrow$ ounces × 28.35 = grams
Grams to ounces	$\Rightarrow$ grams × 0.035 = ounces
Pounds to grams	$\Rightarrow$ pounds × 453.5 = grams
Pounds to kilograms	$\Rightarrow$ pounds × 0.45 = kilograms
Cups to liters	$\Rightarrow$ cups × 0.24 = liters
Fahrenheit to Celsius	$\Rightarrow$ (°F − 32) × 5 ÷ 9 = °C
Celsius to Fahrenheit	$\Rightarrow$ (°C × 9) ÷ 5 + 32 = °F

Linear Measurements

½ inch = 1½ cm
1 inch = 2½ cm
6 inches = 15 cm
8 inches = 20 cm
10 inches = 25 cm
12 inches = 30 cm
20 inches = 50 cm

Volume (Dry) Measurements

¼ teaspoon = 1 milliliter
½ teaspoon = 2 milliliters
¾ teaspoon = 4 milliliters
1 teaspoon = 5 milliliters
1 tablespoon = 15 milliliters
¼ cup = 59 milliliters
⅓ cup = 79 milliliters
½ cup = 118 milliliters
⅔ cup = 158 milliliters
¾ cup = 177 milliliters
1 cup = 225 milliliters
4 cups or 1 quart = 1 liter
½ gallon = 2 liters
1 gallon = 4 liters

Volume (Liquid) Measurements

1 teaspoon = ⅙ fluid ounce = 5 milliliters
1 tablespoon = ½ fluid ounce = 15 milliliters
2 tablespoons = 1 fluid ounce = 30 milliliters
¼ cup = 2 fluid ounces = 60 milliliters
⅓ cup = 2⅔ fluid ounces = 79 milliliters
½ cup = 4 fluid ounces = 118 milliliters
1 cup or ½ pint = 8 fluid ounces = 250 milliliters
2 cups or 1 pint = 16 fluid ounces = 500 milliliters
4 cups or 1 quart = 32 fluid ounces = 1,000 milliliters
1 gallon = 4 liters

Oven Temperature Equivalents, Fahrenheit (F) and Celsius (C)

100°F = 38°C
200°F = 95°C
250°F = 120°C
300°F = 150°C
350°F = 180°C
400°F = 205°C
450°F = 230°C

Weight (Mass) Measurements

1 ounce = 30 grams
2 ounces = 55 grams
3 ounces = 85 grams
4 ounces = ¼ pound = 125 grams
8 ounces = ½ pound = 240 grams
12 ounces = ¾ pound = 375 grams
16 ounces = 1 pound = 454 grams

Recipe Index